The Norton Sampler

The
Norton Sampler
Short Essays
for Composition

Thomas Cooley
The Ohio State University

W · W · NORTON & COMPANY

New York · London

W. W. Norton & Company, Inc., 500 Fifth Avenue, New York, N.Y. 10110
W. W. Norton & Company Ltd., 25 New Street Square, London EC4A 3NT

Library of Congress Cataloging in Publication Data
Cooley, Thomas, 1942–
    The Norton sampler.

    1. College readers.   2. Exposition (Rhetoric)
3. Essays.   I. Title.
PE1417.C655   808'.0427   78–23328
ISBN 0–393–09007–8

        6 7 8 9 0

Acknowledgments

Edward Abbey: "The Great Globe Arizona Wild Pig and Varmint Hunt," from *The Journey Home: Some Words in Defense of the American West* by Edward Abbey. Copyright © 1977 by Edward Abbey. Reprinted by permission of the publishers, E. P. Dutton.

Shana Alexander: "Fashions in Funerals," from *Talking Woman* (New York: Delacorte Press, 1976). Copyright © 1976 by Shana Alexander.

William Allen: "How to Set a World Record" used by permission of the author. The article first appeared in the *Columbus Dispatch*, December 23, 1973. From "Prologue," from *Starkweather* (Boston: Houghton Mifflin, 1976). Copyright © 1976 by William Allen.

Woody Allen: "Slang Origins," from *Without Feathers* by Woody Allen. Copyright © 1972, 1973, 1974, 1975 by Woody Allen. Reprinted by permission of Random House, Inc.

Roger Angell: From "The Interior Stadium," from *The Summer Game* by Roger Angell. Copyright © 1971 by Roger Angell. Originally appeared in *The New Yorker*. Reprinted by permission of the Viking Press.

Isaac Asimov: "What Do You Call a Platypus?" Copyright 1972 by the National Wildlife Federation. Reprinted from the March–April issue of *National Wildlife Magazine* with the permission of Dr. Isaac Asimov.

Ronald Bracewell: "The Colonization of Space," from *The Galactic Club: Intelligent Life in Outer Space*, a volume in the Portable Stanford Series. Copyright © 1974, 1975 by Ronald Bracewell. Reprinted with permission of the Stanford Alumni Association and W. W. Norton & Co., Inc.

Steven Brill: "When Lawyers Help Villains." Reprinted with permission from the March 14, 1978 issue of *Esquire Fortnightly*.

Jacob Bronowski: From *The Common Sense of Science* (Cambridge, Mass.: Harvard University Press, 1966). Reprinted by permission of Harvard University Press and Heinemann Educational Books International, Ltd.

William F. Buckley, Jr.: "Capital Punishment," from *Execution Eve and Other Contemporary Ballads* by William F. Buckley, Jr. Copyright © 1972, 1973, 1974, 1975 by William F. Buckley, Jr. Reprinted by permission of G. P. Putnam's Sons.

Rachel Carson: "The Obligation to Endure," from *Silent Spring* by Rachel Carson. Copyright © 1962 by Rachel L. Carson. Reprinted by permission of Houghton Mifflin Company.

Bruce Catton: "Grant and Lee: A Study in Contrasts," from *The American Story*, edited by Earl Schenck Miers. Copyright © 1956 by Broadcast Music, Inc. Used by permission of the copyright holder.

Barry Curtis: "Two Jews" courtesy of Barry Curtis.

Magda Denes: From the Prologue of *In Necessity and Sorrow: Life and Death in an Abortion Hospital* by Magda Denes. Copyright © 1976 by Magda Denes, Basic Books, Inc., Publishers, New York.

Edwin S. Dethlefsen and Kenneth Jensen: Excerpt from "Social Commentary from the Cemetery." Excerpted from *Natural History Magazine*, June–July, 1977. Copyright © The American Museum of Natural History, 1977.

Annie Dillard: From pp. 13–19 of *Holy the Firm* by Annie Dillard. Copyright © 1977 by Annie Dillard. Reprinted by permission of Harper & Row, Publishers, Inc.

For Jack Neill

Preface

It was Edgar Allan Poe who said that a long poem does not exist. As editor of these readings for composition, I have kept in mind the unity of effect that Poe taught us to value. Most of the essays in this collection, therefore, are only two to four pages long, and even the longest—Alex Haley's "My Furthest-Back Person"—can be easily read in a single sitting.

It is misleading to talk about unity, however, when one is dealing with a fragment. Thus I have taken pains to gather *complete* essays or, in a few cases, *complete* chapters of books. Of the forty-three selections, thirty-three are reprinted in their entirety, including familiar ones like Petrunkevitch's "The Spider and the Wasp" that are usually anthologized with amputations. Seven essays are portions of longer works, but they represent the authors' own self-contained divisions. That leaves three excerpted by the editor (by Ephron, Farb, and Freuchen), and these have been chosen to stand alone without internal omission. In every case, needless to say, my first concern has been to find well-written essays that appeal to students with diverse backgrounds and interests.

The arrangement of selections is not intended to force the teacher into a lockstep but to suggest one way of proceeding. The first chapter provides sample paragraphs for teachers who like to discuss the parts of an essay before examining the kinds, and it also demonstrates the basic technique of explaining by examples. Of the traditional modes of discourse that organize the rest of the volume, narration comes first because these are personal narratives and many teachers may want to have students tell about their own lives in their first complete essays.

The next six chapters, the bulk of the book, illustrate strategies of exposition and can be taken up in any order, though here the plan has been to build from the simple (as I perceive it) to the more complex. For example: Chapter 5 ("Essays That Define") presents extended definitions that draw upon the techniques of classification and analysis discussed earlier.

Description is treated in a single chapter (Chapter 8) because this mode is seldom isolated from the others in practice; the teacher who requires more examples will find them throughout the collection. Chapters 9 and 10 are devoted to persuasion and argumentation, and they observe the classical division of persuasion into *logos, pathos,* and *ethos* (although I have not burdened the student with these terms). Some teachers will want to start here.

The questions after each selection are intended to help students understand what they are reading and especially to aid them in analyzing standard rhetorical strategies and techniques. The comparative questions—which invite students to make connections between essays—are an innovation; and so is the inclusion of student essays in full parity with those of the professionals. The "Essays for Further Reading" are more complicated, and generally longer, than the rest; but they too have been selected from a wide range of subjects. The editor has, therefore, resisted the temptation to make them exclusively—or even largely—"literary."

Many people have helped in the preparation of this reader, and it is a pleasure to name them here. Sheila P. Cooley, John Lauritsen, Paula Thompson, and members of the staff of W. W. Norton—especially my talented, long-suffering editor Barry Wade, Karen Fischer, and Susan Miller-Coulter—have devoted many hours to this project. The following colleagues, students, and friends at Ohio State have also been most helpful and kind: William Allen, Richard D. Altick, Daniel R. Barnes, Rita Bova, Betsy Brown, Gail Burke, Katherine Burkman, Candis Condo, Edward P. J. Corbett, Barry Curtis, Linda Dever, William Ellis, Ronald Fortune, Ann Forster, David O. Frantz, Paul Fullmer, John B. Gabel, Janet Gabler, Patricia Greiner, James Griffith, Douglas Haneline, Joel Herman, Katharine Hoch, Beth Hunker, Marilyn Kampe, Kathy Kiefer, Julian H. Markels, Susan Miller, Sigrid Milner, Betty Milum, Richard Milum, Patrick Moore, Mildred Munday, Sue Payne, W. N. Protheroe, David Robinson, Joan Samuelson, Arnold Shapiro, Frances Shapiro, Stephen Siegfried,

Pamela Transue, Nancy Tyson, Charles Wheeler, and Christian K. Zacher.

For the criticism and encouragement that guided me in the final stages of writing, I wish to thank the following: Judith Barnet, Cape Cod Community College; Richard Benston, Bakersfield College; Harry Brent, Rutgers University—Camden College of Arts and Sciences; Lois Bueler, Winona State University; Larry Carver, the University of Texas at Austin; John Cope, Western State College of Colorado; Charles B. Dodson, University of North Carolina at Wilmington; Betty Flowers, the University of Texas at Austin; Ramsey Fowler, Memphis State University; Barbara Goff, Rutgers University—Cook College; David Goslee, the University of Tennessee; William Gracie, Miami University; Joan Hartman, the College of Staten Island; Robert W. Hill, Clemson University; John Huxhold, Meramec Community College; Bernetta Jackson, Washington University; H. Gerald Joiner, Clayton Junior College; Russ Larson, Eastern Michigan University; Kristin Lauer, Fordham University; James MacKillop, Onondaga Community College; Catharine McCue, Framingham State College; John Mellon, University of Illinois at Chicago Circle; Tom Miles, West Virginia University; Robin Mitchell, Marquette University; James Murphy, California State University—Hayward; Elizabeth Penfield, University of New Orleans; Richard Poulsen, Brigham Young University; Kenn Sherwood Roe, Shasta College; Charles Schuster, the University of Iowa; Jayana Sheth, Baruch College; Susan Shreve, George Mason University; Lynne Shuster, Erie Community College; Donald Smith, University of New Haven; Tori Haring Smith, University of Illinois at Urbana-Champaign; Craig Snow, the University of Arizona; William Tucker, the University of North Carolina at Greensboro; John L. Vifian, Central Washington State College; and J. Peter Williams, County College of Morris.

Contents

Exposition

2. Essays That Classify and Divide

3. Essays That Analyze a Process

4. Essays That Analyze Cause and Effect   115

Introduction

Suppose that you went on a strenuous camping trip in the mountains, while all your friends decided to relax at the seashore. Suppose, also, that you got bored after two days without company and that you composed a letter inviting your best friend to forsake the surf and join you on the rocks. Your letter might contain the following elements:

— the story of your time on the road, your arrival in camp, and the events of the first two days, including an account of the skunk that got into your provisions;
— directions for getting there and a list of equipment, food, and clothes to bring;
— a description of your campsite, the yellow tent, the beautiful blue valley in the distance, and the crystal lake nearby;
— all the reasons why your friend should join you and why the mountains are preferable to the shore.

The four parts of your letter would conform to the four traditional MODES [1] (or "means") of writing: NARRATION, EXPOSITION, DESCRIPTION, and PERSUASION. The first part would be in the narrative mode. Narration is writing that tells a story; it records events, actions, adventures. It tells, in short, what happened. The part of your letter that gives directions is exposition. This is informative writing, or writing that explains. In this book, exposition receives more attention than the other modes because it is the one you are likely to use most often in the years to come. Examinations, term papers, insurance claims, job and graduate school applications, sales reports, almost every scrap of practical

[1] Terms printed in all capitals are defined in the Glossary.

1

prose you write over a lifetime, including your last will and testament, will demand expository skills.

The third part of your letter, of course, is description. This is the mode that captures how a person, thing, place, or idea looks, feels, sounds, or otherwise impresses the senses or the mind. The last part of your letter, the part designed to convince your friend to join you, is in the persuasive mode. Persuasion is writing that seeks assent, conveys advice, or moves the reader to action. In a sense, all writing is persuasion because the writer must convince the reader that what he or she says deserves to be heeded.

As our hypothetical letter to a friend suggests, the four modes of writing seldom appear in "pure" states. An accomplished writer is not likely to say, "Well I shall produce an expository definition today." The mode (or means) that a writer chooses will vary with his or her purpose (as in our letter). A writer may set out to define something and end up describing it or telling the story of its invention. Writers often mix the modes in actual practice, and you will find more than one essay in this collection that could be placed under a different heading.

Nevertheless, a single mode often dominates the others in any given essay. Furthermore, composing themes that largely narrate, explain, describe, or persuade is a valuable exercise toward learning to write well; and so is concentrating on a single strategy within a mode. A good piece of exposition, for example, may follow several methods of development; but before learning to combine, say, PROCESS ANALYSIS with DEFINITION it is useful to study each of these strategies independently. Therefore, the modes and strategies of writing have been separated in this book.

The narrative mode is exemplified in Chapter 1 ("Essays in the First Person Singular"). The next six chapters (2–7) give examples of the common strategies of exposition: CLASSIFICATION, PROCESS ANALYSIS, CAUSE AND EFFECT, DEFINITION, COMPARISON AND CONTRAST, METAPHOR AND ANALOGY. Chapter 8 ("Essays That Appeal to the Senses") is a collection of descriptive writing. Chapter 9 ("Essays That Appeal to Reason") and Chapter 10 ("Essays That Appeal to Emotion and Ethics") present examples of the different strategies of persuasion. At the end of the book you will find a collection of "Essays for Further Reading."

No one expects you to imitate word for word these highly finished productions of professional writers (though you may well emulate some of the student writing included here). But you can analyze standard rhetorical devices and techniques and so learn to use them in your own writing.

By RHETORIC, as the term will be applied in these pages, we mean "the art of using language effectively"—both in writing and in reading. A skilled writer is usually a skilled reader, in fact. The patterns of words on the written page (and of the sounds those words stand for) lodge themselves in the reader's head. When the writer puts pen to paper, therefore, he or she has a store of patterns to impose upon his or her own black marks. A writer learns some patterns of language by hearing them used orally. But others—such as the printed alphabet—can only be learned by reading.

The purpose of this collection of readings, then, is that set forth by Mark Twain in "The Art of Authorship." Attempting to analyze his own methods of composition, Twain found that "whenever we read a sentence and like it, we unconsciously store it away in our model-chamber; and it goes with a myriad of its fellows to the building, brick, by brick, of the eventual edifice which we call our style. And let us guess that whenever we run across other forms— bricks—whose color, or some other defect, offends us, we unconsciously reject these, and so one never finds them in our edifice."

This is a book of prose forms. Each essay offers proven rhetorical designs that you can store away in your "model-chamber," ready at hand whenever you have a verbal edifice to construct. Such a collection provides this further advantage over reading at random: the defective bricks have already been discarded for you.

Paragraphs for Analysis

Beginning with Chapter 1, this book presents entire essays. Since an essay, like a stereo system, is made up of integrated components, however, you may want to start with the following model paragraphs, included here for two purposes. First, they illustrate the standard ways in which paragraphs function and develop. We begin with an introductory paragraph from the opening of an essay that appears complete in a later chapter. It is followed by a TRANSITION [1] paragraph and a concluding paragraph; but the "parent" essays are not included, so you will have to surmise what has gone before or after. The last four selections, each lifted from the main body of its parent essay, illustrate various methods of paragraph development. They are arranged in order of increasing complexity.

The second purpose of these sample paragraphs is to show how good writers use specific examples to help explain their ideas. When John McPhee says that the history of Florida is measured in freezes, he backs up this claim by citing the good people of Keystone City during the Great Freeze of 1895. When William Allen defines "style" by telling how he combed his hair in high school, this concrete example gives us a tight grip on a slippery subject. Selected for their use of lively examples like these, the following paragraphs isolate, for careful study, a basic strategy of informative and persuasive writing that you will encounter in almost every essay in this book.

The traditional definition of a paragraph is a group of

---

[1] Terms printed in all capitals are defined in the Glossary.

related sentences on the same topic. This definition suggests two important facts about paragraphs in general. One is that paragraphs build up by a process of addition. A paragraph combines two or more statements into a unit of thought. That unit is the sum of its parts, for no single part carries the entire meaning of the paragraph in all its complexity.

The other fundamental aspect of paragraphs is suggested by that word related in our definition. The sentences in a paragraph must stand in some recognizable relation to one another. If you combine the last sentence of each chapter in this book and, after indenting, run them all together on the same page, you will assemble only a cluster of unrelated sentences, hardly a paragraph. A good paragraph develops a topic in some systematic way. It can unfold in chronological order (as in NARRATIVE writing). It can develop spatially (as in DESCRIPTION), ranging over an object from left to right, top to bottom, front to back. Or, in EXPOSITORY writing, a paragraph can progress from step to step of a logical ARGUMENT, by assertion and example, COMPARISON AND CONTRAST, CAUSE AND EFFECT, statement and restatement.

The movement of a paragraph depends upon what it says. However, that movement can be traced through grammatical clues. These are often connecting words like and, but, although, therefore, on the other hand, moreover, now, consequently, and for example. But they may also be verbs (or other parts of speech): conclude, infer, imply, disagree. Such words glance backward to statements that the writer has entertained for a moment and forward to statements that complete, qualify, or deny what has gone before. In the following paragraphs, look for grammatical clues that can help you analyze how each paragraph is organized. An understanding of the basic principles of paragraph structure is a big step toward writing well-organized paragraphs of your own.

Alexander Petrunkevitch

Intelligence vs. Instinct

Alexander Petrunkevitch (1875–1964) was a Yale professor of zoology and one of the world's leading experts on spiders. "Intelligence vs. Instinct" (editor's title) is a paragraph from his essay, "The Spider and the Wasp," reprinted in its entirety and with more information about the author in Chapter 3 ("Essays That Analyze a Process"). This model introductory paragraph comes near the beginning of its parent essay and sets up much of what follows. Notice that it makes a clear general statement of the author's subject but only hints at details. The author is showing his hand and then taking it up again, ready to play his cards one by one. The study questions following this and each selection in these pages should help you to understand not only what an author is saying but how it is said.

In the feeding and safeguarding of their progeny the insects and spiders exhibit some interesting analogies to reasoning and some crass examples of blind instinct. The case I propose to describe here is that of the tarantula spiders and their arch-enemy, the digger wasps of the genus Pepsis. It is a classic example of what looks like intelligence pitted against instinct—a strange situation in which the victim, though fully able to defend itself, submits unwittingly to its destruction.

QUESTIONS

Understanding

1. Why do the wasps and spiders that Petrunkevitch is going to discuss fight each other?
2. What *human* qualities does their combat display?

Strategies and Structure

1. You cannot be sure until you have seen this paragraph in the context of its parent essay, but which sentence appears to be the TOPIC SENTENCE (the one that states the author's main subject most precisely)?
2. Is the author's main topic developed fully here or merely stated for future development? Explain your answer.
3. From this paragraph, we know that the loser in the combat between wasp and spider is destroyed, but we do not know which insect is the victim. Why might the author not want to tell us in an introductory paragraph like this one?

4. What aspect of the "case" of spider and wasp is likely to receive most of the author's attention in the essay to come? How does this paragraph anticipate that interest?

Words and Figures of Speech

1. Consult your dictionary for the definition of *progeny* if you do not already know the word.
2. What is an ANALOGY?

Comparing

1. When you read "The Spider and the Wasp" in Chapter 3 (or you may want to take a peek now), see if your answers to the "Strategies and Structure" questions were reasonably accurate.

Discussion and Writing Topics

1. Write a paragraph describing an insect or animal doing something that seems to exhibit human intelligence. For example: a raccoon opening a garbage can.

Shana Alexander
Fashions in Funerals

Born in New York City in 1925, Shana Alexander is a journalist and broadcaster. Since attending Vassar College, she has worked as an editor for Harper's Bazaar, Flair, Life, McCall's, Newsweek, and other publications. As a radio and television commentator for CBS News, she has appeared on "Spectrum" and "60 Minutes." Her books include The Feminine Eye (1970) and Talking Woman (1976), the source of the following passage. It is a TRANSITION paragraph from an essay comparing the funeral customs of cannibals with those in Nashville, Tennessee, home of the high-rise mausoleum and drive-in funeral. With the aid of the study questions, see if you can read Alexander's clues to what comes before and after.

When word of the feast reached civilization, the authorities concluded that on this occasion justice had literally been served, and perhaps a bit too swiftly, so they hauled the seven cannibals into court, where a wise Australian judge dismissed all the charges, and acquitted the seven men. "The funerary customs of the people of Papua and New Guinea," he explained, "have been, and in many cases remain, bizarre in the extreme."

QUESTIONS

Understanding

1. Why does the Australian judge dismiss the charges against the cannibals?
2. What is Shana Alexander's opinion of the judge's decision?

Strategies and Structure

1. What incident has Alexander probably just described in the essay from which this transition paragraph is taken? Point out the clues by which she suggests what has gone before.
2. You cannot tell from this paragraph that the author will later discuss funeral customs in Nashville, but the paragraph does anticipate a comparison between the customs of "civilized" society and those of primitive society. How? By what signals does it alert us to such a comparison?
3. Do you think the author of this paragraph will go on to write an essay that shows the superiority of modern civilization over primitive "savagery" or one that shows such terms to be relative, open to judgment? Explain your answer by referring to specific words and phrases in the paragraph.

Words and Figures of Speech

1. What are the CONNOTATIONS of *bizarre*?
2. Explain the pun in Alexander's first sentence.

Comparing

1. How does the TONE of this paragraph differ from Petrunkevitch's tone in the preceding paragraph?

Discussion and Writing Topics

1. Write a paragraph explaining a funeral custom you consider bizarre and pointing forward or backward to an example of its observance that you do not actually describe.

Roger Angell

Time Out

> A native of New York City and graduate of Harvard (A.B., 1942), Roger Angell has been a sportswriter and editor for The New Yorker since 1956. Author of The Stone Arbor and Other Stories (1960) and A Day in the Life of Roger Angell (1970), a collection of humorous sketches, he has also written The Summer Game (1972), a book on baseball and the American mind. "Time Out" (editor's title) appears at the end of The Summer Game. It is a model concluding paragraph that recalls and rounds out what has gone before. Again, look for the signals that help us identify its context.

The last dimension is time. Within the ballpark, time moves differently, marked by no clock except the events of the game. This is the unique, unchangeable feature of baseball, and perhaps explains why this sport, for all the enormous changes it has undergone in the past decade or two, remains somehow rustic, unviolent, and introspective. Baseball's time is seamless and invisible, a bubble within which players move at exactly the same pace and rhythms as all their predecessors. This is the way the game was played in our youth and in our fathers' youth, and even back then—back in the country days—there must have been the same feeling that time could be stopped. Since baseball time is measured only in outs, all you have to do is succeed utterly; keep hitting, keep the rally alive, and you have defeated time. You remain forever young. Sitting in the stands, we sense this, if only dimly. The players below us—Mays, DiMaggio, Ruth, Snodgrass—swim and blur in memory, the ball floats over to Terry Turner, and the end of this game may never come.

QUESTIONS

Understanding

1. What is unique about the rules of baseball as Angell describes it? How does baseball differ from football and basketball in this regard?
2. Willie Mays entered the major leagues in 1951; Joseph Paul DiMaggio in 1936; George Herman Ruth in 1914; Fred Carlisle (Snow) Snodgrass in 1908; and Terence Lamont ("Cotton Top") Turner in 1901. Why do you think Angell's paragraph goes backward in time like this?
3. Where does "this game" in the final sentence take place? What implications does such a game hold for the individual baseball fan?

Strategies and Structure

1. What has Angell been discussing prior to these closing remarks? How does he let us know?
2. How does Angell create a sense of an ending in this concluding paragraph? Point to specific words and phrases that suggest finality.
3. What is the effect of Angell's referring to the reader as "you" in the closing sentences of the paragraph?

Words and Figures of Speech

1. What are the CONNOTATIONS of *rustic* (sentence 3)? How does Angell's use of this word help to define *country* two sentences earlier?
2. Why is *floats* (last sentence) appropriate in its context? What other verbs in the sentence does it resemble?
3. Because it is unbroken, Angell likens baseball's time to a "bubble"; what else does this ANALOGY suggest?

Comparing

1. When you read Michael Rogers's "Portrait of the Newlyweds as a Young Hologram" (Chapter 5), compare his treatment of time with Angell's.

Discussion and Writing Topics

1. If successful batting stops time by (theoretically) prolonging a baseball game forever, what is the *pitcher's* role with regard to time? Write a paragraph describing that role.

2. What is the spectator's role at a baseball or football game? Are the players the fans' heroes or their scapegoats?

3. Unlike baseball as Angell describes it, professional football is neither "unviolent" nor "introspective." What does the tremendous popularity of football say about the changes in American culture since "the country days"?

Magda Denes

In an Abortion Hospital

Magda Denes is a clinical psychologist in private practice in New York City. At Yeshiva University (Ph.D., 1961) and New York University, she received training in Gestalt therapy, group therapy, and psychoanalysis. The mother of two children, she has also had first-hand experience with abortion. "In an Abortion Hospital" (editor's title) is from the preface of her recent book, In Necessity and Sorrow: Life and Death in an Abortion Hospital (1976). The paragraph is structured by placing its component sentences "in parallel" with one another, a basic form of paragraph development.

In some ways I am an exceptionally privileged woman of thirty-seven. I am in the room of a private, legal abortion hospital, where a surgeon, a friend of many years, is waiting for me in the operating room. I am only five weeks pregnant. Last week I walked out of another hospital, unaborted, because I had suddenly changed my mind. I have a husband who cares for me. He yells because my indecisiveness makes him anxious, but basically he has permitted the final choice to rest in my hands: "It would be very tough, especially for you, and it is absolutely insane, but yes, we could have another baby." I have a mother who cares. I have two young sons, whose small faces are the most moving arguments I have against going through with this abortion. I have a doctorate in psychology, which, among other advantages, assures me of the professional courtesy of special passes in hospitals, passes that at this moment enable my husband and my mother to stand in my room at a nonvisiting hour and yell at each other over my head while I sob.

QUESTIONS

Understanding

1. Why is the woman described in this paragraph stalling? What is her state of mind?
2. What clues does Denes give to suggest that the woman will not go through with the abortion on the occasion reported here?
3. What is the significance of the patient's having a doctorate in psychology? In what ways are her "privileges" irrelevant?

Strategies and Structure

1. The basic strategy of this paragraph is simple addition; it gives all ideas roughly equal weight by giving them parallel form. Point out (or underline) every use of "I am" or "I have" in the paragraph.
2. In which two sentences does Denes *not* follow this basic sentence pattern?
3. How does she vary the basic pattern (while still maintaining it) in the second and last sentences of the paragraph?
4. Given that the patient here is badly upset, why might Denes choose to relate her thoughts in a seemingly simple order?
5. How does the way the author organizes this paragraph show that she was in a different state of mind when she wrote it than when she was in the hospital?
6. Why is *sob* placed at the end of this paragraph? How would our response to the whole paragraph be different if this one word were placed, say, at the beginning?

Words and Figures of Speech

1. Why is the clinical term *unaborted* more appropriate here than words like *unsullied* or *undefiled*?

2. We are told that the faces of the author's two children are "moving arguments" against abortion. Faces are not literally arguments, but how might they inspire this METAPHOR?

Comparing

1. What fundamental difference do you see between the organization of this paragraph and that of the next one, by Jacob Bronowski?

Discussion and Writing Topics

1. Do you consider abortion an open or closed issue? If you think abortion is permissible under certain circumstances, what are they?
2. Why is the age of a fetus an important consideration in legal, religious, and personal debates about abortion? Should it be?
3. Feminists argue that a woman's body is hers to control. How does the abortion issue enter into this argument?

Jacob Bronowski

The Process of Learning

Polish-born Jacob Bronowski (1908–1974) was trained as a mathematician at Cambridge University. He taught at Oxford and other British universities, and in 1964 became resident fellow and trustee of the Salk Institute for Biological Studies in California. Interested throughout his life in the relation between the arts and science, he was a playwright, a radio commentator, an expert on the poet William Blake, and the author of many books, including Science and Human Values (1958); Insight (1964); and The Identity of Man (1965). The following paragraph (with editor's title) is from The Common Sense of Science (1951); it demonstrates another basic form of paragraph development.

The process of learning is essential to our lives. All higher animals seek it deliberately. They are inquisitive and they experiment. An experiment is a sort of harmless trial run of some action which we shall have to make in the real world; and this, whether it is made in the laboratory by scientists or by fox-cubs outside their earth. The scientist experiments and the cub plays; both are learning to correct their errors of judgement in a setting in which errors are not fatal. Perhaps this is what gives them both their air of happiness and freedom in these activities.

QUESTIONS

Understanding

1. What is an experiment as defined by Bronowski?
2. How do experiments, according to him, contribute to the process of learning?

Strategies and Structure

1. What is the TOPIC SENTENCE of this paragraph?
2. Do the other sentences in the paragraph repeat the idea of the topic sentence or narrow it down? Explain your answer.
3. Point out individual words that help to tie one of Bronowski's sentences to another because they appear in both sentences. How does Bronowski differ from Denes (preceding paragraph) in the use of this device of organization?
4. Given the flow of Bronowski's ideas from one sentence to another, why could he *not* have adopted the parallel form of the paragraph by Denes?

Words and Figures of Speech

1. Look up the root meaning of *experiment* in your dictionary. How does it fit the learning process that Bronowski describes?

Comparing

1. What does the structure of this paragraph have in common with the paragraph by Magda Denes? In what sense do both proceed by addition?
2. How do the "units" that Bronowski is adding together differ from those in Denes's paragraph?

Discussion and Writing Topics

1. Bronowski explains how men and animals test their judgment.
   How do they show their mutual "inquisitiveness" or curiosity?

John McPhee

Orange Freeze

Born in 1931, John McPhee is a native of Princeton, New Jersey,
and a graduate of Princeton University, where he sometimes
teaches creative writing. Most of the time, however, he is a
magazine staff writer and editor for, among others, The New
Yorker, Time, Holiday, National Geographic, and Playboy. Known
for his precise style and wide range of interests, he has written a
number of books, including A Sense of Where You Are (1965);
The Pine Barrens (1968); The Crofter and the Laird (1969); The
Deltoid Pumpkin Seed (1973, a study of experimental aircraft);
The Survival of the Bark Canoe (1975); and Coming into the
Country (1978). "Orange Freeze" (editor's title) appeared in
Oranges (1967). This paragraph has a more complex organization
than the two preceeding paragraphs because it combines the
methods of both.

The history of Florida is measured in freezes. Severe ones, for
example, occurred in 1747, 1766, and 1774. The freeze of February, 1835, was probably the worst one in the state's history. But,
because more growers were affected, the Great Freeze of 1895
seems to enjoy the same sort of status in Florida that the Blizzard
of '88 once held in the North. Temperatures on the Ridge on
February 8, 1895, went into the teens for much of the night. It
is said that some orange growers, on being told what was happen-
ing out in the groves, got up from their dinner tables and left the
state. In the morning, it was apparent that the Florida citrus
industry had been virtually wiped out. The groves around Keystone City, in Polk County, however, went through the freeze of
1895 without damage. Slightly higher than anything around it
and studded with sizable lakes, Keystone City became famous,
and people from all over the Ridge came to marvel at this Garden

of Eden in the middle of the new wasteland. The citizens of
Keystone City changed the name of their town to Frostproof.

QUESTIONS

Understanding

1. Who (besides McPhee) measures the history of Florida in
   freezes? Why?
2. Why does McPhee mention the lakes around Keystone City?
3. What does their choice of a new name tell you about the citizens
   of that town?

Strategies and Structure

1. What is McPhee's TOPIC SENTENCE? How many examples does he
   give in support of it?
2. Point out the three sentences by which McPhee narrows down his
   initial idea (as Bronowski does in "The Process of Learning").
3. How do these three sentences stand in relation to *each other*? Are
   they on a par in meaning and in form (as in the paragraph by
   Magda Denes on abortion) or are some more narrow than others?
   Explain your answer.
4. What proposition, or statement, do sentences 5–7 illustrate?
5. Are the last three complete sentences of this paragraph "in parallel" (as in the Denes paragraph) or "in sequence" (as in the
   Bronowski paragraph)? Explain your answer.
6. How has McPhee shifted his focus by the end of this selection?
   From what to what? Is this a legitimate maneuver? Why or why
   not?

Words and Figures of Speech

1. How does McPhee's calling Keystone City a "Garden of Eden"
   contribute to the sense of the miraculous in the town's escape
   from the great freeze?

Comparing

1. How is McPhee's use of history and the past different from Roger
   Angell's in "Time Out"?

Discussion and Writing Topics

1. How did your hometown or county get its name? Is there an interesting history behind that name or the name of any other town in which you have lived?

William Allen

Haircut

A native of Texas, William Allen is a writer, teacher, and holder of the world's record for stationary broom-balancing. (His mastery of this event is described in "How to Set a World Record" reprinted in Chapter 3 along with more biographical information about Allen.) "Haircut" (editor's title) is from the book, Stark-weather (1976); it recalls the author's coming-of-age in the 1950s. Here is another example of the "mixed" paragraph development that places some sentences "in parallel" and others "in sequence." Most paragraphs, in fact, combine these two basic forms of organization.

My teen-age days were more style than substance. My friends and I realized at an early age the power and status of having an automobile, and I worked hard and saved my money to buy one. Within weeks after I got my 1953 Ford, it was shaved hood and deck, lowered in back, had pinstripes, twin glass-pack mufflers, skirts, Oldsmobile taillights, and a rolled and pleated interior. It was one of the better-looking cars in South Oak Cliff and, by doing things like occasionally skipping school and racking my pipes outside the classroom windows, I built an identity around it. Just as my car looked good but wasn't "hot," I spent more of my energy trying to look cool rather than being tough. We were all fanatics about our hair, working on it in the school restrooms until our arms grew weak. I plastered mine with Brylcreem and combed it in a weird, complicated style that Charlie [1] himself often wore. I can't tell you where the aesthetic sense came from

[1] Charles Starkweather, executed 12:04 A.M., June 25, 1959, for the murder of ten Nebraskans in eight days.

that developed that hairdo, but it was absolute and I was in accord with it. Using my comb and both hands, I would work till I was ready to collapse—then finally it would be just right, a work of art. During those days I walked around like I had a book on my head, and was a master at avoiding areas likely to generate sudden gusts of wind.

QUESTIONS

Understanding

1. What distinction can you make between a hairdo and hair? How might this distinction help you define the concept of style?
2. What does it mean to say that something has more style than substance?
3. Why does Allen end with a reference to the wind?

Strategies and Structure

1. This paragraph develops its topic by use of examples. What is Allen's TOPIC SENTENCE, and what are the two chief examples he uses to illustrate it?
2. Which sentence provides a TRANSITION from one example to the other?
3. Are the sentences explaining the first example arranged "in parallel" or "in sequence"?
4. How are the sentences arranged that explain the second example?
5. If you were breaking up Allen's paragraph into two paragraphs, where would you divide it? Would this division be an improvement? Why or why not?

Words and Figures of Speech

1. What does *style* mean when applied to writing?
2. What is an "aesthetic" sense? Look the word up in your dictionary. How is it different from *ascetic*?

Comparing

1. Both "Haircut" and "In an Abortion Hospital" incorporate ele-

ments of personal NARRATIVE (the kind of writing you will study in Chapter 1). Point out some of the narrative aspects of the two.

Discussion and Writing Topics

1. How was style achieved and measured in your high school?
2. What happened to those who could not keep up with the styles for lack of money or "coolness"?
3. Can you recall classmates who had substance that outweighed style? What were they like? (For an essay on this subject, see Ellen Willis's "Memoirs of a Non-Prom Queen" in Chapter 4.)
4. Do you find any evidence to suggest that the automobile is declining as a status symbol in America? What others seem to be going strong?

Narration

1

Essays in the First Person Singular

NARRATION [1] *is the story-telling mode of writing; it recounts actions and events; it answers the question, "What happened?" The essays in this chapter are written in the narrative mode. They are personal narratives in which each author records experiences from his or her private life.*

One reason for beginning with personal narratives is suggested by Henry David Thoreau's famous opening words in Walden:

In most books, the I, or first person, is omitted; in this it will be retained; that, in respect to egotism, is the main difference. We commonly do not remember that it is, after all, always the first person that is speaking. I should not talk so much about myself if there were anybody else whom I knew as well. . . . Moreover, I, on my side, require of every writer, first or last, a simple and sincere account of his own life. . . .

The common feature of these openly autobiographical selections is the controlling presence of a distinct personality—like yours. You may not think that you know yourself well, but whom do you know better?

Another reason for beginning with personal narratives is that essays have always been personal. Our modern word essay *comes from the French* essayer, *meaning "to try." An essay is your personal trial or attempt to grapple with a subject or problem. Yours and nobody else's. Another person addressing the same subject would necessarily speak in a different voice from a different perspective. Because they*

[1] Terms printed in all capitals are defined in the Glossary.

23

invited readers to listen in (like informal guests in the writer's living room), these modest attempts at self-expression became known as "personal" or "familiar" essays.

Any writer who gives an account of his or her own experiences must understand the difference between events and the telling of events. Think of actions as sounds for a moment—the sounds of a college band playing the national anthem. When the band strikes up "Oh, say can you see," your ear hears trombones, trumpets, and drums all in a single harmonious strain. If you were to look at the written parts of the different instruments in their music-holders, however, you would have to separate them. You might follow a single bar of trombone music, then race over to the trumpet section, then back to the drums. But you would be alternating between parts, as the readers of a book must do when his or her eyes move from left to right and down the printed page. Events in real life often occur simultaneously; in a written narrative, they must be printed in sequence.

The sequence of events in a narrative is called the PLOT; unlike random events in real life, the plot of a narrative must be controlled and directed by the narrator. So must the POINT OF VIEW. Point of view is the vantage from which a narrative is told. It is not a difficult concept to master if you think of the difference between watching a football game in the stadium and watching it on television. The camera controls your point of view on the screen; you see only what the camera focuses upon. In the stands, however, you are free to scan the entire field, to watch the quarterback or the line, to concentrate on the cheerleaders. Your point of view is determined by your eyes alone; your vantage is a high place above the total action.

In narration, point of view is controlled in part by the grammatical PERSON in which an author chooses to write. Many narratives are told "in the third person" or "from the third-person point of view." For example, you might write: "The tornado hit while George was playing cards; he had just drawn a third ace, but when he plunked it down, the table was gone." Here the narrator and George are different persons; the narrator does not say how George felt inside at the crucial moment; the story is told after the fact and from the outside (of George). The essays in this chapter are "first-person" narratives, the point of view you would adopt in an autobiography or an account of your adventures during the first day of your college career. Here the "I" is an actor in each drama, and we see the world of the narrative through the narrator's eyes.

Authors of narrative essays in the first person have great freedom: they may record their personal thoughts on anything that has happened to them. As attested by master essayist E. B. White (whose "Once More to the Lake" appears at the end of this volume), "There is one thing the essayist cannot do, though—he cannot indulge himself in deceit or in concealment, for he will be found out in no time." Modern readers of essays, like Thoreau, require a "simple and sincere account"—the sincerity that comes of personal integrity and the simplicity that comes from discipline. The essayist may wander at will, but may not ramble. He or she may be relaxed, even self-indulgent. But if the reader can not follow along because the essayist writes obscurely or is dishonest, their partnership will be disbanded. And this is what a personal essay amounts to, finally—a friendly partnership between reader and author.

Loren Eiseley

The Angry Winter

Born in Lincoln, Nebraska, in 1907, Loren Eiseley was a distinguished anthropologist and sociologist. After graduate work at
the University of Pennsylvania, he taught there for twelve years
before becoming Franklin Professor of Anthropology and History
of Science in 1961. The recipient of more than a dozen honorary
degrees from universities throughout the U.S. and Canada, he also
taught at the University of Kansas, Oberlin College, Columbia,
Berkeley, and Harvard. Eiseley's major works include The Immense Journey (1957); Darwin's Century (1958); The Firmament
of Time (1960); The Mind as Nature (1962); and The Invisible
Pyramid (1970). The following personal narrative is the complete
Part 1, Chapter 5, of The Unexpected Universe (1969). It recalls
a deep winter's conflict between the author and his dog. The
volume bears the following dedication: "To Wolf, who sleeps
forever with an ice age bone across his heart, the last gift of one
who loved him."

A time comes when creatures whose destinies have crossed
somewhere in the remote past are forced to appraise each
other as though they were total strangers. I had been huddled
beside the fire one winter night, with the wind prowling outside and shaking the windows. The big shepherd dog on the
hearth before me occasionally glanced up affectionately,
sighed, and slept. I was working, actually, amidst the debris
of a far greater winter. On my desk lay the lance point of ice
age hunters and the heavy leg bone of a fossil bison. No remnants of flesh attached to these relics. The deed lay more than
ten thousand years remote. It was represented here by naked
flint and by bone so mineralized it rang when struck. As I

worked in my little circle of light, I absently laid the bone beside me on the floor. The hour had crept toward midnight. A grating noise, a heavy rasping of big teeth diverted me. I looked down.

The dog had risen. That rock-hard fragment of a vanished beast   2
was in his jaws and he was mouthing it with a fierce intensity I had never seen exhibited by him before.

"Wolf," I exclaimed, and stretched out my hand. The dog   3
backed up but did not yield. A low and steady rumbling began to rise in his chest, something out of a long-gone midnight. There was nothing in that bone to taste, but ancient shapes were moving in his mind and determining his utterance. Only fools gave up bones. He was warning me.

"Wolf," I chided again.   4

As I advanced, his teeth showed and his mouth wrinkled to   5
strike. The rumbling rose to a direct snarl. His flat head swayed low and wickedly as a reptile's above the floor. I was the most loved object in his universe, but the past was fully alive in him now. Its shadows were whispering in his mind. I knew he was not bluffing. If I made another step he would strike.

Yet his eyes were strained and desperate. "Do not," something   6
pleaded in the back of them, some affectionate thing that had followed at my heel all the days of his mortal life, "do not force me. I am what I am-and cannot be otherwise because of the shadows. Do not reach out. You are a man, and my very god. I love you, but do not put out your hand. It is midnight. We are in another time, in the snow."

"The *other* time," the steady rumbling continued while I   7
paused, "the other time in the snow, the big, the final, the terrible snow, when the shape of this thing I hold spelled life. I will not give it up. I cannot. The shadows will not permit me. Do not put out your hand."

I stood silent, looking into his eyes, and heard his whisper   8
through. Slowly I drew back in understanding. The snarl diminished, ceased. As I retreated, the bone slumped to the floor. He placed a paw upon it, warningly.

And were there no shadows in my own mind, I wondered. Had   9
I not for a moment, in the grip of that savage utterance, been about to respond, to hurl myself upon him over an invisible haunch ten thousand years removed? Even to me the shadows had whispered—to me, the scholar in his study.

"Wolf," I said, but this time, holding a familiar leash, I spoke   10
from the door indifferently. "A walk in the snow." Instantly from
his eyes that other visitant receded. The bone was left lying. He
came eagerly to my side, accepting the leash and taking it in his
mouth as always.

A blizzard was raging when we went out, but he paid no heed.   11
On his thick fur the driving snow was soon clinging heavily. He
frolicked a little—though usually he was a grave dog—making up
to me for something still receding in his mind. I felt the snow-
flakes fall upon my face, and stood thinking of another time, and
another time still, until I was moving from midnight to midnight
under ever more remote and vaster snows. Wolf came to my side
with a little whimper. It was he who was civilized now. "Come
back to the fire," he nudged gently, "or you will be lost." Automatically I took the leash he offered. He led me safely home and
into the house.

"We have been very far away," I told him solemnly. "I think   12
there is something in us that we had both better try to forget."
Sprawled on the rug, Wolf made no response except to thump his
tail feebly out of courtesy. Already he was mostly asleep and
dreaming. By the movement of his feet I could see he was running
far upon some errand in which I played no part.

Softly I picked up his bone—our bone, rather—and replaced it   13
high on a shelf in my cabinet. As I snapped off the light the white
glow from the window seemed to augment itself and shine with a
deep, glacial blue. As far as I could see, nothing moved in the
long aisles of my neighbor's woods. There was no visible track,
and certainly no sound from the living. The snow continued to
fall steadily, but the wind, and the shadows it had brought, had
vanished.

QUESTIONS

Understanding

1. Who are the "creatures" of Eiseley's first sentence?
2. What "other time" is he talking about in paragraphs 6 and 7?
   Why was the "terrible" snow also "final" (par. 7)?
3. Apparently the dog in Eiseley's narrative is not hungry, because

he goes to sleep easily after playing. Why, then, does he snarl over a fossilized bone that he could not eat even if he wanted to?

4. What is it that both dog and man should try to forget in paragraph 12?

Strategies and Structure

1. The dog's resistance to the man (pars. 5–8) is one of the two principal actions in Eiseley's narrative. What is the other? Where is it narrated?

2. In Eiseley's little drama, setting and lighting effects are very important. What are the chief *places* of his narrative, and how do they serve him? How do the desklamp and the powerful "white glow" of the snow contribute to the real conflict of the drama?

3. Where does that drama actually take place?

4. What is the function of the leash in paragraph 11?

5. How is the man who tells this story different from the man it is told about?

6. As the narrator, Eiseley has the difficult task of portraying the thoughts of an animal. How does he solve this difficulty?

7. Why does Eiseley end by referring to his neighbor's woods and the vanished shadows?

Words and Figures of Speech

1. Why is "Wolf" an appropriate name for the dog in Eiseley's narrative?

2. There are literal shadows on the snow outside the scholar's window, but what are the "shadows" that flit through his mind and the mind of the dog?

3. Why might Eiseley picture himself as "huddled" by the fire while the wind is "prowling" outside (par. 1)? How does this METAPHOR fit in with the rest of the narrative?

4. What are the CONNOTATIONS of "glacial" in paragraph 13? Why do you suppose Eiseley chose this word instead of "diamond" or "ice" blue?

5. He does not use the word, but how might *instinct* be applied in a discussion of Eiseley's narrative?

6. Consult your dictionary for the meanings of any of the following words that are not familiar to you: *destiny* (par. 1), *appraise* (1), *debris* (1), *chide* (4), *visitant* (10), *augment* (13).

Comparing

1. Eiseley's personal narrative tells a story, but it also explains one cause of human (and animal) aggression. When you study CAUSE AND EFFECT essays in Chapter 4, compare Eiseley's essay with Reynolds Price's "Summer Games."

Discussion and Writing Topics

1. Tell the story of an occasion on which you almost "lost your head." Recount the events leading up to the incident in such a way as to suggest *why* you acted as you did.

2. It was once thought that criminals were throwbacks to man's animalistic ancestors. What do you think of this explanation for criminal behavior? Do you suppose Eiseley would accept it? Why or why not?

3. What is the "collective unconscious" posited by some modern psychologists?

4. What is a cultural anthropologist? What does he or she study?

David Dubber

Crossing the Bar on a Fiberglas Pole

David Dubber was a freshman at Indiana University when he wrote this account of breaking a collegiate pole-vaulting record. He graduated in 1967 with a B.S. in business, and now lives with his family in Evansville, Indiana. A professional writer in the public relations and advertising division of a large pharmaceutical company, Dubber recently began working on "an American fictional novel."

A one hundred foot asphalt runway leads to a metal shoot   1
and metal standards and a crossbar. Behind the shoot rises
a pile of foam rubber scraps. This is the pole vaulting field at
the 1963 S. I. A. C. (Southern Indiana Athletic Conference)
Track and Field Meet. The stands are filled.

The meet is over but the crowd has stayed to watch the   2
finish of the pole-vaulting event. There are two television
cameras trying to squeeze in just one more Double Cola com-
mercial before swinging back to tape the last of the vaulting
event. The crossbar has been raised to thirteen feet, six inches,
nearly a foot higher than the old, long-standing record. It is
my job—it seems my duty since I have kept the crowd—to
gather my strength into one single attempt to propel my body
up and over that crossbar with the aid of my fiberglas pole.
Many times lately I have heard people debating whether or
not the pliable fiberglas pole should be allowed in competition. People say that one has only to "hang on to the thing
and it will throw you to any desired height."

These recollections bring me much bitterness as I stand   3 before my trial. I am developing a fatalistic attitude toward this towering height and wish I had never come out for track, or at least I wish I had never heard of this silly "bending" pole. But it is too late to untwine this tightly woven cord; the crowd is waiting. I completely dismiss distracting thoughts and put all my powers, mental and physical, into this one leap.

Mentally I run through the particulars of the vault. I have   4 counted my steps down to the tape mark on the runway where my left foot is to hit the runway for the last time. I must remember to keep my body loose to conserve strength. I must also remember to strike my left foot on the mark hard enough to give me a four-foot jump on the pole before switching my balance and strength to my hands; otherwise I will not get off the ground. It must be a quick and trained reflex that is well routed in the grooves of my mind.

Now the crowd is dead silent. I count ten as I leave the world—   5 seeing only the runway and crossbar directly ahead, believing only that I will succeed in clearing the bar, hearing only the beating of my own heart. Slowly I begin an easy jog down the runway as the pole I cling to bounces slightly in front of me in a syncopation of my steps. Gradually my speed picks up until my body attains a swift glide. The tip of the pole descends as I approach the shoot. Although my main concern is making good contact between the end of my pole and the shoot, I am also watching the tape marking. After a few years practice, a vaulter learns to compensate for any misjudgment the last few strides before he reaches the shoot. Through some inexplicable mechanism the vaulter's sub-conscious tells his body how much to shorten or lengthen the stride in order to hit the take-off mark. Just as the tip of my pole touches the backstop of the shoot, I push the pole straight forward and with one final bound I smack the pavement with the ball of my left foot and straighten my half bent left leg with a great thrust to give me my height on the pole.

All my weight shifts to my hands, and as the angle of the pole   6 increases toward the vertical, my body climbs to about three-fourths the height of the crossbar. As I come up I throw my head back toward the ground causing my hips to sweep upward until my feet pass through my line of vision and on, one foot further, so that I am now completely upside down. The pole bends suddenly to about four feet from the ground, and my body, remaining in the inverted position, falls rapidly with it. In my upside down position, all the stress is put on the abdominal area of the body. The tension wrenches the stomach and the intestines. The pole now stops its bend and starts to reflex back up to a straight position, but my body is still falling straight down. At this moment the strain multiplies as my body is brought to an abrupt stop and then starts back in the opposite direction. The inverted position must be maintained. Unbelievable pressure is put on the abdominal area. My hands and fingers clench the pole like wrenches. Just as the deep-sea pole comes alive in the hands of a fisherman when he has hooked a fighting sailfish, this pole strains to pull away from me as it jiggles violently from side to side. I feel I can't hold on any longer. In my fury to keep from losing the pole I wish the people who had said one merely has to "hang on" to the fiberglas pole for the ride could take my place now and try "hanging on" to this monster. I feel the muscle fibers along my stomach straining to the point of popping, and my numb fingers seem to be slipping off the rising pole; but suddenly, my body ceases to resist and rises upward toward the stars.

I am amazed to realize that I am still on the pole. My body [7] writhes slowly to the left, and my feet come up to the crossbar. My body continues turning as the bar passes under my shins, knees, and thighs, and my body stops in a half-twist as the crossbar stands directly under my waist. At this point I lock my arms in a half-bent position, the pole begins its final slight bend. My waist is approximately three feet higher than my hands and well above the crossbar. The slight bend of the pole lowers my body four to six inches. I keep my arms locked in bent position as again the pressure mounts on my tight, quivering stomach muscles. As the pole becomes a straight line, I straighten my arms out keeping my head forward and down, my body arched into a parabola around the crossbar. I stiffen my arms, and the fingertips, tired and pained, become the only things supporting my weight on the pole. I push off with my stiff fingertips, pulling my elbows up, back, and over; I throw my head back as my weak fingers barely clear the bar. I let go of all tension and let my body fall easily, down, and backward—sinking into the soft white mass, seeing only the dark blue sky. Wait! Not only the dark blue sky, but also a crossbar lying across the tops of two standards up there in the heavens, quivering a bit perhaps, but not falling, not in a thousand years. The hundred or so people who have gathered around the pit rush to pick me up as the masses in the stands exhale a roar. I look back at the pole lying over there alone, still, and I know what a marvelous monster it is to ride.

QUESTIONS

Understanding

1. Dubber's job is to clear the bar at a record height. Why is it also his "duty" (par. 2)?

2. As the pole launches him upward, Dubber wishes that critics of the fiberglas pole could take his place. Why? What does he want them to find out?

3. Dubber is writing about a single event and a relatively unfamiliar sport, but what does his narrative suggest about competition in general?

Strategies and Structure

1. Why does Dubber keep referring to the fiberglas pole? Besides narrating the story of how he broke the record, what *argument* is he developing? What is the counterargument of his opponents?

2. What is the effect of the last sentence in paragraph 1? What difference would it have made if Dubber had written instead, "The stands *were* filled"?

3. If the opening paragraphs of this essay create suspense, does the last paragraph continue the suspense or resolve it? Explain your answer.

4. Dubber mentions the crowd at the beginning and end of his narrative. What happens to the crowd in between? Why?

5. To read the last three paragraphs of this essay takes much longer than an actual pole vault. Dubber could not possibly have formulated all these sensations while he broke the record. Does this mean his account is "untrue"? Why or why not?

Words and Figures of Speech

1. PERSONIFICATION is the device of conferring life on inanimate

objects. Where does Dubber use this figure of speech? Why does he use it?

2. When Dubber starts to "leave the world" (par. 5), he is taking off from the physical earth. In what other sense can these words be understood?

3. If you find anything awkward in the following phrases, suggest ways of changing them: "untwine this tightly woven cord" (par. 3); "abdominal area of the body" (6); "marvelous monster" (7).

Comparing

1. In Chapter 3, you will encounter essays that analyze processes. What process is Dubber explaining as he tells his story? When you read William Allen's "How to Set a World Record" (Chapter 3), ask yourself what emotional attitude his broom-balancer shares with Dubber's pole-vaulter.

Discussion and Writing Topics

1. Has any experience in sports—a tournament competition, a particularly smooth dive, a lucky hook shot—made you understand for a moment how a champion athlete feels? Tell the story of that experience. Try to convey its sensations and the glimpse of mastery that it gave you.

2. Narrate your triumph in a board game (like Monopoly or chess) as if it required all the stamina, skill, and split-second timing of a field sport. Be as dramatic as you please.

3. Do you consider competition to be healthy? Why or why not? To what extent is it avoidable in life?

Nora Ephron

A Few Words about Breasts

The daughter of Hollywood screenwriters, Nora Ephron was born
in New York City in 1941 but grew up in Beverly Hills, California, where she remembers "the smell of mink . . . and the smell
of dollar bills." A graduate of Wellesley College, she has been a
reporter, interviewer, columnist, editor, and contributor to the
New York Post, Esquire, New York, Oui, McCall's, and Cosmo-
politan. Ephron's Wallflower at the Orgy (1970) was followed in
1975 by Crazy Salad, a collection of twenty-five articles on women
and popular culture, her favorite subjects, and in 1978 by Scribble
Scribble. Ephron says that she writes by starting over again whenever she runs into difficulty; thus by the time she finishes an
essay, "every section has been through the typewriter many
times." The following selection is approximately the last third
of an essay, reprinted in Crazy Salad, that originally appeared
in Esquire in 1972. It is a personal narrative that also resembles
the CAUSE AND EFFECT essays you will find in Chapter 4.

"Do you want to marry my son?" the woman asked me.   1
"Yes," I said.   2

I was nineteen years old, a virgin, going with this woman's   3
son, this big strange woman who was married to a Lutheran
minister in New Hampshire and pretended she was Gentile
and had this son, by her first husband, this total fool of a son
who ran the hero-sandwich concession at Harvard Business
School and whom for one moment one December in New
Hampshire I said—as much out of politeness as anything
else—that I wanted to marry.

"*Fine,*" *she said.* "*Now, here's what you do. Always make sure* 4
you're on top of him so you won't seem so small. My bust is
very large, you see, so I always lie on my back to make it look
smaller, but you'll have to be on top most of the time."

I nodded. "*Thank you,*" *I said.* 5

"*I have a book for you to read,*" *she went on,* "*Take it with you* 6
when you leave. Keep it." *She went to the bookshelf, found it,*
and gave it to me. It was a book on frigidity.

"*Thank you,*" *I said.* 7

That is a true story. Everything in this article is a true story, 8
but I feel I have to point out that that story in particular is true.
It happened on December 30, 1960. I think about it often. When
it first happened, I naturally assumed that the woman's son, my
boyfriend, was responsible. I invented a scenario where he had had
a little heart-to-heart with his mother and had confessed that his
only objection to me was that my breasts were small; his mother
then took it upon herself to help out. Now I think I was wrong
about the incident. The mother was acting on her own, I think:
that was her way of being cruel and competitive under the guise
of being helpful and maternal. You have small breasts, she was
saying; therefore you will never make him as happy as I have. Or
you have small breasts; therefore you will doubtless have sexual
problems. Or you have small breasts; therefore you are less woman
than I am. She was, as it happens, only the first of what seems to
me to be a never-ending string of women who have made competitive remarks to me about breast size. "I would love to wear a dress
like that," my friend Emily says to me, "but my bust is too big."
Like that. Why do women say these things to me? Do I attract
these remarks the way other women attract married men or alco-
holics or homosexuals? This summer, for example, I am at a party
in East Hampton [1] and I am introduced to a woman from Washington. She is a minor celebrity, very pretty and Southern and
blonde and outspoken and I am flattered because she has read
something I have written. We are talking animatedly, we have
been talking no more than five minutes, when a man comes up to
join us. "Look at the two of us," the woman says to the man,
indicating me and her. "The two of us together couldn't fill an

[1] A wealthy summer community on Long Island.

A cup." Why does she say that? It isn't even true, dammit, so why? Is she even more addled than I am on this subject? Does she honestly believe there is something wrong with her size breasts, which, it seems to me, now that I look hard at them, are just right. Do I unconsciously bring out competitiveness in women? In that form? What did I do to deserve it?

As for men.   9

There were men who minded and let me know they minded. 10
There were men who did not mind. In any case, I always minded.

And even now, that I have been countlessly reassured that my 11
figure is a good one, now that I am grown up enough to understand that most of my feelings have very little to do with the
reality of my shape, I am nonetheless obsessed by breasts. I cannot help it. I grew up in the terrible Fifties—with rigid stereo-
typical sex roles, the insistence that men be men and dress like
men and women be women and dress like women, the intolerance
of androgyny—and I cannot shake it, cannot shake my feelings of
inadequacy. Well, that time is gone, right? All those exaggerated
examples of breast worship are gone, right? Those women were
freaks, right? I know all that. And yet, here I am, stuck with the
psychological remains of it all, stuck with my own peculiar version
of breast worship. You probably think I am crazy to go on like
this: here I have set out to write a confession that is meant to hit
you with the shock of recognition and instead you are sitting there
thinking I am thoroughly warped. Well, what can I tell you? If I
had had them, I would have been a completely different person.
I honestly believe that.

After I went into therapy, a process that made it possible for 12
me to tell total strangers at cocktail parties that breasts were the
hang-up of my life, I was often told that I was insane to have been
bothered by my condition. I was also frequently told, by close
friends, that I was extremely boring on the subject. And my girl
friends, the ones with nice big breasts, would go on endlessly about
how their lives had been far more miserable than mine. Their bra
straps were snapped in class. They couldn't sleep on their stom-
achs. They were stared at whenever the word "mountain" cropped
up in geography. And *Evangeline*,[2] good God what they went
through every time someone had to stand up and recite the Pro-

[2] Published in 1847 by the American poet Henry Wadsworth Longfellow
(1807–1882).

logue to Longfellow's *Evangeline:* "*. . . stand like druids of eld . . .
/ With beards that rest on their bosoms.*" It was much worse for
them, they tell me. They had a terrible time of it, they assure me.
I don't know how lucky I was, they say.

I have thought about their remarks, tried to put myself in their   13
place, considered their point of view. I think they are full of shit.

QUESTIONS

Understanding

1. Ephron asserts that her "peculiar version of breast worship" (par. 11) has been caused by the sex-role stereotypes of the 1950s. What were they, according to her account?
2. For enforcing those stereotypes, does Ephron seem to put more blame upon women or men? Judging from paragraph 8, what is their motive for acting the way they do?
3. How does Ephron's portrait of her boyfriend's mother bear out what she says about enforced role-playing?
4. In what sense is Ephron's narrative a feminist statement? In what sense could it be seen as antifeminist?

Strategies and Structure

1. Ephron refers to the italicized part of her narrative as a "story" (par. 8). Is this term accurate? What elements of narrative does the segment display?
2. The incident with her boyfriend's mother occurred when Ephron was nineteen years old. Which paragraph of her entire narrative is set at the time of writing? When did she meet the minor celebrity at the East Hampton party (par. 8)? When did the events of paragraph 12 take place?
3. Given what her narrative is intended to prove, how might you justify Ephron's skipping around in time and place?
4. Point out passages in which Ephron seems to *talk* to the reader. How do these passages contribute to the impression that Ephron is writing a "confession" (par. 11)?
5. How does the way in which she tells her story indicate that Ephron is in better psychological health than she claims?

6. What specific incidents in her narrative suggest that Ephron is as much interested in winning sympathy for her inferiority complex as in assigning blame for it?

Words and Figures of Speech

1. The word *stereotype* comes from printing; it refers to a metal plate of type, or other design, cast from a mold. What does the word mean when applied to people, and what is the connection with its original meaning?
2. A *scenario* is the plot outline of a play or other literary work, but today it is more often applied to what kind of imaginative creation? Why is a scenario likely to change?
3. Is the last word in Ephron's essay justified? Why or why not?
4. What is a "heart-to-heart" (par. 8)? With whom, besides her boyfriend's mother, is Ephron having one in her confession?
5. Psychologists speak of a mental fixation as an "obsession." What current SLANG term for this idea does Ephron use in paragraph 12?
6. Find the following words in your dictionary: *guise* (par. 8), *animatedly* (8), *androgyny* (11), *prologue* (12).

Comparing

1. In "Body Ritual Among the Nacirema" (Chapter 8), Horace Miner describes a people who have a "hyper-mammary" hang-up because they think the natural body is ugly. How might his explanation be applied in Ephron's case?
2. How would you expect Ephron to react to Robert Jastrow's argument in "Man of Wisdom" (Chapter 4) that adversity brings about human advancement?

Discussion and Writing Topics

1. Did you find sex roles to be stereotyped during your adolescent years? Relate one or two incidents involving you or your friends that enforced the stereotypes.
2. Can you recall an occasion when a member of your own sex encouraged a form of "chauvinistic" role-playing that is usually

blamed upon the other sex? Describe the experience and try to account for his or her motives.

3. Do you think competition during the years of growing up leads to psychological hang-ups later? Cite real-life incidents to support your opinion.

4. Imagine a patient with delusions of grandeur and tell his story.

Alex Haley

My Furthest-Back Person—
"The African"

When Alex Haley's Roots was published in 1976, it created a
literary stir; and when the film version appeared soon after on
national television, this account of seven generations of an Afro-
American family became part of the American consciousness. A
native of Tennessee, Haley joined the U.S. Coast Guard in 1939
after briefly attending a North Carolina teachers' college. He
taught himself to write at sea, and later the Coast Guard created
the rating "journalist" expressly for him. When Haley retired
from the service in 1959, he began writing for men's adventure
magazines and then for Reader's Digest. One of his Playboy interviews led to his co-authoring The Autobiography of Malcolm X
in 1965. Then began the years of intensive genealogical research
that Haley recalls in "My Furthest-Back-Person—'The African.' "
This is not so much the family story of a descendant of African
slaves as it is the narrative of his personal quest for that story.

My Grandma Cynthia Murray Palmer lived in Henning,   1
Tenn. (pop. 500), about 50 miles north of Memphis. Each
summer as I grew up there, we would be visited by several
women relatives who were mostly around Grandma's age,
such as my Great Aunt Liz Murray who taught in Oklahoma,
and Great Aunt Till Merriwether from Jackson, Tenn., or
their considerably younger niece, Cousin Georgia Anderson
from Kansas City, Kan., and some others. Always after the
supper dishes had been washed, they would go out to take seats
and talk in the rocking chairs on the front porch, and I would

scrunch down, listening, behind Grandma's squeaky chair, with the dusk deepening into the night and the lightning bugs flicking on and off above the now shadowy honeysuckles. Most often they talked about our family—the story had been passed down for generations—until the whistling blur of lights of the southbound Panama Limited train *whooshing* through Henning at 9:05 P.M. signaled our bedtime.

So much of their talking of people, places and events I didn't understand: For instance, what was an "Ol' Massa," an "Ol' Missus" or a "plantation"? But early I gathered that white folks had done lots of bad thing to our folks, though I couldn't figure out why. I guessed that all they talked about had happened a long time ago, as now or then Grandma or another, speaking of someone in the past, would excitedly thrust a finger toward me, exclaiming, "Wasn't big as *this* young 'un!" And it would astound me that anyone as old and gray-haired as they could relate to my age. But in time my head began both a recording and picturing of the more graphic scenes they would describe, just as I also visualized David killing Goliath with his slingshot, Old Pharaoh's army drowning, Noah and his ark, Jesus feeding that big multitude with nothing but five loaves and two fishes, and other wonders that I heard in my Sunday school lessons at our New Hope Methodist Church.

The furthest-back person Grandma and the others talked of— always in tones of awe, I noticed—they would call "The African." They said that some ship brought him to a place that they pronounced " 'Naplis." They said that then some "Mas' John Waller" bought him for his plantation in "Spotsylvania County, Va." This African kept on escaping, the fourth time trying to kill the "hateful po' cracker" slave-catcher, who gave him the punishment choice of castration or of losing one foot. This African took a foot being chopped off with an ax against a tree stump, they said, and he was about to die. But his life was saved by "Mas' John's" brother— "Mas' William Waller," a doctor, who was so furious about what had happened that he bought the African for himself and gave him the name "Toby."

Crippling about, working in "Mas' William's" house and yard, the African in time met and mated with "the big house cook named Bell," and there was born a girl named Kizzy. As she grew up her African daddy often showed her different kinds of things, telling her what they were in his native tongue. Pointing at a banjo, for example, the African uttered, "*ko*"; or pointing at a river near the plantation, he would say, "*Kamby Bolong*." Many of his strange words started with a "*k*" sound, and the little, growing Kizzy learned gradually that they identified different things.

When addressed by other slaves as "Toby," the master's name for him, the African said angrily that his name was "*Kin-tay*." And as he gradually learned English, he told young Kizzy some things about himself—for instance, that he was not far from his village, chopping wood to make himself a drum, when four men had surprised, overwhelmed, and kidnaped him.

So Kizzy's head held much about her African daddy when at age 16 she was sold away onto a much smaller plantation in North Carolina. Her new "Mas' Tom Lea" fathered her first child, a boy she named George. And Kizzy told her boy all about his African grandfather. George grew up to be such a gamecock fighter that he was called "Chicken George," and people would come from all over and "bet big money" on his cockfights. He mated with Matilda, another of Lea's slaves; they had seven children, and he told them the stories and strange sounds of their African great-grandfather. And one of those children, Tom, became a blacksmith who was bought away by a "Mas' Murray" for his tobacco plantation in Alamance County, N.C.

Tom mated there with Irene, a weaver on the plantation. She also bore seven children, and Tom now told them all about their African great-great-grandfather, the faithfully passed-down knowledge of his sounds and stories having become by now the family's prideful treasure.

The youngest of that second set of seven children was a girl, Cynthia, who became my maternal Grandma (which today I can only see as fated). Anyway, all of this is how I was growing up in Henning at Grandma's, listening from behind her rocking chair as she and the other visiting old women talked of that African (never then comprehended as *my* great-great-great-great-grandfather) who said his name was "*Kin-tay*," and said "*ko*" for banjo, "*Kamby Bolong*" for river, and a jumble of other "*k*"-beginning sounds that Grandma privately muttered, most often while making beds or cooking, and who also said that near his village he was kidnaped while chopping wood to make himself a drum.

The story had become nearly as fixed in my head as in Grandma's by the time Dad and Mama moved me and my two younger brothers, George and Julius, away from Henning to be with them at the small black agricultural and mechanical college in Normal, Ala., where Dad taught.

To compress my next 25 years: When I was 17 Dad let me [10] enlist as a mess boy in the U.S. Coast Guard. I became a ship's cook out in the South Pacific during World War II, and at night down by my bunk I began trying to write sea adventure stories, mailing them off to magazines and collecting rejection slips for eight years before some editors began purchasing and publishing occasional stories. By 1949 the Coast Guard had made me its first "journalist"; finally with 20 years' service, I retired at the age of 37, determined to make a full time career of writing. I wrote mostly magazine articles; my first book was "The Autobiography of Malcolm X."

Then one Saturday in 1965 I happened to be walking past the [11] National Archives building in Washington. Across the interim years I had thought of Grandma's old stories—otherwise I can't think what diverted me up the Archives' steps. And when a main reading room desk attendant asked if he could help me, I wouldn't have dreamed of admitting to him some curiosity hanging on from boyhood about my slave forebears. I kind of mumbled that I was interested in census records of Alamance County, North Carolina, just after the Civil War.

The microfilm rolls were delivered, and I turned them through [12] the machine with a building sense of intrigue, viewing in different census takers' penmanship an endless parade of names. After about a dozen microfilmed rolls, I was beginning to tire, when in utter astonishment I looked upon the names of Grandma's parents: Tom Murray, Irene Murray . . . older sisters of Grandma's as well—every one of them a name that I'd heard countless times on her front porch.

It wasn't that I hadn't believed Grandma. You just *didn't* not [13] believe my Grandma. It was simply so uncanny actually seeing those names in print and in official U.S. Government records.

During the next several months I was back in Washington [14] whenever possible, in the Archives, the Library of Congress, the Daughters of the American Revolution Library. (Whenever black attendants understood the idea of my search, documents I requested reached me with miraculous speed.) In one source or another during 1966 I was able to document at least the highlights of the cherished family story. I would have given anything to have told Grandma, but, sadly, in 1949 she had gone. So I went and told the only survivor of those Henning front-porch storytellers: Cousin Georgia Anderson, now in her 80's in Kansas City, Kan. Wrinkled, bent, not well herself, she was so overjoyed, repeating to me the old stories and sounds; they were like Henning echoes: "Yeah, boy, that African say his name was 'Kin-tay'; he say the banjo was 'ko,' an' the river 'Kamby-Bolong,' an' he was off choppin' some wood to make his drum when they grabbed 'im!" Cousin Georgia grew so excited we had to stop her, calm her down, "You go' head, boy! Your grandma an' all of 'em—they up there watching what you do!"

That week I flew to London on a magazine assignment. Since by now I was steeped in the old, in the past, scarcely a tour guide missed me—I was awed at so many historical places and treasures I'd heard of and read of. I came upon the Rosetta stone [1] in the British Museum, marveling anew at how Jean Champollion, the French archaeologist, had miraculously deciphered its ancient demotic and hieroglyphic texts . . .

The thrill of that just kept hanging around in my head. I was on a jet returning to New York when a thought hit me. Those strange, unknown-tongue sounds, always part of our family's old story . . . they were obviously bits of our original African "Kin-tay's" native tongue. What specific tongue? Could I somehow find out?

Back in New York, I began making visits to the United Nations Headquarters lobby; it wasn't hard to spot Africans. I'd stop any I could, asking if my bits of phonetic sounds held any meaning for them. A couple of dozen Africans quickly listened, and took off—understandably dubious about some Tennessean's accent alleging "African" sounds.

My research assistant, George Sims (we grew up together in Henning), brought me some names of ranking scholars of African linguistics. One was particularly intriguing: A Belgian- and English-educated Dr. Jan Vansina; he had spent his early career living in West African villages, studying and tape-recording count-

---

[1] Ancient Egyptian stone tablet. The French archaeologist Champollion (1790–1832) used it to decipher hieroglyphic writing.

less oral histories that were narrated by certain very old African men; he had written a standard textbook, "The Oral Tradition."

So I flew to the University of Wisconsin to see Dr. Vansina. In [19] his living room I told him every bit of the family story in the fullest detail that I could remember it. Then, intensely, he queried me about the story's relay across the generations, about the gibberish of "*k*" sounds Grandma had fiercely muttered to herself while doing her housework, with my brothers and me giggling beyond her hearing at what we had dubbed "Grandma's noises."

Dr. Vansina, his manner very serious, finally said, "These sounds [20] your family has kept sound very probably of the tongue called 'Mandinka.' "

I'd never heard of any "Mandinka." Grandma just told of the [21] African saying "*ko*" for banjo, or "*Kamby Bolong*" for a Virginia river.

Among Mandinka stringed instruments, Dr. Vansina said, one [22] of the oldest was the "*kora*."

"*Bolong*," he said, was clearly Mandinka for "river." Preceded [23] by "*Kamby*," it very likely meant "Gambia River."

Dr. Vansina telephoned an eminent Africanist colleague, Dr. [24] Philip Curtin. He said that the phonetic "*Kin-tay*" was correctly spelled "*Kinte*," a very old clan that had originated in Old Mali. The Kinte men traditionally were blacksmiths, and the women were potters and weavers.

I knew I must get to the Gambia River. [25]

The first native Gambian I could locate in the U.S. was named [26] Ebou Manga, then a junior attending Hamilton College in upstate Clinton, N.Y. He and I flew to Dakar, Senegal, then took a smaller plane to Yundum Airport, and rode in a van to Gambia's capital, Bathurst. Ebou and his father assembled eight Gambia government officials. I told them Grandma's stories, every detail I could remember, as they listened intently, then reacted. " '*Kamby Bolong*' of course is Gambia River!" I heard. "But more clue is your forefather's saying his name was '*Kinte.*' " Then they told me something I would never even have fantasized—that in places in the back country lived very old men, commonly called *griots*, who could tell centuries of the histories of certain very old family clans. As for *Kintes*, they pointed out to me on a map some family villages, Kinte-Kundah, and Kinte-Kundah Janneh-Ya, for instance.

The Gambian officials said they would try to help me. I re- [27]

turned to New York dazed. It is embarrassing to me now, but despite Grandma's stories, I'd never been concerned much with Africa, and I had the routine images of African people living mostly in exotic jungles. But a compulsion now laid hold of me to learn all I could, and I began devouring books about Africa, especially about the slave trade. Then one Thursday's mail contained a letter from one of the Gambian officials, inviting me to return there.

Monday I was back in Bathurst. It galvanized me when the officials said that a *griot* had been located who told the *Kinte* clan history—his name was Kebba Kanga Fofana. To reach him, I discovered, required a modified safari: renting a launch to get upriver, two land vehicles to carry supplies by a roundabout land route, and employing finally 14 people, including three interpreters and four musicians, since a *griot* would not speak the revered clan histories without background music.

The boat Baddibu vibrated upriver, with me acutely tense: Were these Africans maybe viewing me as but another of the pith-helmets? After about two hours, we put in at James Island, for me to see the ruins of the once British-operated James Fort. Here two centuries of slave ships had loaded thousands of cargoes of Gambian tribespeople. The crumbling stones, the deeply oxidized swivel cannon, even some remnant links of chain seemed all but impossible to believe. Then we continued upriver to the left-bank village of Albreda, and there put ashore to continue on foot to Juffure, village of the *griot*. Once more we stopped, for me to see *toubob kolong*, "the white man's well," now almost filled in, in a swampy area with abundant, tall, saw-toothed grass. It was dug two centuries ago to "17 men's height deep" to insure survival drinking water for long-driven, famishing coffles of slaves.

Walking on, I kept wishing that Grandma could hear how her stories had led me to the *"Kamby Bolong."* (Our surviving story-teller Cousin Georgia died in a Kansas City hospital during this same morning, I would learn later.) Finally, Juffure village's playing children, sighting us, flashed an alert. The 70-odd people came rushing from their circular, thatch-roofed, mud-walled huts, with goats bounding up and about, and parrots squawking from up in the palms. I sensed him in advance somehow, the small man amid them, wearing a pillbox cap and an off-white robe—the *griot*. Then the interpreters went to him, as the villagers thronged around me.

And it hit me like a gale wind: every one of them, the whole [31] crowd, was *jet black*. An enormous sense of guilt swept me—a sense of being some kind of hybrid . . . a sense of being impure among the pure. It was an awful sensation.

The old *griot* stepped away from my interpreters and the crowd [32] quickly swarmed around him—all of them buzzing. An interpreter named A. B. C. Salla came to me; he whispered: "Why they stare at you so, they have never seen here a black American." And that hit me: I was symbolizing for them twenty-five millions of us they had never seen. What did they think of me—of us?

Then abruptly the old *griot* was briskly walking toward me. His [33] eyes boring into mine, he spoke in Mandinka, as if instinctively I should understand—and A. B. C. Salla translated:

"Yes . . . we have been told by the forefathers . . . that many [34] of us from this place are in exile . . . in that place called America . . . and in other places."

I suppose I physically wavered, and they thought it was the [35] heat; rustling whispers went through the crowd, and a man brought me a low stool. Now the whispering hushed—the musicians had softly begun playing *kora* and *balafon*, and a canvas sling lawn seat was taken by the *griot*, Kebba Kanga Fofana, aged 73 "rains" (one rainy season each year). He seemed to gather himself into a physical rigidity, and he began speaking the *Kinte* clan's ancestral oral history; it came rolling from his mouth across the next hours . . . 17th-and 18th-century *Kinte* lineage details, predominantly what men took wives; the children they "begot," in the order of their births; those children's mates and children.

Events frequently were dated by some proximate singular physi- [36] cal occurrence. It was as if some ancient scroll were printed indelibly within the *griot's* brain. Each few sentences or so, he would pause for an interpreter's translation to me. I distill here the essence:

The *Kinte* clan began in Old Mali,[2] the men generally black- [37] smiths ". . . who conquered fire," and the women potters and weavers. One large branch of the clan moved to Mauretania from

[2] Haley's branch of the clan apparently moved from mid-western Africa northward into present-day Morocco and Algeria, then southward again into the Senegal region. The ancient names "Mali" and "Mauretania" were revived by modern West African states that gained independence from France in 1960.

where one son of the clan, Kairaba Kunta Kinte, a Moslem Marabout holy man, entered Gambia. He lived first in the village of Pakali N'Ding; he moved next to Jiffarong village; ". . . and then he came here, into our own village of Juffure."

In Juffure, Kairaba Kunta Kinte took his first wife, ". . . a Mandinka maiden, whose name was Sireng. By her, he begot two sons, whose names were Janneh and Saloum. Then he got a second wife, Yaisa. By her, he begot a son, Omoro." 38

The three sons became men in Juffure. Janneh and Saloum went off and found a new village, Kinte-Kundah Janneh-Ya. "And then Omoro, the younger son, when he had 30 rains, took as a wife a maiden, Binta Kebba. 39

"And by her, he begot four sons—Kunta, Lamin, Suwadu, and Madi . . ." 40

Sometimes, a "begotten," after his naming, would be accompanied by some later-occurring detail, perhaps as ". . . in time of big water buffalo." Having named those four sons, now the *griot* stated such a detail. 41

"About the time the king's soldiers came, the eldest of these four sons, Kunta, when he had about 16 rains, went away from this village, to chop wood to make a drum . . . and he was never seen again . . ." 42

Goose-pimples the size of lemons seemed to pop all over me. In my knapsack were my cumulative notebooks, the first of them including how in my boyhood, my Grandma, Cousin Georgia and the others told of the African *"Kin-tay"* who always said he was kidnaped near his village—while chopping wood to make a drum . . . 43

I showed the interpreter, he showed and told the *griot*, who excitedly told the people; they grew very agitated. Abruptly then they formed a human ring, encircling me, dancing and chanting. Perhaps a dozen of the women carrying their infant babies rushed in toward me, thrusting the infants into my arms—conveying, I would later learn, "the laying on of hands . . . through this flesh which is us, we are you, and you are us." The men hurried me into their mosque, their Arabic praying later being translated outside: "Thanks be to Allah for returning the long lost from among us." Direct descendants of Kunta Kinte's blood brothers were hastened, some of them from nearby villages, for a family portrait to be 44

taken with me, surrounded by actual ancestral sixth cousins. More
symbolic acts filled the remaining day.

When they would let me leave, for some reason I wanted to go   45
away over the African land. Dazed, silent in the bumping Land
Rover, I heard the cutting staccato of talking drums. Then when
we sighted the next village, its people came thronging to meet us.
They were all—little naked ones to wizened elders—waving, beam-
ing, amid a cacophony of crying out; and then my ears identified
their words: "*Meester Kinte! Meester Kinte!*"

Let me tell you something: I am a man. But I remember the   46
sob surging up from my feet, flinging up my hands before my face
and bawling as I had not done since I was a baby . . . the jet-black
Africans were jostling, staring . . . I didn't care, with the feelings
surging. If you really knew the odyssey of us millions of black
Americans, if you really knew how we came in the seeds of our
forefathers, captured, driven, beaten, inspected, bought, branded,
chained in foul ships, if you really knew, you needed weeping . . .

Back home, I knew that what I must write, really, was our black   47
saga, where any individual's past is the essence of the millions'.
Now flat broke, I went to some editors I knew, describing the
Gambian miracle, and my desire to pursue the research; Double-
day contracted to publish, and Reader's Digest to condense the
projected book; then I had advances to travel further.

What ship brought Kinte to Grandma's " 'Naplis" (Annapolis,   48
Md., obviously)? The old *griot's* time reference to "king's soldiers"
sent me flying to London. Feverish searching at last identified, in
British Parliament records, "Colonel O'Hare's Forces," dispatched
in mid-1767 to protect the then British-held James Fort whose
ruins I'd visited. So Kunta Kinte was down in some ship probably
sailing later that summer from the Gambia River to Annapolis.

Now I feel it was fated that I had taught myself to write in the   49
U.S. Coast Guard. For the sea dramas I had concentrated on had
given me years of experience searching among yellowing old U.S.
maritime records. So now in English 18th Century marine records
I finally tracked ships reporting themselves in and out of the Commandant of the Gambia River's James Fort. And then early one
afternoon I found that a Lord Ligonier under a Captain Thomas
Davies had sailed on the Sabbath of July 5, 1767. Her cargo: 3,265
elephants' teeth, 3,700 pounds of beeswax, 800 pounds of cotton,

32 ounces of Gambian gold, and 140 slaves; her destination: "Annapolis."

That night I recrossed the Atlantic. In the Library of Congress 50 the Lord Ligonier's arrival was one brief line in "Shipping In The Port Of Annapolis—1748–1775." I located the author, Vaughan W. Brown, in his Baltimore brokerage office. He drove to Historic Annapolis, the city's historical society, and found me further documentation of her arrival on Sept. 29, 1767. (Exactly two centuries later, Sept. 29, 1967, standing, staring seaward from an Annapolis pier, again I knew tears.) More help came in the Maryland Hall of Records. Archivist Phebe Jacobsen found the Lord Ligonier's arriving customs declaration listing, "98 Negroes"—so in her 86-day crossing, 42 Gambians had died, one among the survivors being 16-year-old Kunta Kinte. Then the microfilmed Oct. 1, 1767, Maryland Gazette contained, on page two, an announcement to prospective buyers from the ship's agents, Daniel of St. Thos. Jenifer and John Ridout (the Governor's secretary): "from the River GAMBIA, in AFRICA . . . a cargo of choice, healthy SLAVES . . ."

QUESTIONS

Understanding

1. This essay tells the story of three different kinds of quests. One is a writer's search for material; another is his quest for bits and pieces of personal family history. What is the third? Point out specific paragraphs (for example, par. 46) that contribute to this part of the story.

2. Which of the three kinds of searches in Haley's essay do you consider most important? Why?

3. Why is Haley struck with the color of the Gambians in paragraph 31?

4. What is the significance of the laying-on-of-hands ceremony in paragraph 44?

5. What message does Haley's personal narrative hold for others who might search the distant past for their roots?

Strategies and Structure

1. Through roughly how many years of his life does Haley's narrative carry us? Why does he start with his childhood instead of some later stage; when he retired from the Coast Guard, for example?

2. As Haley's life moves forward in time, his search moves deeper into the past. Where do the two time dimensions of the narrative come together? How does Haley create the impression of relentless pursuit, of past and present inevitably meeting?

3. How do Haley's various accounts of the front-porch storytellers anticipate his account of the *griot* he meets in Gambia. How does the boy's reaction to the family story condition *our* reaction to the *griot*'s words in paragraphs 34–42?

4. Haley could have told us from the beginning who the African was and where he came from. Why does he choose *not* to do this in retelling the story? What effect does he achieve by withholding such information?

5. How is the *language* of Haley's own account of his search different from the language of both the Africans and his relatives in America? What two different kinds of historical evidence does Haley's historian offer us?

6. Why does Haley so often *repeat* the elements of the family legend, the fact that the African was captured while making a drum, for instance?

7. Describe the effect of Haley's "Let me tell you something" at the beginning of paragraph 46.

8. Why do you think Haley omitted paragraph 31 in a version of this essay that appeared in *Reader's Digest,* a magazine intended for a vast general audience?

9. Haley ends his narrative by quoting an advertisement in the *Maryland Gazette* of October 1767. Is this an effective ending to his story? Why or why not?

Words and Figures of Speech

1. What are the implications of the words *roots*? Why is the METAPHOR appropriate to the kind of search that Haley is conducting?

2. What is the effect when Haley's history switches from the word *mated* (as in pars. 6 and 7) to *begot* (in pars. 35, 38, 40, 41)?

3. What is an *odyssey* (par. 46)? Explain the literary ALLUSION implied by the word. Why is the term appropriate to Haley's story?

4. Who are the "pith-helmets" in paragraph 29? What FIGURE OF SPEECH does the term exemplify?

5. Consult your dictionary for the precise meanings of any of the following words you are not sure of: *graphic* (par. 2), *archives* (11), *uncanny* (13), *phonetic* (17), *linguistics* (18), *gibberish* (19), *eminent* (24), *galvanized* (28), *coffles* (29), *proximate* (36), *indelibly* (36), *staccato* (45), *wizened* (45), *cacophony* (45), *saga* (47).

Comparing

1. Both Haley's essay and Loren Eiseley's "The Angry Winter" (at the beginning of this chapter) tell the story of a thoughtful man's return to the past. How do the two narratives *differ* in this regard?

Discussion and Writing Topics

1. Tell the story that emerges from any legends of your own family that you can recall.

2. Relate any events in your family history that have a general social significance. Try to do so without losing their personal flavor.

3. After the publication of *Roots* in book form, a British reporter alleged that Haley's *griot* knew in advance what Haley wanted to hear and stretched the facts to please him. Would Haley's entire search be invalidated if it should turn out that the griot's Kinte was not the same African his aunts talked about? Why or why not?

4. How exclusively "black" do you find Haley's essay to be? Explain your answer.

Essays in the First Person Singular

1. Write an autobiography in which you give a chronological account of the formative events of your life.

2. Which aspects of college have you found most different from high school? Which have you found especially shocking or liberating? Tell the story of your adjustment to a new environment.

3. Have you had a religious or intellectual experience that has *changed* your life? Try to recapture it.

4. Do you have a special skill or talent (like David Dubber's)? Relate how it has served you in past challenges or emergencies.

5. Recount your reaction to the news of a relative's or close friend's death.

6. Describe your reaction to one of the following: an athletic event; an election or political rally; a meeting with a famous person; an impressive building or natural scene; an accident.

7. Recall a childhood journey that you find unusually memorable. Organize your account around the stages of the journey.

8. From your own perspective, tell the story of a family reunion you have attended. Pay special attention to the oldest family members.

9. How do you expect to act at the tenth anniversary of your high school graduating class? The twentieth? Describe the scene.

Exposition

2
Essays That
Classify and Divide

When we divide a group of similar objects, we separate
them from one another. For example, a physiologist divides
human beings according to body types: mesomorph (muscu-
lar and bony), ectomorph (skinny), and endomorph (soft
and fleshy). When we CLASSIFY [1] an object, we place it
within a group of similar objects. The zoologist puts a
monkey and a man in the order Primates because both mammals have nails and opposable thumbs. A librarian classifies
Mark Twain's Adventures of Huckleberry Finn along with
Herman Melville's Moby-Dick because both are works of
prose fiction by nineteenth-century American authors.
Shakespeare's Macbeth would go into a different class, however, because its distinguishing features are different. The
technical definition of a class is a group with the same
distinguishing features.

The simplest classification systems divide things into
those that exhibit a set of distinguishing features and those
that do not. A doctor conducting genetic research among
identical male twins would divide the human race first into
Males and Females; then he would subdivide the Males into
Twins and Non-Twins; and finally he would subdivide the
Twins into the categories, Identical and Nonidentical.

The doctor's simple system has limited uses, but it re-
sembles even the most complicated systems in one respect.
The categories do not overlap. They are mutually exclusive.
A classification system is useless if it "cross-ranks" items.
Suppose, for example, that we classified all birds according to

[1] Terms printed in all capitals are defined in the Glossary.

the following categories: Flightless, Nocturnal, Flat-billed, Web-Footed. Our system might work well enough for owls (nocturnal), but where would a duck (flat-billed, web-footed) fit? Or a penguin (flightless, web-footed)? A system of classifying birds must have one and only one pigeonhole for pigeons. Otherwise it makes a distinction that does not distinguish, a flaw as serious as failing to make a distinction that really does exist. Our faulty system would not differentiate between a penguin and an ostrich since both are flightless, but a naturalist would see a big difference between the two.

The distinguishing features of a class must set its members apart from those of other classes or subclasses. How the features of a given class are defined, however, will vary with who is doing the classifying and for what purpose. A teacher divides a group of thirty students according to scholarship: types A, B, C, D, and F. A basketball coach would divide the same group of students into forwards, guards, and centers. The director of a student drama group would have an entirely different set of criteria. All three sets are valid for the purposes they are intended to serve. And classification must serve some larger purpose, or it becomes an empty game.

When you write a classification theme, keep your purpose firmly in mind. Are you classifying teachers in order to decide what a good teacher is? To demonstrate that different kinds of teachers can be equally instructive? To explain why some teachers fail? Return often to your reasons and conclusions, for classification is a method of organization that should propose as well as arrange.

The following paragraph from an essay on lightning by Richard Orville goes well beyond merely dividing its subject into three categories:

> There are several types of lightning named according to where the discharge takes place. Among them are intracloud lightning, by far the most common type, in which the flash occurs within the thundercloud; air-discharge lightning, in which the flash occurs between the cloud and the surrounding air; and cloud-to-ground lightning, in which the discharge takes place between the cloud and the ground.

This short paragraph names the types of lightning. But it also suggests a basis for defining all three types ("according to where the discharge takes place"); it defines them on that basis; it tells us that intracloud lightning is the commonest type; and it sets up all that follows.

In the next paragraphs of his essay, Orville explains what causes the three kinds of lightning; how much electrical power they generate; how scientists study them, and where such familiar names as "forked, streak, heat, hot, cold, ribbon, and bead" lightning fit into these categories. After discussing the related topic of thunder, Orville ends by explaining why we need to know as much as possible about his subject. The final sentence of his essay reads: "In the end, we hope that our effort will bring the goal of lightning prediction, and perhaps limited control, within the realm of applied technology."

The author of our example has taken the trouble to study lightning, classify it, and explain his system to us because human life and property may depend upon such efforts in the future. You may not be writing about life-and-death matters, but your theme should explain why a particular system of classification is valid, what we can learn from it, and what good that knowledge can do.

Barbara G. Walker

For Women Mostly

Born in Philadelphia, Barbara G. (Jones) Walker was an under-graduate at the University of Pennsylvania when she wrote "For Women Mostly" (which is actually for men also). After graduat-ing from Penn with a B.A. and a Phi Beta Kappa key, she has worked as a journalist, a teacher of modern dance, and a profes-sional designer of knitwear. The author of ten books on creative knitting, she now lives in New Jersey with her husband and son. "For Women Mostly" is a tongue-in-cheek (and cheeky) break-down of the six "most objectionable" types of college men.

With all the controversy about the relative uselessness of   1
Penn men and Penn women, there seems to be a need for a
certain amount of field work in the subject. Apparently each
side is judged by the most objectionable of its kind, so—girls—
here is submitted a carefully compiled report on Penn Men
You Need to Avoid. If referred to before you accept dates,
it may save you a lot of bitterness and gnashing of teeth.

Type 1. The Party-Boy. This one simply isn't himself until   2
he gets outside of a little alcohol. Then he manages to be so
much himself that you are bored to death. His conversation is
either quiet or loud; when quiet, it consists of long accounts
of drinking bouts, in which he took part: and when loud, it
is usually carried on with his buddy across the room who
wants everybody to sing the "Whiffenpoof Song," while our
joyboy favors "Roll Me Over in the Clover." For these occasions he is conveniently equipped with a foghorn voice that
makes everybody turn around and look. If you happen to be
sitting next to him you cringe and wilt and feel about two

inches high. You gaze up at him with a sick smile that you hope will make everybody think you're having as much fun as he is.

There may be occasions in the course of the evening when he   3
feels like dancing. Dancing, to him, consists of zooming around ricocheting off walls, other couples, moose heads, etc. They ought to jail him for flying low.

Then the fire-eater creeps up on him and he commences to be   4
morose. In the life of every party-boy there is an unrequited love; and furthermore given even less than half a chance, he will tell you all about it. It sounds vaguely like *True Confessions*. But because you have nothing better to do at the moment, you listen, and sympathize—outwardly, with him; inwardly, with the girl.

Finally he quietly passes out, wrapped comfortably around a   5
chandelier or something, and one of his less enthusiastic brothers takes you home. All this is very interesting, provided you can hold him up long enough to get through the party. And he really isn't useless; he always makes a good bar rag.

Type 2. The Lover. He is a ball of fire with the women—the   6
sultry, slow-burning kind, of course. He overwhelms you with attentions. He leans so close to you when you talk that you get the impression he is concerned about the condition of your wisdom teeth. He has a special hungry sick-dog look which he uses for gazing deeply into eyes. When you go away and talk to somebody else, he sulks. He may even follow you and turn you around to face him, and look silently at you. He is hurt. You have crushed him. You are ashamed. You monster.

An evening with him is like a nice quiet session with a boa con-   7
strictor. No amount of hinting around that, as far as he's concerned, you are of the let's-just-be-friends school of thought, will do; you have to pick up a bottle or something and slug him before he gets the idea. Then, kid, you're washed up. Your name is mud. Not only are you nasty, ungrateful, and a terrible date—but to top it all off, you're an icebox—and this is the sin unforgivable.

Type 3. The Great Mind. You have to prepare ahead of time   8
for a date with one of these. If you're not read up on your Nietzsche and Schopenhauer,[1] you've got two strikes against you before you start. You and Junior will sit down together, cozy-like,

---

[1] Friedrich Wilhelm Nietzsche (1844–1900) and Arthur Schopenhauer (1788–1860), German philosophers.

in a corner and solve world problems. Then for the sake of variety you might go on to metaphysics. You toss Absolutes and Causes and Effects back and forth for a whole evening. I won't say any more on this subject. There's nothing more to say.

Type 4. The Bohemian. This one's theme song is "I Don't   9
Care." He dreams of a garret for two on the Left Bank and a Jug of Wine, a Loaf of Bread—and Thou; [2] and if Thou isn't crazy about the idea, Thou is inhibited, repressed, suppressed, a slave to convention, a conformist, and a louse. The boy knows he's a genius, but just because he dyes his hair pale green and wears a purple satin shoestring for a necktie, people don't appreciate him.

He has moods. Blue moods, black moods, red moods—all kinds.   10
If he's having mood number 157E, keep away from him. Keep away from him anyway. Unless you've reserved a bunk at Byberry,[3] that is.

Type 5. The Dud. He gives you a fleeting impression of a hor-   11
rible, sticky, gray nothingness. He doesn't smoke, drink, dance, drive, stay out late, or raise his voice. He isn't funny—he isn't interesting—he isn't clever. You talk into a vacuum. He is probably very good to his mother, but every time he comes out with that slightly hysterical giggle you feel like slapping him. He sits there like a rock in mid-stream and the party eddies around him. He has a wonderful time. You go home and get a nice big ax and go hunting for the person who got you the date.

Watch the aftereffects of this. He'll call you up, sure as next   12
week. He'll call you again. He'll call you nine or ten times more. If you happen to be wandering around on campus with somebody whom you'd like to impress, he'll pop up out of his hole in the lawn and greet you like a long-lost sister. He's the world's best argument for mercy killing.

Type 6. The Missing Link. Not that we object to muscles, but   13
there is a type that has too much of a good thing. He has an amazing supply of every kind of matter but gray. He looks like

---

[2] An allusion to *The Rubáiyat of Omar Khayyám*, translated by Edward Fitzgerald (1809–1883). The twelfth stanza of the poem reads (in the fourth edition): "A Book of Verses underneath the Bough,/A Jug of Wine, a Loaf of Bread—and Thou/Beside me singing in the Wilderness—/Oh, Wilderness were Paradise enow!" The Left Bank (of the Seine River) is the artist and student quarter of Paris.
[3] Psychiatric hospital in Philadelphia.

something out of the Old Stone Age—and talks surprisingly like it, too. His knuckles drag on the ground. He grunts occasionally to show he's alive. You expect him to stand up and hammer on his chest at any minute. He majors in-duh-phys ed, and takes Advanced Pencil Sharpening on the side.

He's a charming date if you're taking anthropology. Or if you 14
have to write a criticism of *The Man with the Hoe* or *Of Mice and Men*.[4] You couldn't find a better case study.

Of course you have to watch these creatures. If he gets playful 15
you're liable to end up mashed into dog food. It's best to take along a whip and a light metal chair and be able to say "Back, Sultan," in an authoritative voice. Once your nerve fails, you're done.

Well, there they are. Now the object of the game is to go out 16
and find one that doesn't fall into one of these categories. Then, if it's got blood and skin and if it moves around, you're set. Hang onto it. It must be a man.

QUESTIONS

Understanding

1. Barbara Walker's six types are divisions of a single class of Penn men. What is the distinguishing feature of that class? Where does she define it?

2. Into how many classes does she CLASSIFY *all* the undergraduate men at her university? What distinguishes the class or classes that she does not divide into types?

3. How fair and accurate do you consider Walker's assessments to be? Explain your answer.

4. Judging from the opening paragraph, what may have provoked Walker into writing this field guide to the Penn dating game?

Strategies and Structure

1. Like most essays in classification, Walker's is concerned both with

---

[4] The poem by Edwin Markham (1852–1940) and the novel by John Steinbeck (1902–1968) describe men as brutes.

classifying (putting items in a class) and with dividing (separat-ing the items in a class from one another). Point out where she is engaging in each of these two related operations.

2. Which do you find more original and interesting, the details with which Walker fleshes out her examples or her categories them-selves? Explain your answer.

3. What is Barbara Walker's larger purpose in classifying Penn men? She is doing it for fun, presumably; but what purpose does she humorously offer her field guide to serve?

4. Who is Walker's immediate audience, and why does she address her reader as "you" most of the time?

5. How does the author of this essay indicate that she is not a "man-hater," that she takes the game seriously enough to play it with care and discrimination?

6. The general organization of Walker's essay is simple, even me-chanical; but the discussion within each unit is carefully struc-tured. Take a close look at how she ends each segment. What do these endings have in common?

7. Describe the effect that Walker achieves with the four short sentences at the end of paragraph 6.

8. Given its subject, this essay could have become spiteful, even bitter; but Walker softens her criticisms with humor. Point to several examples that you find most amusing. Why is it especially necessary to keep your temper and balance when adding fuel to a "controversy" (par. 1)?

Words and Figures of Speech

1. Walker sometimes uses CLICHES: "feel about two inches high" (par. 2), "you've got two strikes against you" (par. 8). Point out other examples: Do they mar Walker's essay or help it along? Why?

2. What are the implications of the rock-in-the-stream METAPHOR in paragraph 11?

3. A *Bohemian* (type 4) really has nothing to do with Bohemia, the region in western Czechoslovakia. The English word comes from a French name for gypsies (thought originally to have come from Bohemia) that applied to artists and students in Paris. What are the CONNOTATIONS of the term, and how do you suppose a name for gypsies came to be applied to students and artists?

4. In the reference room of your college or university library, look up *The Rubáiyat of Omar Khayyám* in the *Oxford Companion to English Literature* or other standard reference work. Who was Omar Khayyám and why is the allusion fitting?

Comparing

1. Compare and contrast the "compiler" of Walker's report on college men with the speaker in Nora Ephron's "A Few Words about Breasts" in Chapter 1.

2. Where in her classification scheme would Walker probably put the pole-vaulter of David Dubber's "Crossing the Bar on A Fiberglas Pole" (Chapter 1)?

Discussion and Writing Topics

1. Write your own field guide to the opposite sex on your campus. Try to think of types that Walker's essay does not include.

Peter Farb

The Levels of Sleep

An expert on American Indians and on insects, father of two sons, and husband of a museum curator, Peter Farb was born in New York City in 1929. A graduate of Vanderbilt University, he attended graduate school at Columbia and has taught at Yale. Since 1953 he has been primarily a free-lance author of books on the science and natural history of North America. Among his many publications are Living Earth (1959); The Insects (1962); The Story of Life (1962); Face of North America (1963—presented by President Kennedy to one hundred foreign heads of state); Man's Rise to Civilization (1968); and Word Play (1974). "The Levels of Sleep" (editor's title) is an excerpt from "The Intelligent Senses," a chapter in Farb's latest work, Humankind (1978). It classifies human sleep into periods and stages according to eye movements; and it explains, incidentally, why students who cram for tests should get at least some sleep before an exam.

The modern understanding of sleep began quite by accident   1
in 1952, when a graduate student was assigned to observe the eyelids of sleeping volunteers to see whether any movement occurred. He observed that at certain times during the night the eyeballs of sleepers darted about furiously beneath the closed lids. (Eye movements are very easy to detect, even when the lids are closed; ask someone to perform these movements and see for yourself.) Such activity was totally unexpected, since sleep had long been thought to be a time of quiescence, not one in which the brain was actively generating eye movements that were often faster than could be produced

by a waking person. Since then, much more has been learned about rapid eye movement (technically known as "REM") during certain stages of sleep. REM sleep is always accompanied by very distinctive brain-wave patterns, a marked increase in blood flow and in the temperature of the brain, irregular breathing, convulsive twisting of the face and fingertips, and the erection of the penis and clitoris. REM sleep is active sleep, even though the large muscles of the body are completely relaxed. The other kind of sleep is known as "NREM" (that is, non-REM). During this state, breathing is regular, body movement is generally absent, and brain activity is low. Perception shuts down because the senses are no longer gathering information and communicating it to the brain. NREM sleep is sometimes called "quiet sleep" but in one respect that is not so; snoring occurs during this state.

A number of curious experiences occur at the onset of sleep. A [2] person just about to go to sleep may experience an electric shock, a flash of light, or a crash of thunder—but the most common sensation is that of floating or falling, which is why "falling asleep" is a scientifically valid description. A nearly universal occurrence at the beginning of sleep (although not everyone recalls it) is a sudden, uncoordinated jerk of the head, the limbs, or even the entire body. Most people tend to think of going to sleep as a slow slippage into oblivion, but the onset of sleep is not gradual at all. It happens in an instant. One moment the individual is awake, the next moment not.

The first period of sleep is always NREM. It consists of four [3] stages, during each of which the sleeper becomes more remote from the sensory environment. Children in particular are virtually unwakenable at the fourth stage. Even if they can finally be roused, it may be several minutes before they return to awareness. This deepest fourth stage is the period during which most of the talking in one's sleep, sleep-walking, night terrors, and bed-wetting by children take place. After the fourth stage, the sleeper retraces all the stages back to lighter sleep. The downward progression into the first deep sleep is smooth, but the upward progression is marked by irregular jumps from one stage to the other. The first REM period begins about seventy or eighty minutes after a person has fallen asleep and usually lasts for only about ten minutes. The entire NREM–REM cycle averages about ninety minutes, but with some individuals it is as short as seventy minutes and with others as long as 110. The two kinds of sleep—as different from each other as sleep is from wakefulness—continue to alternate throughout the night. With each cycle, the amount of REM sleep gradually increases, to the degree that it may become as long as sixty minutes just before awakening, whereas the amount of NREM sleep decreases markedly. An adult who sleeps seven and a half hours spends from one and a half to two hours of that period in REM sleep, mostly toward the end of the sleep period.

The new view of sleep that has emerged in the past few decades   4
from numerous laboratories is not one of sleep as "death's counter-feit," as Shakespeare [1] put it. Sleep is not passive in the sense that it is the absence of something characteristic of wakefulness. Rather, it is an active state in which the brain is never at rest. One theory about human sleep assigns different functions to the two kinds of sleep. NREM sleep apparently does the things that have traditionally been assigned by common sense to all sleep: growth, repair to the body's tissues, and the synthesis of proteins. NREM sleep is a biological necessity; without it, an individual eventually would collapse. When someone is deprived of sleep, NREM sleep is usually made up first. And until the deprivation is compensated for, that person feels lethargic and less able than usual to carry out physical tasks.

REM sleep, in contrast, apparently restores the neural processes   5
underlying consciousness; it is mental rather than physical. People deprived of it are not physically lethargic but emotionally irritable; they usually perform poorly in concentration and learning tests. REM sleep appears to be essential to integrate recently learned material into long-term memory. Students who stay up all night cramming for an examination the next day usually do not do as well as those who have had some sleep. The explanation is that the students have momentarily learned a lot of new facts, but these facts cannot be remembered unless they have been processed dur-ing sleep for incorporation into the memory. REM sleep also seems to help people cope with day-to-day stress. Experiments have shown that volunteers who were exposed to stressful situations had a sharply increased need for REM sleep, during which time they

[1] In *Macbeth*, Act 2, Scene 3.

apparently made peace with the traumatic experiences. Such experiments offer fresh evidence that sleep is one of the most active parts of a person's day.

QUESTIONS

Understanding

1. What are the respective functions of REM and NREM sleep, according to Farb?
2. In the light of new research, why is sleep no longer to be regarded as "death's counterfeit"?
3. Why do students who have crammed all night for an examination usually perform less well than those who have had some sleep?
4. When, toward morning, a person's REM sleep lasts for sixty minutes, approximately how long is the period of NREM sleep that follows it?

Strategies and Structure

1. Into what two categories does Farb CLASSIFY human sleep? What is the distinguishing feature of each class?
2. Into how many periods does he *divide* the human sleep-cycle? To which class does the sleep in each period belong?
3. Into how many stages does Farb *divide* the first period of human sleep? Why does he *not* divide the second period into stages?
4. What is the distinguishing feature of each stage of sleep in the first period? Its distance from what?
5. With some justification, Farb's essay could be placed in Chapter 5, among essays that *define*. Why? What is Farb defining? How do CLASSIFICATION and DEFINITION work together in his essay?
6. Farb is dividing sleep into periods and stages, but he is also analyzing the sleep cycle. (In the next chapter you will examine essays in PROCESS ANALYSIS.) How does the peculiar cyclical nature of his subject complicate the classifying operation? How does he solve these difficulties?

7. What is the ultimate purpose to be served by Farb's classification of human sleep?

Words and Figures of Speech

1. Why is the METAPHOR "falling asleep" scientifically accurate, according to Farb?
2. What is an "acronym"? What acronyms does Farb use here?
3. Look up any of the following words you do not know: *quiescence* (par. 1), *convulsive* (1), *oblivion* (2), *virtually* (3), *synthesis* (4), *proteins* (4), *deprivation* (4), *lethargic* (4), *neural* (5).

Comparing

1. Compare Farb's division of a cyclical process with Walker's division of Penn-men-to-avoid in "For Women Mostly," the preceding essay. In what sense is Walker's method a "straight-line" method of division?
2. When you read Desmond Morris's "Barrier Signals" in Chapter 5 ("Essays That Define"), analyze how Farb's classification with the aid of definition departs from Morris's definition with the aid of division.

Discussion and Writing Topics

1. All primates share the need for sleep and many other biological characteristics. Write a classification essay in which you explain why men and apes belong in the same kingdom (Animals), phylum (Chordates), class (Mammals), and order (Primates).
2. Farb points out that REM sleep is necessary "to integrate recently learned material into long-term memory" (par. 6). Write an essay in which you classify the operations of human memory according to length of retention and in which you divide the process of remembering into stages.
3. Classify the basic functions of the human body according to whether they are voluntary or involuntary. (Digestion would be involuntary, for example; but eating is voluntary.)

Isaac Asimov

What Do You Call a Platypus?

Isaac Asimov was born in Petrovichi, Russia, in 1920, entered the
United States at age three, and became a naturalized citizen in
1928. After attending undergraduate and graduate school at
Columbia (Ph.D. in chemistry, 1948), he began teaching bio-
chemistry at the Boston University School of Medicine. His two
hundred books deal with an astounding range of subjects: bio-
chemistry, the human body, ecology, mathematics, physics,
astronomy, genetics, history, the Bible, and Shakespeare—to name
only a few. Asimov's first real acclaim came with a short story,
"Nightfall," in 1941; he continues to be best known, perhaps, for
his science fiction, including I, Robot (1950); the "Foundation"
trilogy (1951–53); and The Caves of Steel (1954). More recently,
he has published The Stars in Their Courses (1976) and The
Gods Themselves (1977). "What Do You Call a Platypus?" is an
essay on taxonomy, the science of classification, that shows both
the limitations of that science and how it can help provide new
knowledge of the world.

In 1800, a stuffed animal arrived in England from the newly   1
discovered continent of Australia.

The continent had already been the source of plants and   2
animals never seen before—but this one was ridiculous. It was
nearly two feet long, and had a dense coating of hair. It also
had a flat rubbery bill, webbed feet, a broad flat tail, and a
spur on each hind ankle that was clearly intended to secrete
poison. What's more, under the tail was a single opening.

Zoologists stared at the thing in disbelief. Hair like a mam-   3
mal! Bill and feet like an aquatic bird! Poison spurs like a
snake! A single opening in the rear as though it laid eggs!

There was an explosion of anger. The thing was a hoax. Some 4
unfunny jokester in Australia, taking advantage of the distance
and strangeness of the continent, had stitched together parts of
widely different creatures and was intent on making fools of innocent zoologists in England.

Yet the skin seemed to hang together. There were no signs of 5
artificial joining. Was it or was it not a hoax? And if it wasn't a
hoax, was it a mammal with reptilian characteristics, or a reptile
with mammalian characteristics, or was it partly bird, or *what?*

The discussion went on heatedly for decades. Even the name 6
emphasized the ways in which it didn't seem like a mammal
despite its hair. One early name was *Platypus anatinus* which is
Graeco-Latin [1] for "Flat-foot, ducklike." Unfortunately, the term,
platypus, had already been applied to a type of beetle and there
must be no duplication in scientific names. It therefore received
another name, *Ornithorhynchus paradoxus*, which means "Bird-
beak, paradoxical."

Slowly, however, zoologists had to fall into line and admit that 7
the creature was real and not a hoax, however upsetting it might
be to zoological notions. For one thing, there were increasingly
reliable reports from people in Australia who caught glimpses of
the creature alive. The *paradoxus* was dropped and the scientific
name is now *Ornithorhynchus anatinus.*

To the general public, however, it is the "duckbill platypus," 8
or even just the duckbill, the queerest mammal (assuming it is a
mammal) in the world.

When specimens were received in such condition as to make it 9
possible to study the internal organs, it appeared that the heart
was just like those of mammals and not at all like those of reptiles.
The egg-forming machinery in the female, however, was not at all
like those of mammals, but like those of birds or reptiles. It
seemed really and truly to be an egg-layer.

It wasn't till 1884, however, that the actual eggs laid by a crea- 10
ture with hair were found. Such creatures included not only the
platypus, but another Australian species, the spiny anteater. That
was worth an excited announcement. A group of British scientists
were meeting in Montreal at the time, and the egg-discoverer, W.
H. Caldwell, sent them a cable to announce the finding.

[1] Combination of Greek and Latin; many scientific names put Latin endings
on Greek roots.

It wasn't till the twentieth century that the intimate life of the [11] duckbill came to be known. It is an aquatic animal, living in Australian fresh water at a wide variety of temperatures—from tropical streams at sea level to cold lakes at an elevation of a mile.

The duckbill is well adapted to its aquatic life, with its dense [12] fur, its flat tail, and its webbed feet. Its bill has nothing really in common with that of the duck, however. The nostrils are differently located and the platypus bill is different in structure, rubbery rather than duckishly horny. It serves the same function as the duck's bill, however, so it has been shaped similarly by the pressures of natural selection.

The water in which the duckbill lives is invariably muddy at the [13] bottom and it is in this mud that the duckbill roots for its food supply. The bill, ridged with horny plates, is used as a sieve, dredging about sensitively in the mud, filtering out the shrimps, earthworms, tadpoles and other small creatures that serve it as food.

When the time comes for the female platypus to produce [14] young, she builds a special burrow, which she lines with grass and carefully plugs. She then lays two eggs, each about three quarters of an inch in diameter and surrounded by a translucent, horny shell.

These the mother platypus places between her tail and abdo- [15] men and curls up about them. It takes two weeks for the young to hatch out. The new-born duckbills have teeth and very short bills, so that they are much less "birdlike" than the adults. They feed on milk. The mother has no nipples, but milk oozes out of pore openings in the abdomen and the young lick the area and are nourished in this way. As they grow, the bills become larger and the teeth fall out.

Yet despite everything zoologists learned about the duckbills, [16] they never seemed entirely certain as to where to place them in the table of animal classification. On the whole, the decision was made because of hair and milk. In all the world, only mammals have true hair and only mammals produce true milk. The duckbill and spiny anteater have hair and produce milk, so they have been classified as mammals.

Just the same, they are placed in a very special position. All the [17] mammals are divided into two subclasses. In one of these subclasses ("Prototheria" or "first-beasts")are the duckbill and five species of the spiny anteater. In the other ("Theria" or just "beast") are all the other 4,231 known species of mammals.

But all this is the result of judging only living species of mammals. Suppose we could study extinct species as well. Would that help us decide on the place of the platypus? Would it cause us to confirm our decision—or change it? [18]

Fossil remnants exist of mammals and reptiles of the far past, but these remnants are almost entirely of bones and teeth. Bones and teeth give us interesting information but they can't tell us everything. [19]

For instance, is there any way of telling, from bones and teeth alone, whether an extinct creature is a reptile or a mammal? [20]

Well, all living reptiles have legs splayed out so that the upper part above the knee is horizontal (assuming they have legs at all). All mammals, on the other hand, have legs that are vertical all the way down. Again, reptiles have teeth that all look more or less alike, while mammals have teeth that have different shapes, with sharp incisors in front, flat molars in back, and conical incisors and premolars in between. [21]

As it happens, there are certain extinct creatures, to which have been given the name "therapsids," which have their leg bones vertical and their teeth differentiated just as in the case of mammals. —And yet they are considered reptiles and not mammals. Why? Because there is another bony difference to be considered. [22]

In living mammals, the lower jaw contains a single bone; in reptiles, it is made up of a number of bones. The therapsid lower jaw is made up of seven bones and because of that those creatures are classified as reptiles. And yet in the therapsid lower jaw, the one bone making up the central portion of the lower jaw is by far the largest. The other six bones, three on each side, are crowded into the rear angle of the jaw. [23]

There seems no question, then, that if the therapsids are reptiles they are nevertheless well along the pathway towards mammals. [24]

But how far along the pathway are they? For instance, did they have hair? It might seem that it would be impossible to tell whether an extinct animal had hair or not just from the bones, but let's see— [25]

Hair is an insulating device. It keeps body heat from being lost too rapidly. Reptiles keep their body temperature at about that of the outside environment. They don't have to be concerned over loss of heat and hair would be of no use to them. [26]

Mammals, however, maintain their internal temperature at [27] nearly 100° F. regardless of the outside temperature; they are "warm-blooded." This gives them the great advantage of remaining agile and active in cold weather, when the chilled reptile is sluggish. But then the mammal must prevent heat loss by means of a hairy covering. (Birds, which also are warm-blooded, use feathers as an insulating device.)

With that in mind, let's consider the bones. In reptiles, the [28] nostrils open into the mouth just behind the teeth. This means that reptiles can only breathe with their mouths empty. When they are biting or chewing, breathing must stop. This doesn't bother a reptile much, for it can suspend its need for oxygen for considerable periods.

Mammals, however, must use oxygen in their tissues constantly, [29] in order to keep the chemical reactions going that serve to keep their body temperature high. The oxygen supply must not be cut off for more than very short intervals. Consequently mammals have developed a bony palate, a roof to the mouth. When they breathe, air is led above the mouth to the throat. This means they can continue breathing while they bite and chew. It is only when they are actually in the act of swallowing that the breath is cut off and this is only a matter of a couple of seconds at a time.

The later therapsid species had, as it happened, a palate. If they [30] had a palate, it seems a fair deduction that they needed an uninterrupted supply of oxygen that makes it look as though they were warm-blooded. And if they were warm-blooded, then very likely they had hair, too.

The conclusion, drawn from the bones alone, would seem to be [31] that some of the later therapsids had hair, even though, judging by their jawbones, they were still reptiles.

The thought of hairy reptiles is astonishing. But that is only [32] because the accident of evolution seems to have wiped out the intermediate forms. The only therapsids alive seem to be those that have developed *all* the mammalian characteristics, so that we call them mammals. The only reptiles alive are those that developed *none* of the mammalian characteristics.

Those therapsids that developed some but not others seem to [33] be extinct.

Only the duckbill and the spiny anteater remain near the border [34] line. They have developed the hair and the milk and the single-boned lower jaw and the four-chambered heart, but not the nipples or the ability to bring forth live young.

For all we know, some of the extinct therapsids, while still having their many-boned lower jaw (which is why we call them reptiles instead of mammals), may have developed even beyond the duckbill in other ways. Perhaps some late therapsids had nipples and brought forth living young. We can't tell from the bones alone. 35

If we had a complete record of the therapsids, flesh and blood, as well as teeth and bone, we might decide that the duckbill was on the therapsid side of the line and not on the mammalian side. —Or are there any other pieces of evidence that can be brought into play? 36

An American zoologist, Giles T. MacIntyre, of Queens College, has taken up the matter of the trigeminal nerve, which leads from the jaw muscles to the brain. 37

In all reptiles, without exception, the trigeminal nerve passes through the skull at a point that lies between two of the bones making up the skull. In all mammals that bring forth living young, without exception, the nerve actually passes *through* a particular skull bone. 38

Suppose we ignore all the matter of hair and milk and eggs, and just consider the trigeminal nerve. In the duckbill, does the nerve pass through a bone, or between two bones? It has seemed in the past that the nerve passed through a bone and that put the duckbill on the mammalian side of the dividing line. 39

Not so, says MacIntyre. The study of the trigeminal nerve was made in adult duckbills, where the skull bones are fused together and the boundaries are hard to make out. In young duckbills, the skull bones are more clearly separated and in them it can be seen, MacIntyre says, that the trigeminal nerve goes between two bones. 40

In that case, there is a new respect in which the duckbill falls on the reptilian side of the line and MacIntyre thinks it ought not to be considered a mammal, but as a surviving species of the otherwise long-extinct therapsid line. 41

And so, a hundred seventy years after zoologists began to puzzle out the queer mixture of characteristics that go to make up the duckbill platypus—there is still argument as to what to call it. 42

Is the duckbill platypus a mammal? A reptile? Or just a duckbill platypus? 43

QUESTIONS

Understanding

1. What are the chief distinguishing features of mammals as reported by Asimov? Of reptiles?
2. Which mammalian features does the platypus lack? Which reptilian characteristics does it possess?
3. How does the example of the platypus show the limitations of the zoological CLASSIFICATION system?
4. What new evidence does Asimov cite for reclassifying the platypus? How convincing do you find it? Why?

Strategies and Structure

1. Why do you think Asimov begins his case for reclassifying the platypus by recounting the confused history of how the animal got its name?
2. Why does it matter what we *call* a platypus? For what ultimate purpose is Asimov concerned with the creature's name?
3. Why does Asimov refer to extinct creatures beginning with paragraph 18? What is the function of the therapsids (par. 22) in his line of reasoning?
4. This essay in reclassification ends with three alternatives (par. 43). Why three instead of just two?
5. The logic of paragraph 32 depends upon an unstated assumption about the order of evolution. Which does Asimov assume came first, reptiles or mammals? How does this assumption influence his entire ARGUMENT? Is the assumption valid?

Words and Figures of Speech

1. Why was "paradoxical" (par. 6) an appropriate part of the platypus's name? How does it differ in precise usage from "ambiguous" and "ambivalent"?
2. Asimov refers to the "egg-forming machinery" (par. 9) of the female platypus. How technical is this term? What does it suggest about the audience for whom Asimov intends this essay?
3. What is meant by "the pressures of natural selection" (par. 12)?

4. Asimov's essay is an exercise in "taxonomy," although he does not use the word. What does it mean according to your dictionary?

Comparing

1. Asimov's essay has some features of a logical argument of the sort you will encounter in Chapter 9. What is he attempting to prove or disprove? When you read William Buckley's "Capital Punishment" (Chapter 9), *contrast* the kind of evidence presented in his logical argument with that presented in Asimov's.

Discussion and Writing Topics

1. What would *you* call a platypus? Why?
2. Explain why a whale is classified as a mammal instead of a fish.
3. A classification system provides a means of arranging information about the known world. Using Asimov's train of thought or some other example, explain how classification systems also help us gain *new* knowledge.

Essays That Classify and Divide

Write an essay on one of the following subjects that uses classification or division as its organizing principle. Remember that a good classification essay not only assigns members to a class but also gives interesting reasons for the divisions it makes and draws interesting conclusions about its subject:

1. Your teachers in high school or college

2. Blind dates

3. Drugs and drug-abusers

4. Moral codes

5. Fraternities or sororities

6. Neighborhoods, high schools, or churches in your hometown

7. Landlords in the campus area

8. Fast-food restaurants

9. Food in the dining facilities on your campus

10. Attitudes toward getting a college education

11. Cameras, bicycles, or motorcycles

12. Modern families

13. Movies you have seen in the last year

14. Television soap operas

15. Styles of rock, folk, country and western, or classical music

16. Ways of seeing (for the first time) a city, museum, or foreign country

17. Ways of reacting to personal disappointment or tragedy

18. Life-styles among people under thirty

3

Essays That
Analyze a Process

Analysis breaks its object into components. It differs from
CLASSIFICATION [1] *by attending to a particular member of a
class rather than the class in general. When we classify an
artichoke, for example, we put it in the category of "thistle-
like plants." When we analyze an artichoke, we pull apart
an individual specimen and note that it is made up of layer
upon layer of fibrous green scales. If we analyze the growth
of an artichoke from a seed, we are analyzing a process
(which tends to be in motion) rather than an object (which
tends to be stable). Most how-to-do-it essays analyze processes, as do most accounts of how something works (a
typewriter, a city transit system, gravity). The selections in
this chapter are essays in* PROCESS ANALYSIS.

*In the following analysis, John McPhee tells how orange
juice concentrate is made from fresh oranges:*

As the fruit starts to move along a concentrate plant's assembly
line, it is first culled. In what some citrus people remember as
"the old fresh-fruit days," before the Second World War,
about forty per cent of all oranges grown in Florida were
eliminated at packinghouses and dumped in fields. Florida milk
tasted like orangeade. Now, with the exception of split and
rotten fruit, all of Florida's orange crop is used. Moving up a
conveyer belt, oranges are scrubbed with detergent before they
roll on into juicing machines. There are several kinds of juicing
machines, and they are something to see. One is called the
Brown Seven Hundred. Seven hundred oranges a minute go into
it and are split and reamed on the same kind of rosettes that

---

[1] Terms printed in all capitals are defined in the Glossary.

are in the centers of ordinary kitchen reamers. The rinds that come pelting out the bottom are integral halves, just like the rinds of oranges squeezed in a kitchen. Another machine is the Food Machinery Corporation's FMC In-line Extractor. It has a shining row of aluminum teeth. When an orange tumbles in, the upper jaw comes crunching down on it while at the same time the orange is penetrated from below by a perforated steel tube. As the jaws crush the outside, the juice goes through the perforations in the tube and down into the plumbing of the concentrate plant. All in a second, the juice has been removed and the rind has been crushed and shredded beyond recognition.

From either machine, the juice flows on into a thing called the finisher, where seeds, rag, and pulp are removed. The finisher has a big stainless-steel screw that steadily drives the juice through a fine-mesh screen. From the finisher, it flows on into holding tanks. . . .

The first thing to notice about this analysis is that it combines several processes into one. McPhee describes the journey of fresh oranges from the time they enter the conveyor belt until the juice reaches the holding tanks. But because all companies do not use the same machines, he must digress to explain the differences between the Brown Seven Hundred and the In-line Extractor. The discussion returns from its divergent branches in the beginning of the second paragraph, "From either machine. . . ." McPhee picks up the flow so smoothly that we hardly notice any interruption; but, like many accounts of a complex process, his is a composite. The author has reduced the complexities to their elements and takes care of inconsistencies in brief asides to the reader. (The business of extracting "chilled juice" from fresh oranges is so different from making concentrate that McPhee has to describe it in a separate segment of his account.)

One aside in our example, however, has little to do with the process of making orange concentrate. This is the author's reference to the days before World War II when all Florida milk tasted like orangeade. To keep our interest, McPhee is laying out many things at once, including the changing history of Florida's citrus industry. Process analysis often draws upon other strategies of EXPOSITION and upon the other MODES OF DISCOURSE. When McPhee switches from what happened in "the old fresh-fruit days" to what happens "now," he slips into NARRATION. Process analysis might even be regarded as a specialized form of narration that tells what happens from one stage of a process to another. But the ultimate purpose of process analysis is to explain how rather than to tell what. And although process analysis often describes the parts of an operation, it focuses upon their function rather than their appearance (the business of DESCRIPTION).

Perhaps the most important lesson to be learned from McPhee's analysis is that he divides the process of making concentrate into stages: (1) culling, (2) scrubbing, (3) extracting, (4) straining, (5) storing. When you begin an essay in process analysis, make a list of the stages of the operation you are describing or the directions you are giving. Once you have a rough list of stages, make sure that they are separate and distinct. (McPhee does not isolate the movement of oranges up the conveyor belt as a stage because the conveyor is involved in more than one stage of the process of making concentrate.) When you are satisfied that none of the items on your list repeat others and that you have omitted no essential items, you are ready to decide upon the order in which your steps will be presented to the reader.

The usual order of a process analysis is chronological, beginning with the earliest stage of the process and ending with the last or with the finished product. If you are describing a cyclical rather than a linear process, however, you will have to break into the cycle at an arbitrary point, proceed through the cycle, and return to your starting place. For example, you might describe the circulation of the blood by starting as it leaves the heart, tracing it through the arteries and vessels, and concluding as it flows back into the heart. If the order of the process you are describing is controlled by a piece of mechanism, let that mechanism work for you. The first part of McPhee's analysis is organized as much by that conveyor belt as by time. Whatever order you choose, do not digress from it so long that the reader loses the sequence. Sequence is the backbone of process analysis, and it must be flexible yet strong.

Peter Passell

How to Grow an Avocado

The son of an investor, Peter Passell grew up in Pittsburgh, attended Swarthmore College and Yale (Ph.D., 1970), and joined the Department of Economics, Columbia University, at the age of twenty-six. An economist who specializes in witty guides to unusual consumer goods and services, including inexpensive wines, he is best known for The Best (1974, with Leonard Ross). "How to Grow an Avocado" is a complete entry in How To, a manual of advice and instructions for, among other things, avoiding shark bite, keeping a pipe lit, buying an island, controlling inflation. (On this last item Passell advises us to stay healthy: "the chemicals in your body, which sold for just 98 cents in 1936, are now worth $5.60.")

W hen shopping, remember that larger, rougher, dark-skinned Florida avocados are usually better-behaved house-plants than the smaller California variety. Any kind of avocado will sprout and give forth leaves, however, if you allow it to germinate and plant it in decent soil. Sometimes roots start to sprout even before you get the pit out of the fruit. If so, wash the pit in warm water and proceed. If not, either peel it or just leave it in a warm place for a day or so until the skin dries up and falls off.

From here, there are two schools of thought on avocado culture. Some like to skewer the naked pit and suspend it in a glass of warm water on a tripod of toothpicks while the roots develop. This method allows supervision of root growth; it may amuse, but only postpones the day when you must bury the little darling.

It's faster then, and more efficient, just to plant the pit in   3
a medium-sized pot (about six inches across will do for the first
year) in a mix of two thirds potting soil and one third humus
or garden dirt. Avocados prefer rich, loamy soil. Plant base (wider
part) down, and cover about two thirds of the way up.

Then water frequently. With warm water, please. If your house   4
is dry you may invert a clear cup over the pit to create a humid
environment. Eventually it will split and germinate; almost every
pit cooperates, but it may take up to three months, so be patient.
Your avocado is busy underground.

Once sprouted, an avocado grows fast, a prime reason for its   5
popularity with the brown-thumb set. The first shoot will be
straight and tender. You must be cruel and determined. When the
new stalk reaches six inches in height, snip it off halfway, straight
across. The result will look miserable at first, but your clipped
avocado seedling will fight back with new shoots and more leaves.
Now you should bury the pit completely.

From here on, you are in charge. Feed the avocado often, keep   6
it well watered, and prune in any direction you fancy. Unless you
do prune it will follow a natural inclination to be tall and gawky,
but ruthless shears can force it into a bushy globe. After a year or
so, you will probably need to repot—the general rule is that a
plant's height should not exceed the diameter of the pot by more
than five times. New soil every two years is a good idea also.

Naming your avocado is strictly optional, but we feel it pro-   7
motes healthy identification with weak, green things. . . .

QUESTIONS

Understanding

1. Why, according to Passell's school of avocado care and culture, is
   it better to bury the pit at once instead of dangling it in a glass
   of water?
2. How do you know when it is time to repot your avocado plant?

Strategies and Structure

1. Into how many stages does Passell analyze the process of growing
   an avocado plant? What are they?

2. Throughout most of his analysis, Passell proceeds in a straight line. Where is he forced to digress and why?

3. In paragraph 6, Passell says that the reader is in charge "from here on." Who has been in charge up to this point?

4. It is possible to read "it will split" in paragraph 4 so as to make the pronoun refer to the clear cup instead of the avocado pit. How might the sentence be rewritten to avoid this possible confusion?

5. Describe the TONE of Passell's essay. Cite specific passages that help to set that tone.

Words and Figures of Speech

1. Passell treats avocados as if they had human characteristics. Point out several examples of this PERSONIFICATION. Does his use of this FIGURE OF SPEECH promote "healthy identification" (par. 7) with green things, or do you find it too cute? Explain your opinion.

2. What exactly does a plant do when it *germinates* (par. 1)?

3. Members of the "brown-thumb set" (par. 5) are to be distinguished from whom?

Comparing

1. How do the purpose and organization of Passell's PROCESS ANALYSIS differ from those of Peter Farb's CLASSIFICATION in "The Levels of Sleep" (preceding chapter).

Discussion and Writing Topics

1. Write a PROCESS ANALYSIS in which you explain how to do one of the following: plant a garden, grow roses, make a compost heap, select and plant a tree from a nursery.

Katie Kelly

Garbage

Katie Kelly, a free-lance writer, lives in New York City, but her hometown is Albion (Boone Co.), Nebraska (population: 2010), to which she returns once a year or so. A former contributing editor of Time *and an editor and contributor to women's magazines, she is the author of* The Wonderful World of Women's Wear Daily *(1972). The following essay is Kelly's analysis of how New York City processes its enormous flow of garbage. Soon after writing this piece for the* Saturday Review, *she published a book-length investigation of the same subject,* Garbage: The History and Future of Garbage in America *(1973).*

New Yorkers are a provincial lot. They wear their city's [1] accomplishments like blue ribbons. To anyone who will listen they boast of leading the world in everything from Mafia murders to porno moviehouses. They can also boast that their city produces more garbage than any other city in the world. In fact, it produces more than many countries.

In its 1970–71 garbage season—a boffo season if there ever [2] was one—New York City produced an average of 28,900 tons per day, as against a mere 4,800 tons per day for Los Angeles and a paltry 2,000 tons per day for San Francisco. But it is not only in quantity that New York excels. Fully 20 per cent of the city's garbage consists of quality paper: canceled checks, rough drafts of Broadway hits, executive memos, IBM punch cards, and so on. On Mondays alone seven million pounds of the Sunday *New York Times* are donated to New York garbage cans.

Then there's the packaging. According to the city's flam- [3]

boyant environmental protection administrator, Jerome Kretchmer, in the rest of the country packaging accounts for under 20 per
cent of the total garbage; in New York, for 40 per cent. Much of
this whopping total consists of flip tops, snack paks, variety packs,
plastic cases, bottles, tin cans, and other containers. Another big
chunk is aluminum. If the aluminum that New Yorkers throw out
every day were converted into Reynolds Wrap, it would make a
sheet more than 7,500 miles long—roughly the distance from New
York to Samoa.

The remaining 40 per cent of Fun City's garbage consists of   4
such mundane leavings as egg shells, coffee grounds, wilted lettuce
leaves, and pot scrapings, together with such odds and ends as tex-
tile scraps, tires, wood, glass, plastics, etc. (The 73,000 cars abandoned on New York City streets last year constitute a separate class
of garbage. Though some find their way to the dump, most of
these wrecks are bought up by scrap dealers.)

If New York produces more garbage than any other city in the   5
world, it stands to reason that the cost of getting rid of it must be
correspondingly prodigious. It is. Last year the bill for pickup,
processing, and delivery came to $176,246,604. Though one would
expect innovation from the undisputed leader in the field of garbage, New York is forced to dispose of its trash in ways familiar to
every small town in the country: It burns the stuff in incinerators—
about 30 per cent of New York City garbage is incinerated—and/or
buries it in landfills.

The largest of the city's seven incinerators, the Brooklyn incin-   6
erator is a yellow-brick building with high walls, few windows, and
two 200-foot-tall smoke stacks, one of which is equipped with an
electrostatic precipitator to reduce pollution. (Although a cut
above the average in cleanliness, New York's incinerator stacks still
spew thousands of pounds of soot over the city every day.) Garbage trucks parade up to the Brooklyn plant, dumping their loads
into a pit capable of holding 12,500 tons of garbage. A crane
moves back and forth over this pit, periodically clanking down to
gouge out a one-ton bite. The crane then drops the garbage onto
conveyor belts, which in turn feed it into the incinerator ovens.

Measuring thirty by seven by two hundred feet, each of the   7
Brooklyn incinerator's four ovens is capable of burning up ten tons
of garbage an hour at temperatures averaging 1,600° to 1,800° F.
The towering stacks create such an upward draft that, upon look-

ing into one of the iron grates, I felt as if, if I didn't hold on, I would be sucked into that fiery furnace.

After the garbage has been burned, the cooled residue is dumped [8] onto barges, which are towed off by tugboats to one of five landfill sites around the city. The largest of these is the 3,000-acre Fresh Kills site on Staten Island.

Fresh Kills, which daily receives about 11,000 tons of garbage, [9] is a strange place. Much of this former swampland resembles the ash heaps of *The Great Gatsby*.[1] Vast, forlorn, endless. A vision of death. In the foreground, a discarded funeral wreath. A doll with outstretched arms. A man's black sock. A nylon stocking. And, beyond, refrigerators, toilets, bathtubs, stoves.

Yet Fresh Kills is also—in places and in its own way—unexpect- [10] edly beautiful. Thousands of gulls wheel in the air. Banking sharply, they dip down one by one to settle in for a good feast. In areas where the garbage is fresh, there is an overpowering stench, but where it is older, its blanket of earth is covered with grass, bushes, shrubs, trees. Summertime in Fresh Kills is a time of flowers and birdsong. A volunteer vegetable garden flourishes in the landfill. Here, in the world's largest compost heap, the seeds and sprouts of kitchen scraps thrive. Come fall, offices all around New York's City Hall are decorated with gourds and pumpkins harvested at Fresh Kills. In the fall, too, quail and pheasants scurry through Fresh Kills' underbrush, creating a problem for the De- partment of Sanitation: Hunters try to poach on this municipal game preserve.

"Fresh Kills turns me on," Jerome Kretchmer said a few days [11] after my visit to the site. Recently, he went on, he had taken his seven-year-old daughter's class out to Fresh Kills for a field trip. Even the sight of the barges heading off for the landfill sites excited him: "You can stand on the shore on Monday morning and watch the barges going out. And you know what went on in New York City over the weekend. There are fetuses and dead cats. Packages, boxes, cartons from fancy stores, dress scraps. Wow, man! Whatever went on in the city is going out to Fresh Kills. You can see it all. What we used. What we wasted."

Opened in 1948, Fresh Kills is already almost full to the brim, [12]

---

[1] Novel by F. Scott Fitzgerald published in 1925; it compares modern life to a wasteland of ashes near a Long Island railroad track.

for New York City, like every other city in this country, has more garbage than it can cope with. The city is, in fact, due to run out of landfill space—preferably swampland or a sandpit or gulley—in 1985. The solution: Pile it higher. But even here there are limits. As one city official put it: "We have to leave some room between the sea gulls and the planes."

"It sure has changed out here," one worker, who has been at   13
Fresh Kills for years, told me. "Why, there used to be fresh natural springs over there." He gestured out over the hundreds of acres of garbage. Natural crab beds once flourished in the area. Now they, too, are gone, buried under tons of garbage.

QUESTIONS

Understanding

1. In what two ways does New York City's garbage differ from that of other cities? What about the process of handling that garbage? How different is *it*?
2. Why does Fresh Kills "turn on" (par. 11) Administrator Kretchmer? What story does he read in the city's garbage?
3. New York's great garbage dump is a place of death for Kelly (par. 9). What other associations does it hold for her? In which direction does the last paragraph (13) tip the balance?

Strategies and Structure

1. Kelly divides the process of handling New York's garbage into three main stages. If the first is collection, what are the other two? Where are they explained?
2. To which stage does Kelly pay least attention? Should she have paid more? Why or why not?
3. Abandoned cars are a substantial form of garbage that Kelly leaves out of her process analysis. Why does she do so?
4. Point out specific details (for example, the money figures in paragraph 5) by which Kelly establishes her authority as an expert in the "field" she is explaining to us.
5. What is the purpose of the last sentence in paragraph 7?

6. What is the role of environmental protectionist Kretchmer in Kelly's essay?
7. How effective do you find the example of the giant aluminum roll in paragraph 3? Explain your answer.
8. What is the effect of including "fetuses" in the list of items in paragraph 11? How interesting do you find most of the "catalogues" of garbage in Kelly's essay?

Words and Figures of Speech

1. "Fresh Kills" may sound like a well-chosen name for a garbage graveyard, but in American place-names "Kill" has nothing to do with death. What geographical meaning does the word have, according to your dictionary?
2. Describe the TONE of Kelly's essay as set by SLANG words like *boffo* (par. 2) and *Fun City* (4).
3. Look up any of the following words you do not already know: *provincial* (par. 1), *paltry* (2), *flamboyant* (3), *mundane* (4), *prodigious* (5), and *innovation* (6).

Comparing

1. What hints of a PERSUASIVE ARGUMENT about ecology can you find in Kelly's PROCESS ANALYSIS? How does the evidence set forth in her essay confirm Rachel Carson's argument (in "The Obligation to Endure," "Essays For Further Reading") that we are adding new substances to the environment faster than it can adapt to them?
2. How does Kelly's tone resemble William Allen's in the next essay?

Discussion and Writing Topics

1. How does your hometown or city dispose of its garbage? Of cars abandoned on the streets? Explain either process step by step.
2. Some cities (Cleveland, Ohio, for example) are experimenting with garbage as a source of fuel. Conceive and analyze such an ideal recycling process.

3. Cities in many parts of the U.S. must cope with the problem of snow removal in winter. How well does your town handle the job? What steps are taken after a snowfall? What additional steps would you recommend to the mayor?

4. A town's history may often be read in its refuse. Describe a dump you have visited as the end product of some sequence of human events.

William Allen

How to Set a World Record

William Allen teaches creative writing at the Ohio State University. He was born in Dallas, Texas, in 1940 and attended the high school he describes in "Haircut ("Paragraphs For Analysis"). A graduate of California State University, Long Beach, he studied creative writing at the University of Iowa (M.F.A., 1970). Editor of the Ohio Journal, he has contributed stories and essays to the New York Times, Saturday Review, Antioch Review, Reader's Digest, and other publications. He is the author of Starkweather (1976), the story of a mass-murderer, and To Tojo from Billy-Bob Jones (1977), a novel. Allen considers himself a regional writer, and he thinks that "every good story should have at least one chicken in it." "How to Set a World Record" explains how even a college bookworm can become a champion.

Absolutely anyone can set a world record. The key to doing [1] something better, longer, faster, or in larger quantity than anyone else is *desire*. Desire fostered by proper attitude.

Before I set my world record, I was a great fan of *The* [2] *Guinness Book of World Records* and read each new edition from cover to cover. I liked knowing and being able to tell others that the world's chug-a-lug champ consumed 2.58 pints of beer in 10 seconds, that the world's lightest adult person weighed only 13 pounds, that the largest vocabulary for a talking bird was 531 words, spoken by a brown-beaked budgerigar named Sparky. There is, of course, only a fine line between admiration and envy, and for awhile I had been secretly desiring to be in that book myself—to astonish others just as I had been astonished. But it seemed hopeless. How could a nervous college sophomore, an anonymous bookworm, perform any of those wonderful feats? The open-throat technique necessary for chug-a-lugging was incomprehensible to my trachea— and I thought my head alone must weigh close to 13 pounds.

One day I realized what was wrong. Why should I want to *break* a record at all? Why not blaze a trail of my own? Now, as you can see, I definitely had desire, but more than that I discovered I had talent. This is where we may differ. You may have no talent at all. If not, you can still go on to set a world record that will be well worth setting. It requires no talent to wear a sock longer than anyone else has ever worn a sock. It requires no talent to wear a nickel taped to your forehead longer than anyone else— it requires desire fostered by proper attitude.

First, though, search long and hard for that hidden talent you may possess. Let me offer one important guideline. Don't follow the beaten path. Look for your own personal gift, the little something that you've always had a knack for, a certain way with. It could conceivably be anything at all—sewing on buttons efficiently, waxing a car fast yet well, or speed-rolling your hair.

My own gift—broom-balancing—was developed in my back yard when I was a child. When I remembered the unusual ability, I immediately wrote the editors of the Guinness book in London.

Dear Sirs:

I have read with enjoyment *The Guinness Book of World Records* and want you to know that I intend to contribute to your next edition.

Thinking back today, I recalled that as a child I had an uncanny talent for balancing a common house broom on the end of my forefinger. Rushing to the kitchen, I found that I have retained this gift over the years. Since almost everyone must have at some time attempted this feat, I think it would be an appropriate addition to your book.

I would like to know exactly what must be done to establish a record—how many witnesses, what sort of timing device, etc. If you will provide me with this information, I will provide you with a broom-balancing record that should astonish your readers and last for years to come.

Sincerely,
William Allen

The reply came the next week.

Dear Mr. Allen:

In order to establish a world record of broom-balancing, we would like to have the confirmation of a newspaper report and an affidavit from one or more witnesses. With regard to the timing device, I think that a good wrist watch with a second hand would prove sufficient for this purpose.

Please let us know the duration of your best effort.

Sincerely,
Andrew Thomas
Assistant Editor

It sounds simple, but a lot of preparation must go into setting a world record. You can't just set it. You must advertise, generate public interest. The purpose of this is to lure in the news media. It's absolutely necessary to have a write-up if your record is going to stick. And, of course, you will want the article for your scrapbook later on. Imagine what would happen if you just went into the bathroom and brushed your teeth for eight hours and then called the newspapers. They would think you were crazy. But if you generated interest beforehand—involved a local drugstore chain, got a name-brand toothpaste to sponsor you—then you wouldn't be crazy at all. You might even come to be something of an authority and make a career out of promoting things to do with teeth.   6

I took a slightly different tack. I ran an ad in the college newspaper which read, in part: "FREE BEER! FREE BEER! Come one, come all, to Bill Allen's Broom-Balancing Beer Bust! Yes, friends, Bill will attempt to balance a common house broom on his forefinger for at least one hour to establish a world record. The editors of *The Guinness Book of World Records* in London are anxiously awaiting the outcome. The evening will be covered by the press. Ties will not be necessary. Come one, come all, to this historic event!"   7

May I suggest you find yourself a good manager before you try to set your record. My roommate, Charlie, was mine and he proved to be invaluable. On the big night, he drew with chalk a small circle on the living room floor so I would have a place to stand. He cunningly scattered copies of the Guinness book on the coffee table. He had the good sense to make me wear a coat and tie: "You don't want to go down in history looking like a bum, do you? Of course not. You want to make a good impression."   8

The ad in the paper paid off, naturally. Over 50 people showed   9
up, filling our apartment and spilling out onto the lawn. Some
left after their two-beer limit, but most remained to see the outcome. There was some problem, though, in holding the group's
interest. For the first 10 minutes or so, they were fine, placing bets,
commenting on my technique. After that, their minds tended to
stray. They began to talk of other matters. One couple had the
nerve to ask if they could put music on and dance in the kitchen.

Charlie handled the situation like a professional. He began to   10
narrate the event, serving as a combination sportscaster and master
of ceremonies. "Ladies and gentlemen, give me your attention
please. We are at mark 15 minutes. At this time, I would like you
to look at Bill's feet. You will notice that they are not moving.
This is an indication of his skill. If you've ever tried broom-balancing yourself, you know that the tendency is to run around the
room in an effort to maintain stability."

Someone said, "He's right. I tried it today and that's exactly   11
what you do."

At the 20-minute mark, Charlie said, "Ladies and gentlemen, I   12
have an announcement. Bill's previous top practice time was 20
minutes. He has just beaten his own record! Anything can happen
from here on in, folks. Pay attention."

You might be wondering about my emotions at this point. I   13
hadn't slept well the night before, and all day I had been a nervous
wreck. I hadn't been able to eat. I had a horrible sinking feeling
every time I thought about what was coming up. But once I
started, I found I wasn't nervous at all. Not a trace of stage fright.
In fact, I blossomed under the attention. I realized this was where
I had belonged all along—in the center. Someone began to strum
a guitar and I foolishly began to bob my broom in time to the
music. "Don't get cocky," my manager warned. "You've got a long
way to go yet."

At mark 30 minutes, Charlie held up his hands for silence. "Lis-   14
ten to this, folks! The halfway point has been passed! We're halfway to history! And I want you people to know that Bill is feeling
good! He's not even sweating! I swear I don't understand how he
does it. How many people can even stand in one place that long?"

I had no clear idea who was in the room, or what they were   15
doing. In order to balance a broom, you have to stare right at the

straw. I'm not sure why this is, but it's certainly the case. You can't look away for even a second. By using peripheral vision, I was able to see a vague sea of heads but it wasn't worth the effort and I gave up. While in this awkward position, I heard the low, sinister voice of a stranger address me: "You know everyone here thinks you're crazy, don't you? I think I'll just step on your feet and see how you like that. You couldn't do anything about it. You wouldn't even know who did it because you can't look down."

"Charlie!" I called. "Come here!"   16

My manager had the situation under control in seconds. After   17
he had hustled the character out the door, he said, "Don't worry, folks. Just a heckler. One in every crowd, I guess."

I must say that Charlie's earlier remark that I was in good shape   18
was a lie—and I was feeling worse by the second. At mark 45 minutes, my neck seemed to have become locked in its upward arch. My legs were trembling and the smaller toes on each foot were without feeling. My forefinger felt like it was supporting a length of lead pipe. But more startling, I think, was the strain on my mind. I felt giddy. Strange that I have this gift, I reflected. I can't even walk around the block without occasionally wobbling off to one side. It suddenly seemed as though all the balance normally spread throughout the human body had somehow converged in my forefinger. Wouldn't it be ironic, I thought dizzily, if I just toppled over? I sniggered, seeing myself flat on my back with the broom still perfectly poised on my finger. Then I began to observe the broomstraw in incredible detail. Each stick seemed huge, like trees . . . logs . . . telephone poles. . . .

"Are you okay?" Charlie asked. I snapped out of it and reported   19
my condition. He turned to the crowd. "Folks! With only ten minutes to go, I would like us to reflect on the enormous physical and mental strain Bill is suffering right before our eyes. It's the price all champions pay, of course, when they go the distance, when they stretch the fibers of their being to the breaking point." His voice became lower, gruffer. "You may as well know. Bill has been hallucinating for some time now. But think of it, folks. While all over this country of ours, people are destroying their minds with dangerous drugs, Bill here is achieving the ends they seek—" his voice rose: he cried, "—with *no chance* of dangerous after-effects!"

Even in my condition, I knew he was going too far. I called him over to loosen my shoelaces and whispered, "Cut the speeches, okay? Just let them watch for awhile."

The hour mark came amazingly fast after that. There was a loud 10-second countdown, then the press's flashbulbs and strobes began going off like starbursts. Everybody began clapping and cheering. Using my peripheral vision, I saw that the crowd was on its feet, jumping around. I saw the happy, grinning faces.

I kept balancing. Charlie conferred with me, then yelled, "Folks! Bill is not going to stop! He says he will balance till he drops! Isn't he something? Take your seats, ladies and gentlemen. You're witnessing history tonight. Relax and enjoy it." The group was for seeing me drop, all right, but they didn't want to wait around all night for it. They became louder and harder to handle. They wanted more beer. At mark one hour, 15 minutes, I was on the verge of collapse anyway, so I gave in and tossed the broom in the air. With a feeble flourish, I caught it with the other hand and the record was set.

But no world record is *truly* set until someone has tried and failed to break it. After the congratulations, the interviews, the signing up of witnesses, it was time for everybody else to try. They didn't have a chance, of course. Most lasted only a pitiful few seconds, and the two best times were seven and 10 minutes. These two had talent but lacked the rest of the magic combination.

My record never appeared in *The Guinness Book of World Records*. I'm not sure why. Maybe they thought I should have gone longer. Maybe the plane carrying the news went down in the Atlantic. At any rate, they never wrote back and I never bothered to check on it. I knew by then that it didn't matter. The record had still been set. I had the write-up—and this alone brought me all the acclaim I could handle.

You, too, can enjoy the same success. And don't worry if you don't have a talent such as mine. There is a man in Iowa who collects dirty oil rags. He has over a thousand so far—more than anyone else in the world. He's not in the Guinness book, either, but people still stop by almost daily to see his collection and ask his opinion about this or that. His picture often appears in the local papers.

All it takes is desire fostered by proper attitude.

QUESTIONS

Understanding

1. Allen gives his entire analysis of how to set a record in the single phrase "desire fostered by proper attitude"—which sounds like an advertising slogan. What other process is he actually illustrating?
2. Who is even better at this operation than Allen's broom-balancer? How does he show *his* talent?
3. Why does Allen's broom-balancer continue past "mark one hour"?
4. Does Allen's essay suffer because his record never appeared in the Guinness book? Why or why not?

Strategies and Structure

1. Point out each stage into which Allen analyzes the process of promoting the broom-balancing event.
2. How do the language and TONE of Allen's advertisement in paragraph 7 reflect the language and tone of the essay as a whole?
3. "Desire fostered by proper attitude" makes a distinction without a real difference. How does this redundancy fit in with the general spirit of Allen's essay?
4. Why does Allen quote word for word his correspondence with the Guinness editor instead of just giving an excerpt or a summary?
5. What is the effect of Allen's aside to Charlie in paragraph 20, "Cut the speeches, okay"?
6. What is the effect of the broom-balancer's getting caught up in his own promotion after "mark one hour"? How does Charlie get similarly carried away?
7. Allen's champion did not inquire why his time was never recorded because he already had "all the acclaim I could handle" (par. 24). How is this explanation in keeping with the way Allen has portrayed his character earlier, especially in paragraphs 2 and 13?
8. Allen's comic PROCESS ANALYSIS is helped along by NARRATION. Which parts are in the narrative mode? How do they contribute to the analysis?

9. From whose POINT OF VIEW is the incident in paragraph 15 told? How do you know?

Words and Figures of Speech

1. Why does Allen compare the flash bulbs and strobes to "star-bursts" in paragraph 21?
2. The prefix *in* often means "not" (*invalid*, for example); but look up *invaluable* (par. 8) in your dictionary.
3. Why does Allen prefer to call broom-balancing his "gift" rather than his "skill"?

Comparing

1. Compare the tone of Allen's essay with Peter Passell's tone in "How to Grow an Avocado" earlier in this chapter. In which is the tone more complicated? How so?
2. In what ways does Allen's broom-balancer resemble the pole-vaulter in David Dubber's "Crossing the Bar on a Fiberglas Pole" (Chapter 1)?

Discussion and Writing Topics

The following is Allen's list of "10 World Records Waiting to Be Set." Make up your own somewhat more serious list (churning, cow milking, chimney sweeping, canoe rowing, for example) and write a PROCESS ANALYSIS explaining how to set a record in one of them:

1. How many pennies can you fit in your mouth?

2. How far can you throw an ostrich feather, standing at ground level with zero wind velocity?

3. How much weight can you gain in one week?

4. How many beers can you pour in before they begin to pour out?

5. How long can you look at yourself in the mirror, with eyelids taped open to avoid blinking?

6. How many pairs of black and navy blue socks can you mate in one hour under artificial light?

7. How many milkweed seeds can you pile up on a plate 10 inches in diameter?

8. How long can you carry a brick?

9. How many *New York Times*es can you eat at one sitting?

10. How many world record possibilities can you think of in 10 minutes?

Alexander Petrunkevitch

The Spider and the Wasp

Alexander Petrunkevitch (1875–1964), a native of Russia who
came to the United States in his late twenties, was a world-
renowned zoologist. After lecturing briefly at Harvard, he taught
at Indiana University and then Yale for many years. Author of
learned books on insects and a treatise in German on free will, he
also translated poems by Byron (into Russian) and Pushkin (from
Russian into English). Beginning in 1911, with an index to the
species in Central and South America, Petrunkevitch devoted
more than fifty years to the study of spiders. (His second book
on amber spiders appeared in the year of his death.) "The Spider
and the Wasp," which analyzes a natural process of life-out-of
death, is a product of that life-long fascination.

To hold its own in the struggle for existence, every species of   1
animal must have a regular source of food, and if it happens
to live on other animals, its survival may be very delicately
balanced. The hunter cannot exist without the hunted; if the
latter should perish from the earth, the former would, too.
When the hunted also prey on some of the hunters, the matter may become complicated.

This is nowhere better illustrated than in the insect world.   2
Think of the complexity of a situation such as the following:
There is a certain wasp, *Pimpla inquisitor*, whose larvae feed
on the larvae of the tussock moth. *Pimpla* larvae in turn serve
as food for the larvae of a second wasp, and the latter in
their turn nourish still a third wasp. What subtle balance
between fertility and mortality must exist in the case of each
of these four species to prevent the extinction of all of them!

An excess of mortality over fertility in a single member of the group would ultimately wipe out all four.

This is not a unique case. The two great orders of insects, Hymenoptera and Diptera, are full of such examples of interrelationship. And the spiders (which are not insects but members of a separate order of arthropods) also are killers and victims of insects.

The picture is complicated by the fact that those species which are carnivorous in the larval stage have to be provided with animal food by a vegetarian mother. The survival of the young depends on the mother's correct choice of a food which she does not eat herself.

In the feeding and safeguarding of their progeny the insects and spiders exhibit some interesting analogies to reasoning and some crass examples of blind instinct. The case I propose to describe here is that of the tarantula spiders and their arch-enemy, the digger wasps of the genus Pepsis. It is a classic example of what looks like intelligence pitted against instinct—a strange situation in which the victim, though fully able to defend itself, submits unwittingly to its destruction.

Most tarantulas live in the Tropics, but several species occur in the temperate zone and a few are common in the southern U.S. Some varieties are large and have powerful fangs with which they can inflict a deep wound. These formidable looking spiders do not, however, attack man; you can hold one in your hand, if you are gentle, without being bitten. Their bite is dangerous only to insects and small mammals such as mice; for a man it is no worse than a hornet's sting.

Tarantulas customarily live in deep cylindrical burrows, from which they emerge at dusk and into which they retire at dawn. Mature males wander about after dark in search of females and occasionally stray into houses. After mating, the male dies in a few weeks, but a female lives much longer and can mate several years in succession. In a Paris museum is a tropical specimen which is said to have been living in captivity for 25 years.

A fertilized female tarantula lays from 200 to 400 eggs at a time; thus it is possible for a single tarantula to produce several thousand young. She takes no care of them beyond weaving a cocoon of silk to enclose the eggs. After they hatch, the young walk away, find convenient places in which to dig their burrows and spend the rest of their lives in solitude. Tarantulas feed mostly on insects and millepedes. Once their appetite is appeased, they digest the food for several days before eating again. Their sight is poor, being limited to sensing a change in the intensity of light and to the perception of moving objects. They apparently have little or no sense of hearing, for a hungry tarantula will pay no attention to a loudly chirping cricket placed in its cage unless the insect happens to touch one of its legs.

But all spiders, and especially hairy ones, have an extremely 9 delicate sense of touch. Laboratory experiments prove that tarantulas can distinguish three types of touch: pressure against the body wall, stroking of the body hair and riffling of certain very fine hairs on the legs called trichobothria. Pressure against the body, by a finger or the end of a pencil, causes the tarantula to move off slowly for a short distance. The touch excites no defensive response unless the approach is from above where the spider can see the motion, in which case it rises on its hind legs, lifts its front legs, opens its fangs and holds this threatening posture as long as the object continues to move. When the motion stops, the spider drops back to the ground, remains quiet for a few seconds and then moves slowly away.

The entire body of a tarantula, especially its legs, is thickly 10 clothed with hair. Some of it is short and woolly, some long and stiff. Touching this body hair produces one of two distinct reactions. When the spider is hungry, it responds with an immediate and swift attack. At the touch of a cricket's antennae the tarantula seizes the insect so swiftly that a motion picture taken at the rate of 64 frames per second shows only the result and not the process of capture. But when the spider is not hungry, the stimulation of its hairs merely causes it to shake the touched limb. An insect can walk under its hairy belly unharmed.

The trichobothria, very fine hairs growing from disklike mem- 11 branes on the legs, were once thought to be the spider's hearing organs, but we now know that they have nothing to do with sound. They are sensitive only to air movement. A light breeze makes them vibrate slowly without disturbing the common hair. When one blows gently on the trichobothria, the tarantula reacts with a quick jerk of its four front legs. If the front and hind legs are stimulated at the same time, the spider makes a sudden jump. This reaction is quite independent of the state of its appetite.

These three tactile responses—to pressure on the body wall, to   12
moving of the common hair and to flexing of the trichobothria—
are so different from one another that there is no possibility of
confusing them. They serve the tarantula adequately for most of
its needs and enable it to avoid most annoyances and dangers. But
they fail the spider completely when it meets its deadly enemy,
the digger wasp Pepsis.

These solitary wasps are beautiful and formidable creatures.   13
Most species are either a deep shiny blue all over, or deep blue
with rusty wings. The largest have a wing span of about four
inches. They live on nectar. When excited, they give off a pungent
odor—a warning that they are ready to attack. The sting is much
worse than that of a bee or common wasp, and the pain and swell-
ing last longer. In the adult stage the wasp lives only a few
months. The female produces but a few eggs, one at a time at
intervals of two or three days. For each egg the mother must provide one adult tarantula, alive but paralyzed. The tarantula must
be of the correct species to nourish the larva. The mother wasp
attaches the egg to the paralyzed spider's abdomen. Upon hatch-
ing from the egg, the larva is many hundreds of times smaller than
its living but helpless victim. It eats no other food and drinks no
water. By the time it has finished its single gargantuan meal and
become ready for wasphood, nothing remains of the tarantula
but its indigestible chitinous skeleton.

The mother wasp goes tarantula-hunting when the egg in her   14
ovary is almost ready to be laid. Flying low over the ground late
on a sunny afternoon, the wasp looks for its victim or for the
mouth of a tarantula burrow, a round hole edged by a bit of silk.
The sex of the spider makes no difference, but the mother is
highly discriminating as to species. Each species of Pepsis requires
a certain species of tarantula, and the wasp will not attack the
wrong species. In a cage with a tarantula which is not its normal
prey the wasp avoids the spider, and is usually killed by it in the
night.

Yet when a wasp finds the correct species, it is the other way   15
about. To identify the species the wasp apparently must explore
the spider with her antennae. The tarantula shows an amazing
tolerance to this exploration. The wasp crawls under it and walks
over it without evoking any hostile response. The molestation is
so great and so persistent that the tarantula often rises on all

eight legs, as if it were on stilts. It may stand this way for several minutes. Meanwhile the wasp, having satisfied itself that the victim is of the right species, moves off a few inches to dig the spider's grave. Working vigorously with legs and jaws, it excavates a hole 8 to 10 inches deep with a diameter slightly larger than the spider's girth. Now and again the wasp pops out of the hole to make sure that the spider is still there.

When the grave is finished, the wasp returns to the tarantula to complete her ghastly enterprise. First she feels it all over once more with her antennae. Then her behavior becomes more aggressive. She bends her abdomen, protruding her sting, and searches for the soft membrane at the point where the spider's leg joins its body—the only spot where she can penetrate the horny skeleton. From time to time, as the exasperated spider slowly shifts ground, the wasp turns on her back and slides along with the aid of her wings, trying to get under the tarantula for a shot at the vital spot. During all this maneuvering, which can last for several minutes, the tarantula makes no move to save itself. Finally the wasp corners it against some obstruction and grasps one of its legs in her powerful jaws. Now at last the harassed spider tries a desperate but vain defense. The two contestants roll over and over on the ground. It is a terrifying sight and the outcome is always the same. The wasp finally manages to thrust her sting into the soft spot and holds it there for a few seconds while she pumps in the poison. Almost immediately the tarantula falls paralyzed on its back. Its legs stop twitching; its heart stops beating. Yet it is not dead, as is shown by the fact that if taken from the wasp it can be restored to some sensitivity by being kept in a moist chamber for several months.

After paralyzing the tarantula, the wasp cleans herself by dragging her body along the ground and rubbing her feet, sucks the drop of blood oozing from the wound in the spider's abdomen, then grabs a leg of the flabby, helpless animal in her jaws and drags it down to the bottom of the grave. She stays there for many minutes, sometimes for several hours, and what she does all that time in the dark we do not know. Eventually she lays her egg and attaches it to the side of the spider's abdomen with a sticky secretion. Then she emerges, fills the grave with soil carried bit by bit in her jaws, and finally tramples the ground all around to hide any trace of the grave from prowlers. Then she flies away, leaving her descendant safely started in life.

In all this the behavior of the wasp evidently is qualitatively different from that of the spider. The wasp acts like an intelligent animal. This is not to say that instinct plays no part or that she reasons as man does. But her actions are to the point; they are not automatic and can be modified to fit the situation. We do not know for certain how she identifies the tarantula—probably it is by some olfactory or chemo-tactile sense—but she does it purposefully and does not blindly tackle a wrong species. [18]

On the other hand, the tarantula's behavior shows only confusion. Evidently the wasp's pawing gives it no pleasure, for it tries to move away. That the wasp is not simulating sexual stimulation is certain, because male and female tarantulas react in the same way to its advances. That the spider is not anesthetized by some odorless secretion is easily shown by blowing lightly at the tarantula and making it jump suddenly. What, then, makes the tarantula behave as stupidly as it does? [19]

No clear, simple answer is available. Possibly the stimulation by the wasp's antennae is masked by a heavier pressure on the spider's body, so that it reacts as when prodded by a pencil. But the explanation may be much more complex. Initiative in attack is not in the nature of tarantulas; most species fight only when cornered so that escape is impossible. Their inherited patterns of behavior apparently prompt them to avoid problems rather than attack them. For example, spiders always weave their webs in three dimensions, and when a spider finds that there is insufficient space to attach certain threads in the third dimension, it leaves the place and seeks another, instead of finishing the web in a single plane. This urge to escape seems to arise under all circumstances, in all phases of life and to take the place of reasoning. For a spider to change the pattern of its web is as impossible as for an inexperienced man to build a bridge across a chasm obstructing his way. [20]

In a way the instinctive urge to escape is not only easier but more efficient than reasoning. The tarantula does exactly what is most efficient in all cases except in an encounter with a ruthless and determined attacker dependent for the existence of her own species on killing as many tarantulas as she can lay eggs. Perhaps [21] in this case the spider follows its usual pattern of trying to escape, instead of seizing and killing the wasp, because it is not aware of its danger. In any case, the survival of the tarantula species as a whole is protected by the fact that the spider is much more fertile than the wasp.

QUESTIONS

Understanding

1. In which paragraph does Petrunkevitch announce his main topic? When does he actually begin to discuss it? How do the wasp larvae of paragraph 2 anticipate his main "case"?
2. If the digger wasp's favorite kind of tarantula always loses the deadly struggle between them, why does that species not disappear?
3. What might happen to the digger wasp if it were a more prolific breeder? What delicate natural balance do spider and wasp together illustrate?
4. What opposing kinds of behavior do spider and wasp respectively represent?
5. The first half of paragraph 8 is a miniature process analysis. What process does it analyze?

Strategies and Structure

1. Petrunkevitch begins his process analysis with its end result and then returns to the first step, the wasp's hunt for her prey. What is that end result? In which paragraph is it explained?
2. Point out the six stages—from hunting to burying—into which Petrunkevitch analyzes the wasp's conquest of the spider.
3. Petrunkevitch enlarges the combat between spider and wasp to human scale by calling the wasp "her" and by referring to the wasp as the spider's "arch-enemy" (par. 5). Point out other similar techniques by which he minimizes the difference in scale between our world and the world of the insects.
4. Petrunkevitch's process analysis incorporates elements of the COMPARISON AND CONTRAST essay (Chapter 6). Does his compari-

son alternate point by point between spider and wasp, or does he concentrate on one for a while and then concentrate on the other? Explain your answer by referring to several specific passages.

5. Paragraph 12 is a TRANSITION paragraph. Which sentences look backward? Which look forward?
6. Which sentence in paragraph 19 sets up the remainder of the essay?
7. How does paragraph 4 fit in with the rest of Petrunkevitch's essay?

Words and Figures of Speech

1. Such words as *Hymenoptera, Diptera, arthropods,* and *trichobothria* (pars. 3, 9, 11) show that Petrunkevitch, a distinguished zoologist, was comfortable with the technical vocabulary of science; but this essay is sprinkled with nontechnical terms as well, for example: *wasphood* (par. 13), *pops out of the hole* (15), *shot* (16), *prowlers* (17). Give several other examples of your own.
2. From the range of Petrunkevitch's DICTION, what conclusions can you draw about the make-up of the readership of *Scientific American,* the magazine in which this essay appeared?
3. Consult your dictionary for the exact meanings of any of the following words you cannot define precisely: *subtle* (par. 2), *carnivorous* (4), *progeny* (5), *formidable* (6, 13), *appeased* (8), *tactile* (12), *pungent* (13), *gargantuan* (13), *chitinous* (13), *molestation* (15), *exasperated* (16), *secretion* (17, 19), *qualitatively* (18), *instinct* (5, 18), *olfactory* (18), *simulating* (18), *anesthetized* (19).

Comparing

1. According to "The Spider and the Wasp," Loren Eiseley's "The Angry Winter" (Chapter 1), and Robert Jastrow's "Man of Wisdom" (next chapter), how do all creatures acquire their distinctive patterns of behavior? In terms of the capacity it emphasizes, is Petrunkevitch's essay more like Eiseley's or Jastrow's?
2. In its treatment of the relationship between the human world and the insect world, how does the scale of Petrunkevitch's essay resemble that of Annie Dillard's "Transfiguration" (Chapter 7)?

Discussion and Writing Topics

1. Describe the process by which an insect or animal that you have observed feeds its young and starts them off in life.

2. Analyze the stages of maturation that bring a human being to adulthood.

3. Develop a parallel between two insects and two people (or types of people) with whom you are familiar.

4. Do you have a pet that has shown signs of true intelligence over and beyond mere instinct? Describe his or her behavior.

Essays That Analyze a Process

Write an essay analyzing one of the following processes or giving directions for one of the following operations:

1. How to play chess
2. How to change a tire
3. How to install an electric circuit in a house
4. How to make wine, beer, or mead
5. How to milk a cow
6. How to keep bees
7. How to thread and operate a sewing machine
8. How to make butter
9. How a piano works
10. How a solar heating system works
11. How to conserve energy in a house
12. How to install and operate a CB radio
13. How to meet a girl or guy
14. How to make a good (or bad) impression on your boyfriend's or girlfriend's parents
15. How to excel in school
16. How to take and develop photographs
17. How iron ore is made into steel
18. How a fuel injection system (or carburetor) works
19. How an internal combustion engine works
20. How to sail a boat
21. How to buy a used car
22. How to buy a horse or other livestock
23. How to buy stocks, bonds, or other securities
24. How to beat inflation in small ways
25. How to get rich

4

Essays That Analyze Cause and Effect

PROCESS ANALYSIS [1] (Chapter 3) is concerned with sequence in time and space. Sequence is one kind of relationship among objects and events; another is causation. When we confuse the two, we are reasoning as Mark Twain's hero does in Adventures of Huckleberry Finn. Alone in the woods one night, Huck sees an evil omen:

Pretty soon a spider went crawling up my shoulder, and I flipped it off and it lit in the candle; and before I could budge it was all shriveled up. I didn't need anybody to tell me that that was an awful bad sign and would fetch me some bad luck, so I was scared and most shook the clothes off of me. I got up and turned around in my tracks three times and crossed my breast every time; and then I tied up a little lock of my hair to keep witches away. But I hadn't no confidence.

Huck is right to be scared; all sorts of misadventures are going to befall him and Jim in Mark Twain's masterpiece. But Huck commits the blunder of thinking that because the misadventures follow the burning of the spider, they were necessarily caused by it: he confuses mere sequence with causation. This mistake in logic is commonly known as the post hoc, ergo propter hoc fallacy—Latin for "after this, therefore because of this."

Huck Finn does not realize that two conditions have to be met to prove causation:

B can not have happened without A;
Whenever A happens, B must happen.

[1] Terms printed in all capitals are defined in the Glossary.

The chemist who observes again and again that a flammable substance burns (B) only when combined with oxygen (A) and that it always burns when so combined, may infer that oxidation causes combustion. The chemist has discovered in oxygen the "immediate" cause of combustion. The flame necessary to set off the reaction and the chemist himself, who lights the match, are "ultimate" causes.

Often the ultimate causes of an event are more important than the immediate causes, especially when we are dealing with psychological and social rather than purely physical factors. Let us raise the following question about a college freshman: Why does Mary smoke? Depending upon whom we asked, we might get responses like these:

Mary:	"I smoke because I need something to do with my hands."
Mary's boyfriend:	"Mary smokes because she thinks it looks sophisticated."
Medical doctor:	"Because Mary has developed a physical addiction to tobacco."
Psychologist:	"Because of peer pressure."
Sociologist:	"Because 30 percent of all female Americans under 20 years of age now smoke. Mary is part of a trend."
Advertiser:	"Because she's come a long way, baby."

Each of these explanations tells only part of the story. For a full answer to our question about why Mary smokes, we must take all of these answers together. Together they form what is known as the "complex" cause of Mary's behavior.

Most essays in CAUSE AND EFFECT that you will be asked to read or to write will examine the complex cause of an event or phenomenon. There are two reasons for addressing all the contributing causes. The first is to avoid over-simplification. Interesting questions are usually complex, and complex questions probably have complex answers. The second reason is to anticipate objections that might be raised against your argument.

Often a clever writer will run through several causes to show that he or she knows the ground before making a special case for one or two. When a clergyman asked journalist Lincoln Steffens to name the ultimate cause of corruption in city government, Steffens replied with the following analysis:

> Most people, you know, say it was Adam. But Adam, you remember, he said that it was Eve, the woman; she did it. And Eve said no, no, it wasn't she; it was the serpent. And that's where you clergy have stuck ever since. You blame the serpent, Satan. Now I come and I am trying to show you that it was, it is, the apple.

Steffens was giving an original answer to the old question of original sin. Man's fallen state, he said, is due not to innate depravity but to economic conditions.

When explaining causes, be as specific as you can without oversimplifying. When explaining effects, be even more specific. Here is your chance to display the telling fact or colorful detail that can save your essay from the ho-hum response. Consider this explanation of the effects of smoking written by England's King James I (of the King James Bible). His Counter-Blaste to Tobacco (1604) found smoking to be

> A custom lothsome to the eye, hatefull to the Nose, harmefull to the braine, dangerous to the Lungs, and in the blacke stinking fume thereof, neerest resembling the horrible Stigian smoke of the pit that is bottomelesse.

In a more recent essay on the evils of tobacco, Erik Eckholm strikes a grimmer note. "But the most potentially tragic victims of cigarettes," he writes, "are the infants of mothers who smoke. They are more likely than the babies of nonsmoking mothers to be born underweight and thus to encounter death or disease at birth or during the initial months of life."

In singling out the effects of smoking upon unwitting infants, Eckholm has chosen an example that might be just powerful enough to convince some smokers to quit. Your examples need not be so grim, but they must be specific to be powerful. And they must be selected with the interests of your audience in mind. Eckholm is addressing the young women who are smoking more today than ever before. When writing for a middle-aged audience, he points out that smoking causes cancer and heart disease at a rate

70 percent higher among pack-a-day men and women than among nonsmokers.

Your audience must be taken into account because writing a cause and effect analysis is much like constructing a persuasive argument. It is a form of reasoning that carries the reader step by step through a "proof." Your analysis may be instructive, amusing, or startling; but first it must be logical.

Robert Jastrow

Man of Wisdom

Born in 1925, Robert Jastrow is professor of earth science at Dartmouth College and professor of astronomy and geology at Columbia University. A resident and native of New York City, he was educated at Columbia (Ph.D., 1948) and taught briefly at Yale. He served as the head of the theoretical division of the Goddard Space Flight Center, NASA, from 1958 until 1961, when he became director of the Goddard Institute for Space Studies. In 1968, NASA presented him with a medal for exceptional scientific achievement. Jastrow has written books on astronomy and evolution, including Red Giants and White Dwarfs *(1967). "Man of Wisdom" is a chapter from his latest book,* Until the Sun Dies *(1977); it explains what caused Homo sapiens to become the brainiest of all creatures.*

Starting about one million years ago, the fossil record shows   1
an accelerating growth of the human brain. It expanded at
first at the rate of one cubic inch [1] of additional gray matter
every hundred thousand years; then the growth rate doubled;
it doubled again; and finally it doubled once more. Five hundred thousand years ago the rate of growth hit its peak. At
that time the brain was expanding at a phenomenal rate of
ten cubic inches every hundred thousand years. No other
organ in the history of life is known to have grown as fast as
this.[2]

[1] One cubic inch is a heaping tablespoonful. [Author's footnote.]
[2] If the brain had continued to expand at the same rate, men would be
far brainier today than they actually are. But after several hundred
thousand years of very rapid growth the expansion of the brain slowed
down and in the last one hundred thousand years it has not changed
in size at all. [Author's footnote.]

What pressures generated the explosive growth of the human   2
brain? A change of climate that set in about two million years ago
may supply part of the answer. At that time the world began its
descent into a great Ice Age, the first to afflict the planet in
hundreds of millions of years. The trend toward colder weather
set in slowly at first, but after a million years patches of ice began
to form in the north. The ice patches thickened into glaciers as
more snow fell, and then the glaciers merged into great sheets of
ice, as much as two miles thick. When the ice sheets reached their
maximum extent, they covered two-thirds of the North American
continent, all of Britain and a large part of Europe. Many mountain ranges were buried entirely. So much water was locked up on
the land in the form of ice that the level of the earth's oceans
dropped by three hundred feet.

These events coincided precisely with the period of most rapid   3
expansion of the human brain. Is the coincidence significant, or is
it happenstance?

The story of human migrations in the last million years provides   4
a clue to the answer. At the beginning of the Ice Age Homo [3]
lived near the equator, where the climate was mild and pleasant.
Later he moved northward. From his birthplace in Africa [4] he mi-
grated up across the Arabian peninsula and then turned to the
north and west into Europe, as well as eastward into Asia.

When these early migrations took place, the ice was still con-   5
fined to the lands in the far north; but eight hundred thousand
years ago, when man was already established in the temperate
latitudes, the ice moved southward until it covered large parts of
Europe and Asia. Now, for the first time, men encountered the
bone-chilling blasts of freezing winds that blew off the cakes of
ice to the north. The climate in southern Europe had a Siberian
harshness then, and summers were nearly as cold as European
winters are today.

In those difficult times, the traits of resourcefulness and inge-   6
nuity must have been of premium value. Which individual first
thought of stripping the pelt from the slaughtered beast to wrap
around his shivering limbs? Only by such inventive flights of the

[3] Latin for "man."
[4] Until recently, the consensus among anthropologists placed the origin of man
in Africa. However, some recent evidence suggests that Asia may have been
his birthplace. [Author's footnote.]

imagination could the naked animal survive a harsh climate. In every generation, the individuals endowed with the attributes of strength, courage, and improvisation were the ones more likely to survive the rigors of the Ice Age; those who were less resourceful, and lacked the vision of their fellows, fell victims to the climate and their numbers were reduced.

The Ice Age winter was the most devastating challenge that 7 Homo had ever faced. He was naked and defenseless against the cold, as the little mammals had been defenseless against the dinosaurs one hundred million years ago. Vulnerable to the pressures of a hostile world, both animals were forced to live by their wits; and both became, in their time, the brainiest animals of the day.

The tool-making industry of early man also stimulated the 8 growth of the brain. The possession of a good brain had been one of the factors that enabled Homo to make tools at the start. But the use of tools became, in turn, a driving force toward the evolution of an even better brain. The characteristics of good memory, foresight, and innovativeness that were needed for tool-making varied in strength from one individual to another. Those who possessed them in the greatest degree were the practical heroes of their day; they were likely to survive and prosper, while the individuals who lacked them were more likely to succumb to the pressures of the environment. Again these circumstances pruned the human stock, expanding the centers of the brain in which past experiences were recorded, future actions were contemplated, and new ideas were conceived. As a result, from generation to generation the brain grew larger.

The evolution of speech may have been the most important 9 factor of all. When early man mastered the loom of language, his progress accelerated dramatically. Through the spoken word a new invention in tool-making, for example, could be communicated to everyone; in this way the innovativeness of the individual enhanced the survival prospects of his fellows, and the creative strength of one became the strength of all. More important, through language the ideas of one generation could be passed on to the next, so that each generation inherited not only the genes of its ancestors but also their collective wisdom, transmitted through the magic of speech.

A million years ago, when this magic was not yet perfected, and 10 language was a cruder art, those bands of men who possessed the new gift in the highest degree were strongly favored in the struggle for existence. But the fabric of speech is woven out of many threads. The physical attributes of a voice box, lips, and tongue were among the necessary traits; but a good brain was also essential, to frame an abstract thought or represent an object by a word.

Now the law of the survival of the fittest began to work on the   11
population of early men. Steadily, the physical apparatus for speech improved. At the same time, the centers of the brain devoted to speech grew in size and complexity, and in the course of many generations the whole brain grew with them. Once more, as with the use of tools, reciprocal forces came into play in which speech stimulated better brains, and brains improved the art of speech, and the curve of brain growth spiraled upward.

Which factor played the most important role in the evolution   12
of human intelligence? Was it the pressure of the Ice-Age climate? Or tools? Or language? No one can tell; all worked together, through Darwin's [5] law of natural selection, to produce the dramatic increase in the size of the brain that has been recorded in the fossil record in the last million years. The brain reached its present size about one hundred thousand years ago, and its growth ceased. Man's body had been shaped into its modern form several hundred thousand years before that. Now brain and body were complete. Together they made a new and marvelous creature, charged with power, intelligence, and creative energy. His wits had been honed by the fight against hunger, cold, and the natural enemy; his form had been molded in the crucible of adversity. In the annals of anthropology his arrival is celebrated by a change in name, from Homo erectus—the Man who stands erect—to Homo sapiens—the Man of wisdom.

The story of man's creation nears an end. In the beginning   13
there was light; then a dark cloud appeared, and made the sun and earth. The earth grew warmer; its body exhaled moisture and gases; water collected on the surface; soon the first molecules struggled across the threshold of life. Some survived; others perished; and the law of Darwin began its work. The pressures of the environment acted ceaselessly, and the forms of life improved.

The changes were imperceptible from one generation to the   14

[5] British naturalist Charles Darwin (1809–1882) theorized that all species of life evolved from lower forms through "natural selection."

next. No creature was aware of its role in the larger drama; all felt only the pleasure and pain of existence; and life and death were devoid of a greater meaning.

But to the human observer, looking back on the history of life   15 from the perspective of many eons, a meaning becomes evident. He sees that through the struggle against the forces of adversity, each generation molds the shapes of its descendants. Adversity and struggle lie at the root of evolutionary progress. Without adversity there is no pressure; without pressure there is no change.

These circumstances, so painful to the individual, create the   16 great currents that carry life forward from the simple to the complex. Finally, man stands on the earth, more perfect than any other. Intelligent, self-aware, he alone among all creatures has the curiosity to ask: How did I come into being? What forces have created me? And, guided by his scientific knowledge, he comes to the realization that he was created by all who came before him, through their struggle against adversity.

QUESTIONS

Understanding

1. The "complex" cause of an event is the sum of all causes contributing to it. According to Jastrow, what was the complex cause of the human brain's growing to its present imposing size? Which single factor may have been most important?

2. During the Ice Age, which was the immediate (or direct) cause of human brain growth and which was the ultimate (or remote) cause: lower temperatures, the formation of ice, man's imagining the warmth of animal skins?

3. Over long time periods, as Jastrow understands the process, CAUSE AND EFFECT act reciprocally (par. 11) upon each other. Explain the continuing interaction of cause and effect as exemplified by Jastrow's account of language (pars. 9–11).

4. Jastrow refers to "the law of the survival of the fittest" (par. 11). What is the meaning of this rule or principle?

5. Under what single generalized condition, in Jastrow's view, is improvement in any species likely to occur?

6. What does Jastrow interpret *improvement* to mean? The dino-

saurs have never been improved upon for size, but they clearly do not represent the kind of perfection Jastrow has in mind. What is his ultimate standard of perfection?

7. If Jastrow's optimistic analysis is correct, why has the human brain stopped growing? What cause for the slow-down is implied in paragraph 12?

Strategies and Structure

1. Jastrow's essay is organized by clearly visible signals into readily recognizable divisions. Which sentence in paragraph 2 signals what the rest of the essay is about? What is the function of paragraph 3? What are the three main divisions of the body of Jastrow's essay?

2. What is the function of paragraph 12 of this essay? Where does the conclusion begin?

3. Paragraph 2 is a miniature PROCESS ANALYSIS. Of what? Through what stages does the process operate?

4. In which paragraph does Jastrow give a scientist's capsule version of the story of Genesis? How is that paragraph related to paragraphs 15 and 16?

5. Why do you think Jastrow calls attention to Homo's change of name (par. 12)? Where has Homo "arrived" when he deserves a new name?

6. The last paragraph of Jastrow's essay attributes to intelligent man alone the power to ask, "How did I come into being?" How is this statement prepared for earlier in the essay? What does it suggest about Jastrow's conception of the scientific historian's role?

Words and Figures of Speech

1. From what field of endeavor does Jastrow derive the METAPHOR, "pruned the human stock" (par. 8)? What does it mean? How apt is the metaphor when applied to human evolution?

2. What is a "crucible" (par. 12)? Who uses them? Is this an original metaphor or a CLICHE?

3. How effective do you find Jastrow's reference to language as a "loom" (par. 9)? How does this metaphor fit in with his earlier references to tools? Which paragraph develops it further?

4. Look up any of the following words you do not already know: *happenstance* (par. 3), *consensus* (footnote to par. 4), *ingenuity* (6), *improvisation* (6), *innovativeness* (8), *reciprocal* (11), *honed* (12), *annals* (12), *anthropology* (12), *imperceptible* (14), *devoid* (14), *eons* (15), and *adversity* (15).

Comparing

1. Judging from the vocabulary and frequent FIGURES OF SPEECH, do you think Jastrow's essay is intended for an audience more or less scientifically inclined than the intended audience of Petrunkevitch's "The Spider and the Wasp" (Chapter 3)? Explain your answer.

2. Jastrow says (par. 1) that we can learn about the brain from fossils. Judging from the way Asimov "reads" fossilized bones and teeth in "What Do You Call a Platypus?" (Chapter 2), how might fossils provide evidence about the long-vanished gray matter?

Discussion and Writing Topics

1. Social Darwinism is the application of the scientific law of the survival of the fittest to human institutions and customs. How might Jastrow's essay be interpreted to encourage the belief that human society is always progressing?

2. Do recent events in American history confirm or deny the idea of steady social progress through time? Explain your answer.

3. Do modern evolutionists believe that only the strong lion survives the battle, or that the winner bequeaths strong genes to later generations? What is the difference?

4. What is *entropy* (the reverse, almost, of evolution)? If our universe is moving toward this state, as some scientists believe, what long-range effects will entropy cause?

Ellen Willis

Memoirs of a Non-Prom Queen

Ellen Willis is a journalist who was born in New York City in 1941 and attended a large "semisuburban" high school in Queens, before going on to Barnard College and Berkeley. She is now a critic of rock music for The New Yorker and for Rolling Stone, where she writes a column entitled "Alternating Currents." (Her fellow "AC" columnist, Michael Rogers, is represented in Chapter 5.) Willis has been an associate or contributing editor of Cheetah magazine, US magazine, and Ms.; she is a staff member of the Home Front, a center for antiwar soldiers. "Memoirs of a Non-Prom Queen" is a review essay inspired by Ralph Keyes's Is There Life After High School? (1976). It analyzes the lasting psychological effects of Willis's own less than ideal high school years.

There's a book out called *Is There Life after High School?* 1
It's a fairly silly book, maybe because the subject matter is the kind that only hurts when you think. Its thesis—that most people never get over the social triumphs or humiliations of high school—is not novel. Still, I read it with the respectful attention a serious hypochondriac accords the lowliest "dear doctor" column. I don't know about most people, but for me, forgiving my parents for real and imagined derelictions has been easy compared to forgiving myself for being a teenage reject.

Victims of high school trauma—which seems to have af- 2
flicted a disproportionate number of writers, including Ralph Keyes, the author of this book—tend to embrace the ugly duckling myth of adolescent social relations: the "innies"

(Keyes's term) are good-looking, athletic mediocrities who will never amount to much, while the "outies" are intelligent, sensitive, creative individuals who will do great things in an effort to make up for their early defeats. Keyes is partial to this myth. He has fun with celebrity anecdotes: Kurt Vonnegut receiving a body-building course as a "gag prize" at a dance; Frank Zappa yelling "fuck you" at a cheerleader; Mike Nichols,[1] as a nightclub comedian, insulting a fan—an erstwhile overbearing classmate turned used-car salesman. In contrast, the ex-prom queens and kings he interviews slink through life, hiding their pasts lest someone call them "dumb jock" or "cheerleader type," perpetually wondering what to do for an encore.

If only it were that simple. There may really be high schools   3
where life approximates an Archie comic, but even in the Fifties, my large (5000 students), semisuburban (Queens, New York), heterogeneous high school was not one of them. The students' social life was fragmented along ethnic and class lines; there was no universally recognized, schoolwide social hierarchy. Being an athlete or a cheerleader or a student officer didn't mean much. Belonging to an illegal sorority or fraternity meant more, at least in some circles, but many socially active students chose not to join. The most popular kids were not necessarily the best looking or the best dressed or the most snobbish or the least studious. In retrospect, it seems to me that they were popular for much more honorable reasons. They were attuned to other people, aware of subtle social nuances. They projected an inviting sexual warmth. Far from being slavish followers of fashion, they were self-confident enough to set fashions. They suggested, initiated, led. Above all—this was their main appeal for me—they knew how to have a good time.

True, it was not particularly sophisticated enjoyment—dancing,   4
pizza eating, hand holding in the lunchroom, the usual. I had friends—precocious intellectuals and bohemians—who were consciously alienated from what they saw as all that teenage crap. Part of me identified with them, yet I badly wanted what they

[1] Vonnegut, American novelist, author of *Cat's Cradle* (1963); *God Bless You, Mr. Rosewater* (1964); *Slaughterhouse-Five* (1969); and *Breakfast of Champions* (1973). Zappa was the leader of the rock music group, Mothers of Invention. Nichols is a former night club and television comedian, now a film and stage director.

rejected. Their seriousness engaged my mind, but my romantic and sexual fantasies, and my emotions generally, were obsessively fixed on the parties and dances I wasn't invited to, the boys I never dated. I suppose what says it best is that my "serious" friends hated rock & roll; I loved it.

If I can't rationalize my social ineptitude as intellectual rebel-   5
lion, neither can I blame it on political consciousness. Feminism has inspired a variation of the ugly duckling myth in which high school wallflower becomes feminist heroine, suffering because she has too much integrity to suck up to boys by playing a phony feminine role. There is a tempting grain of truth in this idea. Certainly the self-absorption, anxiety and physical and social awk-wardness that made me a difficult teenager were not unrelated to my ambivalent awareness of women's oppression. I couldn't charm boys because I feared and resented them and their power over my life; I couldn't be sexy because I saw sex as a mine field of con-flicting, confusing rules that gave them every advantage. I had no sense of what might make me attractive, a lack I'm sure involved unconscious resistance to the game girls were supposed to play (particularly all the rigmarole surrounding clothes, hair and cos-metics); I was a clumsy dancer because I could never follow the boy's lead.

Yet ultimately this rationale misses the point. As I've learned   6
from comparing notes with lots of women, the popular girls were in fact much more in touch with the reality of the female condi-tion than I was. They knew exactly what they had to do for the rewards they wanted, while I did a lot of what feminist organizers call denying the awful truth. I was a bit schizy. Desperate to win the game but unwilling to learn it or even face my feelings about it, I couldn't really play, except in fantasy; paradoxically, I was consumed by it much more thoroughly than the girls who played and played well. Knowing what they wanted and how to get it, they preserved their sense of self, however compromised, while I lost mine. Which is why they were not simply better game players but genuinely more likable than I.

The ugly duckling myth is sentimental. It may soothe the   7
memory of social rejection, but it falsifies the experience, evades its cruelty and uselessness. High school permanently damaged my self-esteem. I learned what it meant to be impotent; what it meant to be invisible. None of this improved my character, spurred my

ambition, or gave me a deeper understanding of life. I know people who were popular in high school who later became serious intellectuals, radicals, artists, even journalists. I regret not being one of those people. To see my failure as morally or politically superior to their success would be to indulge in a version of the Laingian [2] fallacy—that because a destructive society drives people crazy, there is something dishonorable about managing to stay sane.

QUESTIONS

Understanding

1. What was the effect of her high school experience upon the author? In which sentence does she formulate that effect most directly?
2. What specific difficulties during Willis's high school years caused the aftereffects that she describes?
3. Explain the basic idea behind the ugly duckling myth (or the Cinderella story—the two are fundamentally the same). What does the myth have to do with Ralph Keyes's theory (in *Is There Life after High School?*) about the "innies" and the "outies" (par. 2)?
4. Willis agrees that high school can scar its victims for life, but she thinks Keyes's theory about "innies" and "outies" is wrong. Why? What fallacies does she see in Keyes's reasoning?
5. How, according to Willis, has the feminist movement "inspired a variation of the ugly duckling myth" (par. 5)? Who is the swan in this version? How might Willis's essay be interpreted as a more complicated feminist statement?

Strategies and Structure

1. Does Willis devote more attention to causes or to effects in this essay? Assuming that paragraph 1 and 2 constitute her introduction, which specific paragraphs deal with causes? Which deal with effects?

[2] R. D. Laing, the Scottish psychiatrist, argues that personality division is a predictable result of modern life.

2. How efficient do you find the first sentence in paragraph 3 as a TRANSITION sentence? Explain your answer.

3. In paragraph 1 Willis introduces herself as a "serious" hypochondriac, and we smile at the joke. By the end of the essay, how has the non-prom queen's TONE of voice changed?

4. Sentimentality is emotional response out of all proportion to the conditions · that produce it. Willis criticizes the ugly duckling myth for emotional bloat in paragraph 7. Do you think her "memoirs" successfully avoid sentimentality? Why or why not?

5. Why does Willis mention "Archie" comics and the example of her own high school in paragraph 3?

6. In paragraph 3, Willis tells what her high school days look like "in retrospect." What word in the title of her essay alerts us to this backward glance?

Words and Figures of Speech

1. A *rationale* (par. 6) explains the reasons for some course of action. Rationales may turn out to be accurate or inaccurate. *Rationalizations* (par. 5) are always inaccurate. Why? What does the term mean?

2. *Schizy* (par. 6) is short for *schizophrenic*. What psychological condition does the word DENOTE? How does it apply to Willis's state of mind in high school?

3. Willis's vocabulary is sophisticated, even learned; but it includes a smattering of slang and profanity. How might such language be considered appropriate, given the fact that Willis's essay first appeared in *Rolling Stone* magazine?

4. Look up any unfamiliar words in the following list: *thesis* (par. 1), *derelictions* (1), *trauma* (2), *mediocrities* (2), *anecdotes* (2), *erstwhile* (2), *heterogeneous* (3) *hierarchy* (3), *retrospect* (3), *nuances* (3), *slavish* (3), *precocious* (4), *bohemians* (4), *ineptitude* (5), *ambivalent* (5), *impotent* (7).

Comparing

1. How does Nora Ephron's "A Few Words about Breasts" (Chapter 1) deny the validity of the ugly duckling myth of adolescent social development?

2. Willis says (par. 2) that writers seem especially vulnerable to the traumas of adolescence, and her essay might be seen as a writer's attempt to put a traumatic past into perspective. How does this therapeutic motive compare with the motive Annie Dillard assigns to the writer in "Transfiguration" (Chapter 7)?

Discussion and Writing Topics

1. Have your high school days left any psychological scars? What traumas caused them?

2. Do you now question any standards or values that you accepted without a second thought in high school? What were they? What caused you to change your mind?

3. Did you know people in high school who were popular for some of the "honorable" reasons Willis mentions in paragraph 3? How did they behave?

4. What is a myth? What kinds of belief do myths reveal within a society or a culture?

Reynolds Price
Summer Games

Reynolds Price grew up in North Carolina and studied at Duke
University and Merton College, Oxford, where he was a Rhodes
Scholar. Since 1958, he has taught literature and creative writing
at Duke and has visited numerous other universities as a writer-
in-residence. Price's fiction and poems have appeared in magazines
and journals throughout this country and England. His novels
including A Long and Happy Life (1962); A Generous Man (1967);
Love and Work (1968); and The Surface of Earth (1975). "Summer Games" is one of the essays collected in Permanent Errors
(1971); it recalls a hot summer's day in Price's childhood when
he almost killed a playmate. In this essay, the author attempts to
explain to the reader and to himself why he committed an error
that has taken its permanent place in his memory.

Outside, in our childhood summers—the war. The summers 1
of 1939 to '45. I was six and finally twelve; and the war was
three thousand miles to the right where London, Warsaw,
Cologne crouched huge, immortal under nights of bombs or,
farther, to the left where our men (among them three cousins
of mine) crawled over dead friends from foxhole to foxhole
towards Tokyo or, terribly, where there were children (our
age, our size) starving, fleeing, trapped, stripped, abandoned.

Far off as it was, still we dreaded each waking hour that 2
the war might arrive on us. A shot would ring in the midst
of our play, freezing us in the knowledge that here at last
were the first Storm Troopers [1] till we thought and looked—

---

[1] Nazi soldiers feared for their terrorist methods.

Mrs. Hightower's Ford. And any plane passing overhead after dark seemed pregnant with black chutes ready to blossom. There were hints that war was nearer than it seemed—swastikaed subs off Hatteras or the German sailor's tattered corpse washed up at Virginia Beach with a Norfolk movie ticket in his pocket.[2]

But of course we were safe. Our elders said that daily. Our 3 deadly threats were polio, being hit by a car, drowning in pure chlorine if we swam after eating. No shot was fired for a hundred miles. (Fort Bragg—a hundred miles.) We had excess food to shame us at every meal, excess clothes to fling about us in the heat of play. So, secure, guilty, savage, we invoked war to us by games which were rites.

All our games ended desperately. Hiding, Prisoner's Base, Sling- 4 Statue, Snake in Gutter, Giant Step, Kick the Can. We would start them all as friends, cool, gentle enough; but as we flung on under monstrous heat, sealed in sweat and dirt, hearts thudding, there would come a moment of pitch when someone would shout "Now *war!*" and it would be war—we separating, fleeing for cover, advancing in stealth on one another in terror, inflicting terror, mock death, surrender, till evening came and the hand of the day relaxed above us and cool rose from the grass and we sank drained into calm again, a last game of Hide in the dusk among bitter-smelling lightning bugs, ghost stories on the dark porch steps; then bath, bed, prayers for forgiveness and long life, sleep.

Only once did we draw real blood in our games; and I was the 5 cause, the instrument at least. One August afternoon we had gone from, say, Tag into War. It was me, my cousins Marcia and Pat, and a Negro boy named Walter (who played with us for a quarter a week) against older, rougher boys. They massed on the opposite side of the creek that split the field behind our house. We had gathered magnolia seed pods for hand grenades; but as the charge began and swept toward us, as Madison Cranford leapt the creek and came screaming at me, he ceased being Madison (a preacher's son), the game ceased, the day rose in me, I dropped my fake grenade, stooped, blindly found a stone (pointed flint) and before retreating, flung it. My flight was halted by sudden silence behind me. I turned and by the creek on the ground in a huddle of boys

2 Price is describing his home town of Macon in north central North Carolina. Cape Hatteras is on the Carolina coast; Virginia Beach and Norfolk are on the Virginia coast.

was Madison, flat, still, eyes shut, blood streaming from the part in his sweaty hair, from a perfect circle in the skin which I had made. Walter, black and dry and powdered with dust, knelt by the head and the blood and looking through the day and the distance, said to me, "What ails you, boy? You have killed *this* child."

I had not, of course. He lived, never went to bed though a doctor did see him and pass on to us the warning that, young as we were, we were already deadly. My rock an inch farther down in Madison's temple would have done the work of a bullet—death. Death was ours to give, mine.

The warning was passed through my mother that night when she came from the Cranfords', having begged their pardon, and climbed to my room where I feigned sleep in a walnut bed under photographs of stars. I "woke" with a struggle, oaring myself from fake drowned depths, lay flat as she spread covers round me and heard her question launched, tense but gentle. "Why on earth did you throw a rock when everyone else was playing harmless?" What I suddenly knew I held back from her—that the others were not playing harmless, were as bent on ruin as I but were cowards, had only not yet been touched hard enough by hate. So I blamed the summer. "It was so hot I didn't know I *had* a rock. I was wild, for a minute. I will try not to do it again next summer." She said "*Ever* again" and left me to sleep which, tired as I was, did not come at once.

I lay in half dark (my sacred familiar objects crouched in horror from me against my walls) and thought through the lie I had told to save my mother—that summer was to blame. Then I said aloud as a promise (to my room, to myself), "I will tame *myself*. When the war is over and I am a man, it will all be peace, be cool. And when it is not, when summer comes, we will go to the water—my children and I—and play quiet games in the cool of the day. In the heat we will rest, separate on cots, not touching but smiling, watching the hair grow back on our legs."

Then sleep came unsought, untroubled to seal that further lie I had told to hide from myself what I knew even then—that I was not wrong to blame the summer, not wholly wrong; that wherever summer strikes (its scalding color), even in years of relative peace, something thrusts from the earth, presses from the air, compresses that in us which sets us wild against ourselves, in work, in games, in worst of all our love. Summer is the time wars live, thrive, on.

QUESTIONS

Understanding

1. What "lie" does Price tell his mother? What "further lie" (par. 9) does he tell himself? Which lie has some truth to it?
2. What does Price mean when he says that "summer" causes adult wars as it caused his younger self to throw the deadly rock?
3. Why is young Price anxious to "hide from myself" (par. 9) this truth about CAUSE AND EFFECT, even though it makes his guilt less personal?
4. From what is Price trying to "save" (par. 8) his mother?
5. What is the difference between a "cause" and an "instrument" (par. 5)? Which is young Price? Explain your answer.

Strategies and Structure

1. Price's basic strategy in this essay is to explain a cause by telling the story of its effect. In which paragraph of his NARRATIVE does the action reach a climax? In which paragraph is it most relaxed?
2. How does Price's handling of time of day affect the tension in the activity of his narrative? At what time is the tension greatest? When is it least intense?
3. How does the build up and release of tension in Price's narrative help to explain the *cause* of the boy's hysterically throwing the rock?
4. How might the long sentence in paragraph 4 be seen to capture the rhythm of Price's entire essay?
5. In his last sentence (par. 9), Price doubles the verb for emphasis and to create a sense of finality. Where else in his essay do you find this verb emphasis-through-repetition? What does this technique indicate about the strength and power of the cause that Price is analyzing?
6. In paragraph 7, Price "oars" himself from the "depths" of sleep when his mother "launches" a question at him. How does this water language look forward to paragraph 8? What effect does it have upon the "temperature" of the entire essay?
7. What is the effect of the example of the movie ticket in paragraph 2?

8. Price shows a novelist's skill at handling narrative POINT OF VIEW. How does he capture the terrified innocence of the children in paragraph 1? In which later paragraph does he recollect a past glimpse of the future?

Words and Figures of Speech

1. What is the literal meaning of the METAPHOR, "the day rose in me" (par. 5)? How does it contribute to Price's explanation of the boy's aggressive act?
2. In the heat of play, Price's boy goes "berserk." Look up the root meaning of this term in your dictionary and explain how it applies to the boy's behavior.
3. Look up *rites* (par. 3) in your dictionary. In what sense are the children's games "rites" of war?
4. What is the purpose of the word *say* in paragraph 5?
5. What example of PERSONIFICATION can you find in paragraph 8?

Comparing

1. How is Price's explanation of the causes of human aggression similar to Loren Eiseley's in "The Angry Winter" (Chapter 1)? Why is pointed flint an appropriate weapon in both essays?
2. How is their treatment of the seasons *different* in the two essays by Price and Eiseley?

Discussion and Writing Topics

1. Try to recall some of the games of your childhood. Explain what forces or causes they expressed.
2. What sort of climate did you grow up in? Recount a specific deed or deeds of yours that can be blamed at least in part upon the climate.
3. Tell the story of an incident that introduced you to a painful adult truth while you were still essentially a child.
4. Price says that children in their innocence try to protect their elders from disturbing truths. Do you agree? Why or why not?

Milton Mayer

On the Passing of the Slug

Milton Mayer was born in 1908 in Chicago, the setting of the essay reprinted here. He attended the University of Chicago, where he claims to have been offered a P.P. degree (Permanent Probation). For years a university professor at Chicago and elsewhere, Mayer has described his departure from the lecture room in an essay called "Chucking It." He has also been a writer and editor for many newspapers and magazines, including the Progressive, Commonweal, and Harper's. Among other books, he has published The Revolution in Education (1958, with Mortimer J. Adler); They Thought They Were Free: The Germans, 1933–45 (1955); What Can a Man Do? (1964); Man. v. the State (1969); If Men Were Angels (1972); and The Nature of the Beast (1975). "On the Passing of the Slug," from this last volume, originally appeared in the Progressive. It analyzes why Chicago citizens once hated the telephone company and why they should not have stopped. It has nothing to do with insects.

When I contemplate the things that happen in Chicago, [1] such as the Fire, the Haymarket Riot, the Eastland Disaster, and Colonel McCormick of the *Chicago Tribune*,[1] I wonder how any man with a mind of his own could ever choose to live anywhere else. This week I have another Chicago phenomenon to report, and it will give you an idea of what I mean.

[1] The great fire destroyed most of the city in October 1871. The riot (May 3, 1886) was a bloody clash in Haymarket Square between police and workers protesting the suppression of anarchist labor leaders. The *Eastland*, an excursion steamer, overturned in the Chicago River in July 1915, killing 812 people. Robert Rutherford McCormick (1880–1955), cantankerous publisher of the *Tribune* from 1914 until his death, made the paper the most widely circulated nontabloid in the country.

137

The use of telephone slugs in public places has been abandoned   2
in my city. I am not positive for sure, but I think that Chicago
was the only city in the U.S. of A. where you could not make a
telephone call from a pay station without first purchasing, for five
cents, a conversation tablet, or slug. Each place had a differently
carved slug, with an apparatus hitched on to the nickel hole of
the telephone so that only that particular breed of slug could be
used.

The idea, obviously, was that Chicagoans were crooks, who, if   3
the nickel hole accommodated nickels, would use nickel-sized slugs
purchased at, say, a penny apiece. The total effect of the slug
system was to make telephoning difficult, and to load down the
jeans of the citizens with slugs which fitted a telephone the loca-
tion of which they had forgotten.

The system had another, more sinister, effect, besides. Like the   4
Prohibition Law,[2] it not only got people mad, it also broke down
their respect for law and order. Chicagoans resented the implication of the slug system, the implication being that Chicagoans, in
contrast, say, with New Yorkers, were not to be trusted. Whether
or not it was the telephone company that invented the slug system, the system bred in the heart of every Chicagoan a violent
resentment toward the company.

This resentment was handed down from generation to genera-   5
tion, as such things are, and by the time it reached my generation
it had taken the form of an unrelenting feud. I was brought up to
fear God and hate the telephone company, and I was forgiven my
derelictions in the former matter if I stood fast in the latter.

By the time I got to college I was an adept at beating the com-   6
pany. I knew, for instance, that if you had a two-party line and
the operator, after you gave her the number you wanted, asked
you what *your* number was, you had only to give her the number
of the other party on your line and she would never know the
difference. Of course, the other party was then charged for your
call, and the company did not lose a farthing. But you had the
blind satisfaction of somehow having deceived the company.

In addition, I knew that you could, every once in a while, get   7
a free call by rousing yourself to a bogus state of fury and insisting

[2] The eighteenth amendment to the U.S. Constitution outlawed the manufacture or sale of alcoholic beverages; it was repealed in 1933.

that you had dropped your nickel when in fact you hadn't. It often worked.

But my bright college years made a finished artist of me. I [8] learned, among other scientific matters not taught in the science department, the dime trick. The dime trick consisted of opening the box that contained the guts of the telephone and touching two adjoining screws with a dime. This contact signaled the operator that a nickel had been deposited, and she gave you your number.

The company had only one way to beat the dime trick. When [9] it found a phone, as it did in the office of the college paper, where a goodly number of calls would normally be made, and approximately three nickles in the box at the end of the month, it put some sort of special operator on the job and, evidence of guilt being established, yanked out the phone. That is why the Chicago *Daily Maroon* had no telephone my last year.

Still another common college prank was the plugged nickel. [10] One end of a piece of thread was tied to the plugged nickel and the other end held scientifically in the hand of the man who was beating the company.

You let the nickel down until it established the contact which [11] signaled the operator, held it on the contact until you finished talking, and then withdrew it. The objection to the plugged nickel system was that a nervous man might jiggle the nickel while he was talking and tip off the company. That is how my fraternity lost its phone.

The best of them all, while it lasted, was the flattened penny. [12] Since the flattened penny device involved not merely the ordinary criminality of the other tricks but, in addition, the violation of the Federal law against beating the life out of U.S. currency, it was especially attractive to those collegians whose view of life was not bounded by the local community, with its petty police ordinances, but embraced the entire sweep of a great nation and challenged the Department of Justice and the Army and the Navy.

The penny had to be flattened with consummate skill. If it was [13] too flat, it would go right through, like sassafras through a blue goose, and come out the coin return chute. It had to be flattened just to the degree that would enable it to rest delicately on the contact screws.

If it was not flattened enough, it would go into the coin box, [14] and there would be the evidence when the man came around at the end of the month. Flattened just right, it lay, as I say, on the contact screws while the call was in operation. At the conclusion of the call, you gave the box a terrific whack and the penny came out.

The flattened penny was a wonder while it lasted, and I would guess, if I were put to it, that it had more devotees than the plugged nickel. It had, besides all the beauties mentioned above, a higher degree of fidelity performance than any of the other tricks, and it demanded a higher degree of skill.

But it did not work forever. One day one of the boys, Jim Cusack, if I remember right, was using the flattened penny. Now Jim was a giant of a man, and a man of quick and stormy temper besides. He whacked the phone at the end of the call, but the penny did not come out. He whacked again, and it didn't come out, and Jim began to get mad. About the fourth or fifth try, he kicked the box, and the box came off the wall. And that, I am sorry to say, is how the office of the Student Honor Commission lost its telephone.

Now the incentive to all the ingenuity I have described has been removed. Why the company discontinued the slug system I no more know than I know why it started it, if indeed it was the company that started it. But it is gone, and Chicagoans, no longer mutely accused by every telephone of being crooks, no longer hate the telephone company.

This is too bad, and not just because the hatred inspired the invention of the flattened penny. It is too bad because the company is still a monopoly, which regulates, instead of being regulated by, the Illinois Commerce Commission. And if you do not like their rates, your only recourse is to communicate with people by Indian runner.

QUESTIONS

Understanding

1. Besides inspiring the dime trick, the plugged nickel, and the flattened penny, what long-range effects does Mayer (humorously)

attribute to the phone company's requiring Chicagoans to use slugs? Why was the requirement a slur on their morality?

2. According to Mayer's prediction, what effect will the passing of the slug have upon the average phone-company hater? Why is this likely effect undesirable?

3. What serious argument does Mayer hint at in paragraph 18?

Strategies and Structure

1. Mayer's humor has a tinge of nostalgia for youthful ingenuity and sentiments that are "passing" away. Point out words and phrases that contribute to this mood, for example "my bright college years" (par. 8) and "while it lasts" (par. 12).

2. How would you describe the TONE of the first sentence in this essay? Which individual sentences in paragraphs 5, 16, and 18 strike the same note? How does the cumulative effect of such passages keep the speaker from seeming heavy-handed or overbearing?

3. The last sentences of paragraphs 9, 12, and 16 build upon each other for humorous effect. Why do you think Mayer placed them in the order they follow here? How would the effect have been different if, for example, he had mentioned the student honor commission first?

4. How does the length and flow of the second sentence in paragraph 12 complement what Mayer is saying in that sentence?

5. The dominant MODE of this essay is EXPOSITION, but what elements of NARRATION can you discover in it—for example, big Jim Cusack's destruction of the pay phone in paragraph 16?

Words and Figures of Speech

1. Mayer spices his commentary with SLANG: "U.S. of A." (par. 2), "jeans" (par. 3), "crooks" (par. 3), "guts" (par. 8), "jiggle" (par. 11). Why is some verbal inventiveness appropriate, given Mayer's subject? From his use of slang, what can you deduce about Mayer's intended audience?

2. The word *devotees* (par. 15) usually applies to people devoted to the worship of a god or practice of a religious faith. How does the context make Mayer's use of the term amusing here? What is

funny, given their contexts, in his use of *artist* (par. 8) and *scientifically* (par. 10)?

3. From Mayer's title alone, what did you expect the subject of his essay to be? Why is it an effective title for a comic essay?

4. Check the dictionary definitions of the following words: *apparatus* (par. 2), *derelictions* (3), *adept* (6), *farthing* (6), *bogus* (7), and *consummate* (13). How should this last word be pronounced?

Comparing

1. Despite a vast difference in tone, "The Passing of the Slug" and the preceding essay by Reynolds Price are both about "hate." What else do they have in common?

2. Like Woody Allen's "Slang Origins" in the next chapter, "The Passing of the Slug" is basically comic. What techniques of humor do the two essays share? Which has the more complex TONE?

Discussion and Writing Topics

1. Does any single utility or transportation company monopolize services, or does a single employer monopolize jobs, in your hometown or city? What effect does this monopoly have upon life there?

2. Most communities have no choice about who provides their telephone service, but the phone company in your area probably does not advertise that it holds a monopoly. What effect on the community does your phone company claim to exert when it advertises on television or elsewhere?

3. Mayer's essay confirms the adage that necessity is the mother of invention. Explain what circumstances or necessities brought about one of the following: the gyroscope, the pocket calculator, the electric toothbrush, the crock pot.

WRITING TOPICS for Chapter Four
Essays That Analyze Cause and Effect

Write an essay analyzing the probable causes or effects (or both) of one of the following:

1. The energy crisis
2. Pollution
3. Urban blight
4. Drug or alcohol abuse
5. Heart disease, sickle cell anemia, or some other disease
6. Divorce within the first year or two of marriage
7. Loss of religious faith
8. Loss of self-esteem
9. Racial discrimination or ethnic jokes and slurs
10. Success in college
11. Student cheating
12. Sibling rivalry
13. The Civil War or other historical event
14. Invention of the assembly line system
15. Dropping out of high school or college
16. A sudden shift in status: from high school senior to college freshman, for example

5

Essays That Define

To make a basic DEFINITION,[1] put whatever you are defining into a class and then list the characteristics that distinguish it from all other members of that class. The Greek philosopher Plato, for example, defined man by putting him in the class "biped." Then Plato thought of a quality that sets man off from other two-legged creatures. "Man," he said, "is a featherless biped."

When the rival philosopher Diogenes heard this definition, he brought a plucked chicken into the lecture room and observed, "Here is Plato's man." Plato responded by adding that man is a featherless biped "having broad nails." The general principle that Plato was obeying holds for the basic definitions you will write. If at first you choose qualities that do not sufficiently distinguish your subject from others in the same class, refine those attributes until they do.

You can tell when a basic definition is essentially complete by testing whether it is true if reversed. "Man is a biped" proves to be an incomplete definition when we turn it around, for it is not true that "all bipeds are men." Likewise, we know that the final version of Plato's definition is sound because it is truly reversible. All featherless bipeds having broad nails (instead of claws) are indeed humans.

When it can be reversed, a basic definition is complete enough to be accurate; but it still may be scanty or undeveloped. One way of developing a basic definition is by listing qualities or attributes of a thing beyond those needed merely to identify it. Food expert Raymond Sokolov defines

[1] Terms printed in all capitals are defined in the Glossary.

the Florida tomato, for example, as a vegetable that is "mass-produced, artificially ripened, mechanically picked, long-hauled" (all qualities or attributes). "It has no taste and it won't go splat" (more qualities, though negative ones). Sokolov advises that we grow our own tomatoes if we want them to be "antique-style, squishable, blotchy, tart, and sometimes green-dappled."

Another common strategy of basic definition is to define the whole by naming its parts. "Ketchup is long-haul tomatoes combined with sugar, vinegar, salt, onion powder, and 'natural' flavoring." Or you might define a word by tracing its origins: "The English ketchup (or catsup) comes from the Malay word kechap, derived in turn from the Chinese word meaning 'fish brine.' " This word history may seem to take us far from the tomatoes at the base of America's favorite sauce, but it suggests where ketchup originally got its salty taste. Such word histories (or ETYMOLOGIES) can be found in parentheses or brackets before many of the definitions in your dictionary. Woody Allen has fun with etymologies in his essay "Slang Origins," included in this chapter.

Yet another way of developing a basic definition is to give synonyms for the word or concept being defined. A botanist might well tell us that the tomato is a plant used as a vegetable. But if pushed, he would add that the tomato is actually a "berry," or "fleshy fruit," akin to the "hesperidium" and the "pepo." His botanical definition would then proceed to explain what these closely related terms have in common, as well as the shades of difference among them. You can find synonyms for the word you are defining in any good desk dictionary or dictionary of synonyms. (The etymologies usually come at the beginning of a dictionary entry; the "synonymies," or lists of synonyms, at the end.)

The definitions we have discussed so far are short and limited to defining a basic word or phrase. When the strategy of an entire essay is to define something, the author produces what is called an extended definition. Extended definitions seek first and last to explain the nature or meaning of a thing, but they often use many of the other strategies of exposition. An extended definition of the detective story, for example, might divide it into types according to the kind of detective involved: the hard-boiled cop, the bumbling private eye, the clever priest. This would be an example of supporting a definition by CLASSIFICATION.

If we distinguished the detective story from the mystery story or the thriller, we might go on to define it by COMPARISON AND CONTRAST with similar forms. If we noted that Edgar Allan Poe invented the detective story and we gave the history of great detectives from Poe's Dupin to Sherlock Holmes to Columbo, we might draw upon NARRATIVE. Or if we speculated that the detective story came into being because Poe wanted to discover a walk of life in which the scientific mind blended with the poetic mind, we would be analyzing CAUSE AND EFFECT.

There is no set formula for writing an extended definition, but here are some questions to keep in mind when working one up: What is the essential nature or purpose of the thing you are defining? What are its qualities? How does it work? How is it different from others like it? Why do we need to know about it? In answering these questions, be as specific as you can. Vivid details make definitions interesting, and interest (after accuracy) is the best test of a good definition. Plato's definition of man surprises us into attention by reducing a lofty concept to the homely term "featherless." The poet Emily Dickinson does the same when she defines Hope as "the thing with feathers." It is the vivid specific detail that startles us here, as Woody Allen well knows when he reduces Dickinson's definition to absurdly specific terms: "The thing with feathers has turned out to be my nephew. I must take him to a specialist in Zurich."

Desmond Morris

Barrier Signals

Born in Wiltshire, England, in 1928, Desmond Morris is a zoologist who applies his knowledge of animal behavior to human beings. Since 1968 he has been a full-time writer, but he maintains an office in the Department of Zoology, Oxford University. An associate of the Tinbergen research group at Oxford, he is also an artist, and once organized a gallery sale in London of abstract paintings by chimpanzees. Morris is best known in this country as the author of The Naked Ape *(1961), a study of the human animal that was filmed by Universal studios in 1973. His other books include* The Human Zoo *(1969);* Intimate Behavior *(1971); and* Manwatching: A Field Guide to Human Behavior *(1977). "Barrier Signals," a complete section from this latest work, is about the gestures we unconsciously use to say no. It is an extended definition, developed largely by the use of examples.*

People feel safer behind some kind of physical barrier. If a   1
social situation is in any way threatening, then there is an immediate urge to set up such a barricade. For a tiny child faced with a stranger, the problem is usually solved by hiding behind its mother's body and peeping out at the intruder to see what he or she will do next. If the mother's body is not available, then a chair or some other piece of solid furniture will do. If the stranger insists on coming closer, then the peeping face must be hidden too. If the insensitive intruder continues to approach despite these obvious signals of fear, then there is nothing for it but to scream or flee.

This pattern is gradually reduced as the child matures. In   2
teenage girls it may still be detected in the giggling cover-up of the face, with hands or papers, when acutely or jokingly em-

barrassed. But by the time we are adult, the childhood hiding which dwindled to adolescent shyness, is expected to disappear altogether, as we bravely stride out to meet our guests, hosts, companions, relatives, colleagues, customers, clients, or friends. Each social occasion involves us, once again, in encounters similar to the ones which made us hide as scared infants and, as then, each encounter is slightly threatening. In other words, the fears are still there, but their expression is blocked. Our adult roles demand control and suppression of any primitive urge to withdraw and hide ourselves away. The more formal the occasion and the more dominant or unfamiliar our social companions, the more worrying the moment of encounter becomes. Watching people under these conditions, it is possible to observe the many small ways in which they continue to 'hide behind their mother's skirts'. The actions are still there, but they are transformed into less obvious movements and postures. It is these that are the Barrier Signals of adult life.

The most popular from of Barrier Signal is the Body-cross. In this, the hands or arms are brought into contact with one another in front of the body, forming a temporary 'bar' across the trunk, rather like a bumper or fender on the front of a motor-car. This is not done as a physical act of fending off the other person, as when raising a forearm horizontally across the front of the body to push through a struggling crowd. It is done, usually at quite a distance, as a nervous guest approaches a dominant host. The action is performed unconsciously and, if tackled on the subject immediately afterwards, the guest will not be able to remember having made the gesture. It is always camouflaged in some way, because if it were performed as a primitive fending-off or covering-up action, it would obviously be too transparent. The disguise it wears varies from person to person. Here are some examples:

The special guest on a gala occasion is alighting from his official limousine. Before he can meet and shake hands with the reception committee, he has to walk alone across the open space in front of the main entrance to the building where the function is being held. A large crowd has come to watch his arrival and the press cameras are flashing. Even for the most experienced of celebrities this is a slightly nervous moment, and the mild fear that is felt expresses itself just as he is halfway across the 'greeting-space'. As he walks forward, his right hand reaches across his body and makes a last-minute adjustment to his left cuff-link. It pauses there momentarily as he takes a few more steps, and then, at last, he is close enough to reach out his hand for the first of the many handshakes.

On a similar occasion, the special guest is a female. At just the   5
point where her male counterpart would have fiddled with his cuff, she reaches across her body with her right hand and slightly shifts the position of her handbag, which is hanging from her left forearm.

There are other variations on this theme. A male may finger a   6
button or the strap of a wristwatch instead of his cuff. A female may smooth out an imaginary crease in a sleeve, or re-position a scarf or coat held over her left arm. But in all cases there is one essential feature: at the peak moment of nervousness there is a Body-cross, in which one arm makes contact with the other across the front of the body, constructing a fleeting barrier between the guest and the reception committee.

Sometimes the barrier is incomplete. One arm swings across but   7
does not actually make contact with the other. Instead it deals with some trivial clothing-adjustment task on the opposite side of the body. With even heavier camouflage, the hand comes up and across, but goes no further than the far side of the head or face, with a mild stroking or touching action.

Less disguised forms of the Body-cross are seen with less ex-   8
perienced individuals. The man entering the restaurant, as he walks across an open space, rubs his hands together, as if washing them. Or he advances with them clasped firmly in front of him.

Such are the Barrier Signals of the greeting situation, where one   9
person is advancing on another. Interestingly, field observations reveal that it is most unlikely that both the greeter *and* the greeted will perform such actions. Regardless of status, it is nearly always the new arrival who makes the body-cross movement, because it is he who is invading the home territory of the greeters. They are on their own ground or, even if they are not, they were there first and have at least temporary territorial 'rights' over the place. This gives them an indisputable dominance at the moment of the greeting. Only if they are extremely subordinate to the new arrival, and perhaps in serious trouble with him, will there be a likelihood of them taking the 'body-cross role'. And if they do, this will mean that the new arrival on the scene will omit it as he enters.

These observations tell us something about the secret language [10] of Barrier Signals, and indicate that, although the sending and receiving of the signals are both unconsciously done, the message gets across, none the less. The message says: 'I am nervous but I will not retreat'; and this makes it into an act of subordination which automatically makes the other person feel slightly more dominant and more comfortable.

The situation is different after greetings are over and people are [11] standing about talking to one another. Now, if one man edges too close to another, perhaps to hear better in all the noise of chattering voices, the boxed-in companion may feel the same sort of threatening sensation that the arriving celebrity felt as he walked towards the reception committee. What is needed now, however, is something more long-lasting than a mere cuff-fumble. It is simply not possible to go fiddling with a button for as long as this companion is going to thrust himself forward. So a more composed posture is needed. The favorite Body-cross employed in this situation is the arm-fold, in which the left and right arms intertwine themselves across the front of the chest. This posture, a perfect, frontal Barrier Signal, can be held for a very long time without appearing strange. Unconsciously it transmits a 'come-no-farther' message and is used a great deal at crowded gatherings. It has also been used by poster artists as a deliberate 'They-shall-not-pass!' gesture, and is rather formally employed by bodyguards when standing outside a protected doorway.

The same device of arm-folding can be used in a sitting rela- [12] tionship where the companion is approaching too close, and it can be amplified by a crossing of the legs *away* from the companion. Another variant is to press the tightly clasped hands down on to the crotch and squeeze them there between the legs, as if protecting the genitals. The message of this particular form of barrier is clear enough, even though neither side becomes consciously aware of it. But perhaps the major Barrier Signal for the seated person is that ubiquitous device, the desk. Many a businessman would feel naked without one and hides behind it gratefully every day, wearing it like a vast, wooden chastity-belt. Sitting beyond it he feels fully protected from the visitor exposed on the far side. It is the supreme barrier, both physical and psychological, giving him an immediate and lasting comfort while he remains in its solid embrace.

QUESTIONS

Understanding

1. What is a "barrier signal" as defined by Morris?
2. Why must barrier signals be disguised? What do they mask?
3. Barrier signals as defined by Morris are part of a "secret language" (par. 10) of gestures or signs. How does a sign differ from an action like screaming or running away?
4. In a greeting situation, according to Morris, why is it usually the new arrival who sets up barriers, even when his status is higher than the greeter's?
5. Why are barrier signals of interest to sociologists and anthropologists? What kind of information can they provide?

Strategies and Structure

1. Which sentence in paragraph 2 signals that the author has been constructing a definition?
2. Is the definition in paragraphs 1 and 2 developed primarily by CLASSIFICATION, PROCESS ANALYSIS, CAUSE AND EFFECT analysis, or some combination of these methods? Explain your answer.
3. This essay refers to several different kinds of barrier signals, but it is not really an essay in classification. Why not?
4. The examples in paragraphs 3–8 illustrate "the Body-cross." What else do they also illustrate?
5. In paragraph 12, Morris says that the desk is "the major Barrier Signal for the seated person." Is a desk really a good example of a "signal"? Why or why not?

Words and Figures of Speech

1. Morris is an "ethologist." Look up the definition of this specialty in an unabridged dictionary. How does "Barrier Signals" help to demonstrate what an ethologist does?
2. When he writes such a phrase as "clothing-adjustment task" (par. 7), Morris might be accused of "excess noun-overusage." Point out other examples and suggest less awkward ways for rewriting these phrases-used-as-nouns.

3. How does Morris's METAPHOR of hiding behind mother's skirts (par. 2) apply to barrier signals as he defines them?

4. If you are not sure of any of these words, see how your dictionary defines them: *colleagues* (par. 2), *suppression* (2), *camouflaged* (3), *gala* (4), *status* (9), *subordination* (10), *ubiquitous* (12).

Comparing

1. When you read Barry Lopez's "My Horse" in Chapter 7, look for barrier signals and other symbolic gestures among the Plains Indians that he describes.

2. How does Morris's essay resemble Peter Farb's "The Levels of Sleep" in Chapter 2?

Discussion and Writing Topics

1. Elsewhere, Morris defines a "tie" signal as a gesture that indicates a close relationship between two or more people (holding hands, for example). Write an extended definition of "tie signals" in which you cite examples that you have actually observed "in the field."

2. Define *language*. In what sense are most written languages sign languages?

Willard Gaylin

What You See Is the Real You

A native of Cleveland, Ohio, Willard Gaylin, M.D., is professor of clinical psychiatry at Columbia University and president of the Institute of Society, Ethics, and the Life Sciences. Deeply concerned with the ethical issues in biology and medicine, he has taught at colleges and universities throughout the country, including the Columbia School of Law, where he is an adjunct professor. Gaylin is a consultant on penal reform, and has written a debate on amnesty, When Can I Come Home? (1972). In addition to essays and books on psychoanalysis, he has published two studies of bias in the judicial system, Partial Justice (1974) and At the Heart of Judgement (1974). What you see in the following essay from the New York Times is a psychiatrist's personal definition of the self, ethics, and the limitations of mental science.

It was, I believe, the distinguished Nebraska financier Father Edward J. Flanagan [1] who professed to having "never met a bad boy." Having, myself, met a remarkable number of bad boys, it might seem that either our experiences were drastically different or we were using the word "bad" differently. I suspect neither is true, but rather that the Father was appraising the "inner man," while I, in fact, do not acknowledge the existence of inner people.

Since we psychoanalysts have unwittingly contributed to this confusion, let one, at least, attempt a small rectifying effort. Psychoanalytic data—which should be viewed as supplementary information—is, unfortunately, often viewed as

[1] (1886–1948), founder of Boys' Town orphanage near Omaha, Nebraska.

alternative (and superior) explanation. This has led to the prevalent tendency to think of the "inner" man as the real man and
the outer man as an illusion or pretender.

While psychoanalysis supplies us with an incredibly useful tool   3
for explaining the motives and purposes underlying human behavior, most of this has little bearing on the moral nature of that
behavior.

Like roentgenology, psychoanalysis is a fascinating, but rela-   4
tively new, means of illuminating the person. But few of us are
prepared to substitute an X-ray of Grandfather's head for the
portrait that hangs in the parlor. The inside of the man represents
another view, not a truer one. A man may not always be what he
appears to be, but what he appears to be is always a significant
part of what he is. A man is the sum total of *all* his behavior.
To probe for unconscious determinants of behavior and then
define *him* in their terms exclusively, ignoring his overt behavior
altogether, is a greater distortion than ignoring the unconscious
completely.

Kurt Vonnegut [2] has said, "You are what you pretend to be,"   5
which is simply another way of saying, you are what we (all of
us) perceive you to be, not what you think you are.

Consider for a moment the case of the 90-year-old man on his   6
deathbed (surely the Talmud [3] must deal with this?) joyous and
relieved over the success of his deception. For 90 years he has
shielded his evil nature from public observation. For 90 years he
has affected courtesy, kindness, and generosity—suppressing all the
malice he knew was within him while he calculatedly and artificially substituted grace and charity. All his life he had been fool-
ing the world into believing he was a good man. This "evil" man
will, I predict, be welcomed into the Kingdom of Heaven.

Similarly, I will not be told that the young man who earns his   7
pocket money by mugging old ladies is "really" a good boy. Even
my generous and expansive definition of goodness will not accom-
modate that particular form of self-advancement.

It does not count that beneath the rough exterior he has a   8
heart—or, for that matter, an entire innards—of purest gold,

[2] American novelist, author of *Cat's Cradle* (1963); *God Bless You, Mr.
Rosewater* (1964); *Slaughterhouse-Five* (1969); and *Breakfast of Champions* (1973).
[3] Book of orthodox Jewish civil and religious law.

locked away from human perception. You are for the most part what you seem to be, not what you would wish to be, nor, indeed, what you believe yourself to be.

Spare me, therefore, your good intentions, your inner sensitivities, your unarticulated and unexpressed love. And spare me also those tedious psychohistories which—by exposing the goodness inside the bad man, and the evil in the good—invariably establish a vulgar and perverse egalitarianism, as if the arrangement of what is outside and what inside makes no moral difference.   9

Saint Francis [4] may, in his unconscious, indeed have been compensating for, and denying, destructive, unconscious Oedipal impulses identical to those which Attila projected and acted on. But the similarity of the unconscious constellations in the two men matters precious little, if it does not distinguish between them.   10

I do not care to learn that Hitler's heart was in the right place. A knowledge of the unconscious life of the man may be an adjunct to understanding his behavior. It is *not* a substitute for his behavior in describing him.   11

The inner man is a fantasy. If it helps you to identify with one, by all means, do so; preserve it, cherish it, embrace it, but do not present it to others for evaluation or consideration, for excuse or exculpation, or, for that matter, for punishment or disapproval.   12

Like any fantasy, it serves your purposes alone. It has no standing in the real world which we share with each other. Those character traits, those attitudes, that behavior—that strange and alien stuff sticking out all over you—*that's the real you!*   13

QUESTIONS

Understanding

1. How does Gaylin DEFINE the self? How is it different from the self that psychoanalysis usually addresses?

---

[4] Probably St. Francis of Assisi (1182?–1226), Italian monk and founder of the Franciscan Order. The term *Oedipal impulses* refers to a son's sexual attraction to his mother; in Greek mythology, Oedipus, king of Thebes, unwittingly killed his father and married his mother. Attila was the fierce leader of the Huns from 434 to 453; invader of the Roman Empire.

2. What are fantasies, according to Gaylin's definition? What relation do they bear to the outer world?

3. What is the business of psychoanalysis, according to Gaylin? What aspect of human behavior is largely beyond its reach?

4. In paragraphs 1 and 11, what standard does Gaylin assume for judging the morality of human behavior?

Strategies and Structure

1. Like the preceding selection, Gaylin's essay is another instance of definition by example. Which examples do you find most effective? Why?

2. How do the examples of X-ray and portrait (par. 4) contribute to the distinction Gaylin is making between our "selves"?

3. Why do you think Gaylin chose to begin with the example of Father Flanagan? How does this example help to set the TONE of the essay?

4. Gaylin's definition is aided by COMPARISON AND CONTRAST, the EXPOSITORY strategy you will study in Chapter 6. For now, simply point out those examples that establish a contrast.

5. In paragraph 5, Gaylin rephrases Kurt Vonnegut's definition to make it conform with his own definition. Is this a legitimate technique? Why or why not?

Words and Figures of Speech

1. What peculiar meaning does *unconscious* (par. 11) have in the language of psychoanalysis?

2. What modern popular saying does Gaylin's title seem to echo? Why does this slogan, in particular, suit his purpose?

3. Gaylin says that he does "not acknowledge the existence of inner people" (par. 1). How can this HYPERBOLE be reconciled with his statement in paragraph 4 that the "inside view of the man represents another view, not a truer one"?

4. In paragraph 13, Gaylin defines *behavior* as "strange and alien stuff." Point out other passages where he seems to prefer ordinary language to technical language. How does Gaylin's care to avoid psychological jargon help to define his audience?

5. Consult your dictionary if you are not familiar with any of the following words: *financier* (par. 1), *rectify* (2), *roentgenology* (4), *affect* (6), *unarticulated* (9), *vulgar* (9), *perverse* (9), *egalitarianism* (9), *Oedipal* (10), *adjunct* (11).

Comparing

1. How does Gaylin's view of the self compare with the view implied in Nora Ephron's "A Few Words about Breasts" (Chapter 1)?
2. How does the psychology of barrier signals, as explained by Desmond Morris in the preceding essay, *deny* Gaylin's definition of the self?

Discussion and Writing Topics

1. Write a definition of the self as your experience of human nature has led you to perceive it.
2. The main components of the self, according to the psychoanalyst Sigmund Freud (whose views are summarized by Carl Jung in "Essays For Further Reading" at the end of this volume), are the *ego*, the *id*, and the *superego*. Define one or more of these concepts.

Michael Rogers

Portrait of the Newlyweds as a Young Hologram

*As a science writer, Michael Rogers is at ease with technology,
but he sometimes worries that mad scientists are perhaps taking
over. His latest book,* Biohazard *(1977), is a report on the controversy surrounding DNA; it asks how far molecular biologists
should go in genetic tampering with living organisms. Rogers is
an associate editor of* Rolling Stone *(in which the following essay
recently appeared) and editor-at-large of* Outside *magazine. His
first novel,* Mindfogger, *was published in 1973. "Portrait of the
Newlyweds as a Young Hologram" defines the three-dimensional
laser photograph that Rogers posed for with his bride; he wonders
what their future great-grandchildren will think of this "primitive" portrait.*

When I was a kid, and reading every science fiction book   1
in the local library, I used to wonder exactly how the future
would happen. By that I don't mean what the future would
be *like*—science fiction already told me that—but rather how
we'd actually get there. Science fiction books seemed to agree,
for example, that in the future there would be no money—all
transactions would be made via identity cards and centralized
computers. But that seemed dubious to me: how, I wondered,
are you going to get everybody to give up money in the
first place?

Well. No one even had to try. By now one can travel across   2
the country with only a few embossed plastic rectangles—each
bearing the thin strip of magnetic tape that will likely soon

talk to, of all things, a central computer. There are other examples—home video terminals, or microprocessors—and the general rule seems clear: the future sneaks up on you, even before you see it coming.

Sometimes, however, you can catch a glimpse. Recently, for example, I got married—an action guaranteed to make a fellow think about the future—and it seemed appropriate to arrange for a wedding portrait. And for some reason I thought of the small group of holographers from whom I'd taken a class, a few years back in San Francisco.

A hologram, of course, is a true three-dimensional picture—one in which there is not only a sense of depth, but actual perspective shift. As the viewer moves his head, an object in the foreground of the image will progressively cover another in the back. A good hologram is a striking thing indeed, but until recently, its artistic utility was limited: it took a laser to make one and another laser to view it.

New techniques, however, have made it possible to create holograms that can be viewed in "white"—noncoherent, garden-variety—light. And some of the San Francisco holographers had, moreover, developed yet another process using white light and regular movie film—which is then converted, using a laser, into holographic form.

The product of those techniques is a cylindrical hologram a little less than a foot high and 16 inches in diameter. The image appears to hover, three-dimensional, within the cylinder walls and, as one walks around it, the subject actually moves through 15 or so seconds of time.

It's a remarkable effect, and moreover makes it possible to conveniently holograph human beings for the first time. An ideal wedding portrait, I thought—but when I picked up the White Pages to find the school, it was no longer listed. Frontier technology, I figured, bites the dust again. But then, as an afterthought, I checked the Yellow Pages—and there it was, the Multiplex Co., right under the appropriate heading: Holography.

The future sneaks up again—this time in the telephone book. I dialed and asked about an appointment for a wedding hologram. No problem: the firm was already averaging five or six portraits a week—many shot in foreign studios, with the film flown to San

Francisco for holographic processing. Lily Tomlin and Ringo Starr, I was assured, were among the early customers.

A few days later we arrived, suitably dressed for our wedding   9
portrait. In the middle of a medium-sized warehouse we were seated on straight-backed chairs in the center of a big black turntable, eight feet in diameter, driven by machinery sunk into the concrete floor. The turntable was surrounded by klieg lights—one old light boom still bearing a brass plaque that read COLUMBIA PICTURES SOUND BOOM #3. In the midst of the lights, aimed at the center of the turntable, was a large 35 mm motion picture camera, also vintage Hollywood.

We'd opted for a 120° portrait—one-third of the turntable's   10
rotation—showing our faces from ear to ear and costing, for the first copy, $150. At more than a buck per degree, we wanted a little action, so we'd planned a passionate kiss, a break, then smiles into the camera.

That's not as easy as it sounds. One slip during that little rou-   11
tine—shifting eyes, a nodding head, a jerky motion—and our final hologram would look weird indeed: "It's this whole strange space/time anomaly," one holographer explained cheerfully—all due to the eccentricities of the movie-to-hologram process. If, for example, we shifted our eyes, it would appear in the hologram that first one eye shifted . . . and then, moments later, the other.

Altogether undesirable, and so we rehearsed our kiss again and   12
again, rotating stiff and silly on the big turntable. When everyone was satisfied that our movements were smooth, the camera ran, for two consecutive 15-second takes.

Two weeks later we saw the result: one-third of a holographic   13
cylinder, mounted in a black cardboard wall display, complete with built-in light source. Deep past the plastic surface were miniature images of ourselves—and as one moved around the semicircle, they looked into each other's eyes, came together, parted, then smiled at the viewer.

The color was odd—something of a dull, shifting rainbow—and   14
we looked a little self-conscious and stiff. But then it was us—truly three-dimensional, moving as in life—and as we watched our six-inch images move through those few seconds of frozen time, I couldn't help but think how our tentative, slightly uncomfortable expressions reminded me of early daguerreotypes. And my

next fantasy was inevitable: great-grandchildren in some mile-high stainless-steel city of the future, hanging an ancient hologram of their forebears—dim, dusty, odd and positively primitive, compared to their own unimaginable technology.

Fantasy indeed. There are a lot of assumptions involved in that image, more than I'd even care to number. But there's one I'll stand by: this is how the future happens—it sneaks up, before you even notice.   15

QUESTIONS

Understanding

1. In which paragraph does Rogers begin to set forth his basic DEFINITION of a hologram? What quality, in particular, distinguishes holograms from other kinds of photographs or movies?
2. In what sense is the newlywed's hologram "young"? How does the hologram affect time?
3. What are some of the "assumptions" (par. 15) involved in Roger's image of his great-grandchildren looking at the "ancient hologram" (par. 14).

Strategies and Structure

1. In which paragraphs does Rogers use PROCESS ANALYSIS to help develop his definition?
2. Rogers skillfully blends the other three MODES OF DISCOURSE with his EXPOSITORY definition of a hologram. Which mode dominates in paragraph 6? In Paragraph 12? In paragraph 15?
3. The hologram that Rogers is defining belongs to the space age. How does he "domesticate" this peculiar object so that it does not seem threatening or even alien?
4. Rogers's essay is set in the present. How does he give us glimpses of a time earlier than the time of writing? What do these traces of the past anticipate?
5. Rogers uses his definition of a hologram to advance a THESIS about the future. What other examples does he use?

6. Rogers states his thesis three times. In which paragraphs? Why are his thesis statements *spaced* as they are?

Words and Figures of Speech

1. According to your dictionary, what is a "daguerreotype"? Who invented it and when?
2. There is an ALLUSION in Rogers's title to works by James Joyce and Dylan Thomas. Identify those works by looking up these two authors in the *Cambridge Bibliography of English Literature* or some other standard reference work in your school library.
3. If you are unfamiliar with the definitions of any of the following words, look them up in your dictionary: *dubious* (par. 1), *embossed* (2), *foreground* (4), *vintage* (9), *tentative* (14).

Comparing

1. In "Time Out" ("Paragraphs For Analysis"), Roger Angell compares baseball's time to a "bubble." How might this notion, as Angell develops it, be applied to Rogers's hologram?
2. How does Rogers's treatment of time differ from that of Loren Eiseley in "The Angry Winter" (Chapter 1)?

Discussion and Writing Topics

1. How would you define a credit card and its use to anyone who had never seen one before? A central computer? A microwave oven? A cash register with a wand that "reads" price tags?
2. Define, by describing and analyzing it, an object or process that has brought the future home to you in the present.
3. Define fantasy writing (or fantasy movies); how does it differ from science fiction?

Woody Allen

Slang Origins

Allen Stewart Konigsberg (Woody Allen) was born in Brooklyn,
New York, in 1935. Comedian, actor, director, and writer, he
began a busy career while still in high school by making up jokes
for other people; Herb Shriner, Sid Caesar, Art Carney, and Jack
Paar were among his early clients at NBC before Allen himself
went on the stage in 1961. He is probably most famous for his
films, including Bananas *(1970);* Play It Again, Sam *(1972); and*
Love and Death *(1975).* Annie Hall *(1977) won Allen the*
academy awards for both directing and screenwriting. Allen's work
has been influenced, he says, by "The Bible, A Boy's Guide to
Forestry, and Advanced Sexual Positions—How to Achieve Them
without Laughing." "Slang Origins," from Without Feathers
(1975), shows how to define words by their etymologies (or lin-
guistic roots). Do not dismiss Allen's ridiculous definitions; they
are funny because they come so close to the standard form.

How many of you have ever wondered where certain slang   1
expressions come from? Like "She's the cat's pajamas," or to
"take it on the lam." Neither have I. And yet for those who
are interested in this sort of thing I have provided a brief
guide to a few of the more interesting origins.

Unfortunately, time did not permit consulting any of the   2
established works on the subject, and I was forced to either
obtain the information from friends or fill in certain gaps by
using my own common sense.

Take, for instance, the expression "to eat humble pie."   3
During the reign of Louis the Fat, the culinary arts flourished
in France to a degree unequaled anywhere. So obese was the

French monarch that he had to be lowered onto the throne with a winch and packed into the seat itself with a large spatula. A typical dinner (according to DeRochet) consisted of a thin crêpe appetizer, some parsley, an ox, and custard. Food became the court obsession, and no other subject could be discussed under penalty of death. Members of a decadent aristocracy consumed incredible meals and even dressed as foods. DeRochet tells us that M. Monsant showed up at the coronation as a wiener, and Étienne Tisserant received papal dispensation to wed his favorite codfish. Desserts grew more and more elaborate and pies grew larger until the minister of justice suffocated trying to eat a seven-foot "Jumbo Pie." *Jumbo* pie soon became *jumble* pie and "to eat a jumble pie" referred to any kind of humiliating act. When the Spanish seamen heard the word *jumble*, they pronounced it "humble," although many preferred to say nothing and simply grin.

Now, while "humble pie" goes back to the French, "take it on the lam" is English in origin. Years ago, in England, "lamming" was a game played with dice and a large tube of ointment. Each player in turn threw dice and then skipped around the room until he hemorrhaged. If a person threw a seven or under he would say the word "quintz" and proceed to twirl in a frenzy. If he threw over seven, he was forced to give every player a portion of his feathers and was given a good "lamming." Three "lammings" and a player was "kwirled" or declared a moral bankrupt. Gradually any game with feathers was called "lamming" and feathers became "lams." To "take it on the lam" meant to put on feathers and later, to escape, although the transition is unclear. [4]

Incidentally, if two players disagreed on rules, we might say they "got into a beef." This term goes back to the Renaissance when a man would court a woman by stroking the side of her head with a slab of meat. If she pulled away, it meant she was spoken for. If, however, she assisted by clamping the meat to her face and pushing it all over her head, it meant she would marry him. The meat was kept by the bride's parents and worn as a hat on special occasions. If, however, the husband took another lover, the wife could dissolve the marriage by running with the meat to the town square and yelling, "With thine own beef, I do reject thee. Aroo! Aroo!" If a couple "took to the beef" or "had a beef" it meant they were quarreling. [5]

Another marital custom gives us that eloquent and colorful ex- [6]

pression of disdain, "to look down one's nose." In Persia it was considered a mark of great beauty for a woman to have a long nose. In fact, the longer the nose, the more desirable the female, up to a certain point. Then it became funny. When a man proposed to a beautiful woman he awaited her decision on bended knee as she "looked down her nose at him." If her nostrils twitched, he was accepted, but if she sharpened her nose with pumice and began pecking him on the neck and shoulders, it meant she loved another.

Now, we all know when someone is very dressed up, we say he looks "spiffy." The term owes its origin to Sir Oswald Spiffy, perhaps the most renowned fop of Victorian England. Heir to treacle millions, Spiffy squandered his money on clothes. It was said that at one time he owned enough handkerchiefs for all the men, women and children in Asia to blow their noses for seven years without stopping. Spiffy's sartorial innovations were legend, and he was the first man ever to wear gloves on his head. Because of extra-sensitive skin, Spiffy's underwear had to be made of the finest Nova Scotia salmon, carefully sliced by one particular tailor. His libertine attitudes involved him in several notorious scandals, and he eventually sued the government over the right to wear earmuffs while fondling a dwarf. In the end Spiffy died a broken man in Chichester, his total wardrobe reduced to kneepads and a sombrero.

Looking "spiffy," then, is quite a compliment, and one who does is liable to be dressed "to beat the band," a turn-of-the-century expression that originated from the custom of attacking with clubs any symphony orchestra whose conductor smiled during Berlioz. "Beating the band" soon became a popular evening out, and people dressed up in their finest clothes, carrying with them sticks and rocks. The practice was finally abandoned, during a performance of the *Symphonie fantastique* [1] in New York when the entire string section suddenly stopped playing and exchanged gunfire with the first ten rows. Police ended the melee but not before a relative of J. P. Morgan's [2] was wounded in the soft palate. After that, for a while at least, nobody dressed "to beat the band."

[1] Symphony composed in 1831 by the Frenchman, Hector Berlioz (1803–1869).
[2] John Pierpont Morgan (1837–1913), American banker and art connoisseur, or his son, J. P. Morgan, Jr. (1867–1943), also an investment banker.

If you think some of the above derivations questionable, you ⁹ might throw up your hands and say, "Fiddlesticks." This marvelous expression originated in Austria many years ago. Whenever a man in the banking profession announced his marriage to a circus pinhead, it was the custom for friends to present him with a bellows and a three-year supply of wax fruit. Legend has it that when Leo Rothschild made known his betrothal, a box of cello bows was delivered to him by mistake. When it was opened and found not to contain the traditional gift, he exclaimed, "What are these? Where are my bellows and fruit? Eh? All I rate is fiddlesticks!" The term "fiddlesticks" became a joke overnight in the taverns amongst the lower classes, who hated Leo Rothschild for never removing the comb from his hair after combing it. Eventually "fiddlesticks" meant any foolishness.

Well, I hope you've enjoyed some of these slang origins and ¹⁰ that they stimulate you to investigate some of your own. And in case you were wondering about the term used to open this study, "the cat's pajamas," it goes back to an old burlesque routine of Chase and Rowe's, the two nutsy German professors. Dressed in oversized tails, Bill Rowe stole some poor victim's pajamas. Dave Chase, who got great mileage out of his "hard of hearing" specialty, would ask him:

CHASE: Ach, Herr Professor. Vot is dot bulge under your pocket? ¹¹

ROWE: Dot? Dot's de chap's pajamas. ¹²

CHASE: The cat's pajamas? Ut mein Gott? ¹³

Audiences were convulsed by this sort of repartee and only a ¹⁴ premature death of the team by strangulation kept them from stardom.

QUESTIONS

Understanding

1. A parody is a take-off on a literary form. What kind of writing is Allen's "study" parodying?

2. Look up *humble pie* in your dictionary. What is the ETYMOLOGY of the phrase? Why do you suppose the name of the main ingredient later got confused with the word *humble*?

3. Many words that we use today have their origins in Latin. Check the front or back of your dictionary for a short history of the English language. When and why did Latin most influence English?

Strategies and Structure

1. How soon in paragraph 1 do you know that Allen is "pulling your leg" (to use a phrase that Allen might have "explained" for us)?

2. Describe Allen's TRANSITIONS from word history to word history. How do they contribute to the humor?

3. Allen is not speaking in his own voice here (the voice of Allen Stewart Konigsberg); he is using a persona or stand-in. What is that persona like? How does Allen characterize him? How would you describe the TONE of his voice?

4. Why does Allen end with Rowe and Chase and their strange demise?

5. Allen calls his essay a "guide" (par. 1); it is a form he often uses—"A Brief, Yet Helpful, Guide to Civil Disobedience," for example. Why? What is a "guide" and why might the form appeal to a humorist?

6. Suppose you were explaining what an etymologist is and does. How might you use the etymology of the word itself to help along your DEFINITION?

Words and Figures of Speech

1. Look up several of Woody Allen's words and phrases and "correct" his word histories.

2. Report on the kinds of information to be found in the Dictionary of American Slang, edited by Harold Wentworth and Stuart Berg Flexner (available in the reference room of your college or university library.)

3. Look up the word buxom in the Oxford English Dictionary. (Try the reference room again.) How has the word changed in meaning over the centuries?

Discussion and Writing Topics

1. Make up your own comic etymologies of the following words and phrases, but adhere as strictly as Allen does to the *form* of definition-by-etymology:

   to fly off the handle
   to go off on a tangent
   squared away
   clean as a whistle
   a horse of another color
   birds of a feather
   a white elephant
   a sacred cow.

Write extended definitions of one or more of the following:

1. Photosynthesis or mitosis
2. Obscenity
3. A liberal education
4. Success
5. A happy marriage
6. A liberated woman
7. A true friend
8. Self-reliance
9. Inertia (physical or spiritual)
10. Non-Euclidian geometry
11. Calculus
12. The big-bang theory of creation
13. Your idea of the ideal society
14. Blues music
15. Tragedy, comedy, romance, novel, satire, or some other literary form

6

Essays That Compare and Contrast

Before you begin an essay in COMPARISON AND CONTRAST,[1] it is a good idea to make a list of the qualities of the two objects or ideas to be compared. Suppose, for example, that our "objects" were all-time basketball greats Wilt ("The Stilt") Chamberlain and Bill Russell. Our lists might look like this:

Chamberlain	Russell
7-feet-3-inches tall	6-feet-9-inches tall
good team	better team
fast	faster
style	discipline
loser (almost)	winner (almost)
Goliath	David

Each of these lists is an abbreviated DESCRIPTION of the player whose attributes it compiles. At this early stage, our comparison and contrast essay seems indistinguishable from descriptive writing. As soon as we bring our two lists together, however, the descriptive impulse yields to the impulse to explain. Consider the following excerpt from an actual comparison of Chamberlain with Russell by sportswriter Jeremy Larner:

Wilt's defenders could claim with justice that Russell played with a better team, but it was all too apparent that Boston was better partly because Russell played better with them. Russell has been above all a team player—a man of discipline, self-

1 Terms printed in all capitals are defined in the Glossary.

denial and killer instinct; in short, a *winner,* in the best American Calvinist tradition. Whereas Russell has been able somehow to squeeze out his last ounce of ability, Chamberlain's performances have been marked by a seeming nonchalance—as if, recognizing his Giantistic fate, he were more concerned with personal style than with winning. "I never want to set records. The only thing I strive for is perfection" Chamberlain has said. When Wilt goes into his routine, his body proclaims from tip to toe, it's not my fault, folks, honestly—and though I've got to lose, if you look close, you'll see I'm beautiful through and through!

Even though it describes the two men in some detail, this passage is EXPOSITION *rather than description. Like most comparative writing, its comparisons are cast as statements or propositions: Russell is more efficient than Chamberlain; Chamberlain is concerned with style, while Russell plays to win. The controlling proposition of Larner's entire essay is that Chamberlain was a Goliath "typecast" by fans to lose to Russell the giant-killer; but Chamberlain broke the stereotype to become the greatest basketball player ever.*

We can take a number of hints from Jeremy Larner about writing comparison and contrast essays. First, stick to two and only two subjects at a time. Second, choose subjects that invite comparison because they belong to the same general class: two athletes, two religions, two sororities, two mammals. (In "The Black and White Truth about Basketball," reprinted in this chapter, another sports enthusiast, Jeff Greenfield, compares two styles of playing the same game.) You might point out many differences between a mattress and a steamboat, but no one is likely to be impressed by this exercise in the obvious. The third lesson is that you do not have to give equal weight to similarities and differences. Larner assumes the similarities between Chamberlain and Russell (both are towering champions), but he works carefully through the differences. An essay that compares a turtle to a tank, on the other hand, might concentrate upon the similarities of the two if it proposes that both belong to the class of moving things with armor.

Our example suggests, finally, that comparison and contrast essays proceed by alternation. From paragraph to paragraph, Larner dispenses his subject in "slices." His assertion that Russell is a team player is followed immediately by the counterassertion that Chamberlain plays to a private standard. Chamberlain's free throws are always uncertain; Russell's are accurate in the clutch. And so on, point by point. Another way of comparing and contrasting is in "chunks." Larner might have said all he had to say about Russell in several paragraphs and then followed up with all of his remarks on Chamberlain. Either method (or a combination of the two) is correct if it works. The aim is to set forth clear alternatives.

Bruce Catton

Grant and Lee:
A Study in Contrasts

A native of Michigan who attended Oberlin College, Bruce Catton was a former newspaper reporter, a one-time editor of American Heritage, and a noted historian of the Civil War. A Stillness at Appomattox (1953) won both the Pulitzer Prize and the National Book Award for history in 1954. It was not, said Catton, "the strategy or political meanings" that fascinated him but the "almost incomprehensible emotional experience which this war brought to our country." Among Catton's many other books are This Hallowed Ground (1956); The Coming Fury (1961); The Army of the Potomac (1962); Terrible Swift Sword (1963); Never Call Retreat (1965); Grant Takes Command (1969); and Michigan: A Bicentennial History (1976). "Grant and Lee: A Study in Contrasts" is reprinted from a collection of essays by distinguished historians.

When Ulysses S. Grant and Robert E. Lee met in the parlor of a modest house at Appomattox Court House, Virginia, on April 9, 1865, to work out the terms for the surrender of Lee's Army of Northern Virginia, a great chapter in American life came to a close, and a great new chapter began. 1

These men were bringing the Civil War to its virtual finish. To be sure, other armies had yet to surrender, and for a few days the fugitive Confederate government would struggle desperately and vainly, trying to find some way to go on living now that its chief support was gone. But in effect it was all 2 over when Grant and Lee signed the papers. And the little room where they wrote out the terms was the scene of one of the poignant, dramatic contrasts in American history.

They were two strong men, these oddly different generals, and   3 they represented the strengths of two conflicting currents that, through them, had come into final collision.

Back of Robert E. Lee was the notion that the old aristocratic   4 concept might somehow survive and be dominant in American life.

Lee was tidewater Virginia, and in his background were family,   5 culture, and tradition . . . the age of chivalry transplanted to a New World which was making its own legends and its own myths. He embodied a way of life that had come down through the age of knighthood and the English country squire. America was a land that was beginning all over again, dedicated to nothing much more complicated than the rather hazy belief that all men had equal rights and should have an equal chance in the world. In such a land Lee stood for the feeling that it was somehow of advantage to human society to have a pronounced inequality in the social structure. There should be a leisure class, backed by ownership of land; in turn, society itself should be keyed to the land as the chief source of wealth and influence. It would bring forth (according to this ideal) a class of men with a strong sense of obligation to the community; men who lived not to gain advantage for themselves, but to meet the solemn obligations which had been laid on them by the very fact that they were privileged. From them the country would get its leadership; to them it could look for the higher values—of thought, of conduct, of personal deportment—to give it strength and virtue.

Lee embodied the noblest elements of this aristocratic ideal.   6 Through him, the landed nobility justified itself. For four years, the Southern states had fought a desperate war to uphold the ideals for which Lee stood. In the end, it almost seemed as if the Confederacy fought for Lee; as if he himself was the Confederacy . . . the best thing that the way of life for which the Confederacy stood could ever have to offer. He had passed into legend before Appomattox. Thousands of tired, underfed, poorly clothed Confederate soldiers, long since past the simple enthusiasm of the early days of the struggle, somehow considered Lee the symbol of everything for which they had been willing to die. But they could not quite put this feeling into words. If the Lost Cause, sanctified by so much heroism and so many deaths, had a living justification, its justification was General Lee.

Grant, the son of a tanner on the Western frontier, was everything Lee was not. He had come up the hard way and embodied nothing in particular except the eternal toughness and sinewy fiber of the men who grew up beyond the mountains. He was one of a body of men who owed reverence and obeisance to no one, who were self-reliant to a fault, who cared hardly anything for the past but who had a sharp eye for the future.

These frontier men were the precise opposites of the tidewater aristocrats. Back of them, in the great surge that had taken people over the Alleghenies and into the opening Western country, there was a deep, implicit dissatisfaction with a past that had settled into grooves. They stood for democracy, not from any reasoned conclusion about the proper ordering of human society, but simply because they had grown up in the middle of democracy and knew how it worked. Their society might have privileges, but they would be privileges each man had won for himself. Forms and patterns meant nothing. No man was born to anything, except perhaps to a chance to show how far he could rise. Life was competition.

Yet along with this feeling had come a deep sense of belonging to a national community. The Westerner who developed a farm, opened a shop, or set up in business as a trader, could hope to prosper only as his own community prospered—and his community ran from the Atlantic to the Pacific and from Canada down to Mexico. If the land was settled, with towns and highways and accessible markets, he could better himself. He saw his fate in terms of the nation's own destiny. As its horizons expanded, so did his. He had, in other words, an acute dollars-and-cents stake in the continued growth and development of his country.

And that, perhaps, is where the contrast between Grant and Lee becomes most striking. The Virginia aristocrat, inevitably, saw himself in relation to his own region. He lived in a static society which could endure almost anything except change. Instinctively, his first loyalty would go to the locality in which that society existed. He would fight to the limit of endurance to defend it, because in defending it he was defending everything that gave his own life its deepest meaning.

The Westerner, on the other hand, would fight with an equal

tenacity for the broader concept of society. He fought so because everything he lived by was tied to growth, expansion, and a constantly widening horizon. What he lived by would survive or fall with the nation itself. He could not possibly stand by unmoved in the face of an attempt to destroy the Union. He would combat it with everything he had, because he could only see it as an effort to cut the ground out from under his feet.

So Grant and Lee were in complete contrast, representing two [12] diametrically opposed elements in American life. Grant was the modern man emerging; beyond him, ready to come on the stage, was the great age of steel and machinery, of crowded cities and a restless burgeoning vitality. Lee might have ridden down from the old age of chivalry, lance in hand, silken banner fluttering over his head. Each man was the perfect champion of his cause, drawing both his strengths and his weaknesses from the people he led.

Yet it was not all contrast, after all. Different as they were—in [13] background, in personality, in underlying aspiration—these two great soldiers had much in common. Under everything else, they were marvelous fighters. Furthermore, their fighting qualities were really very much alike.

Each man had, to begin with, the great virtue of utter tenacity [14] and fidelity. Grant fought his way down the Mississippi Valley in spite of acute personal discouragement and profound military handicaps. Lee hung on in the trenches at Petersburg after hope itself had died. In each man there was an indomitable quality . . . the born fighter's refusal to give up as long as he can still remain on his feet and lift his two fists.

Daring and resourcefulness they had, too; the ability to think [15] faster and move faster than the enemy. These were the qualities which gave Lee the dazzling campaigns of Second Manassas and Chancellorsville and won Vicksburg for Grant.

Lastly, and perhaps greatest of all, there was the ability, at the [16] end, to turn quickly from war to peace once the fighting was over. Out of the way these two men behaved at Appomattox came the possibility of a peace of reconciliation. It was a possibility not wholly realized, in the years to come, but which did, in the end, help the two sections to become one nation again . . . after a war whose bitterness might have seemed to make such a reunion wholly impossible. No part of either man's life became him more than the part he played in this brief meeting in the McLean house

at Appomattox. Their behavior there put all succeeding generations of Americans in their debt. Two great Americans, Grant and
Lee—very different, yet under everything very much alike. Their
encounter at Appomattox was one of the great moments of
American history.

QUESTIONS

Understanding

1. Catton writes that generals Lee and Grant represented two opposing currents (par. 3) of American culture. What were they?
   Describe the contrasting qualities and ideals that Catton associates
   with each man.

2. What qualities, according to Catton, did Grant and Lee have in
   common?

3. With Lee's surrender, says Catton, "a great new chapter" (par.
   1) of American history began. He is referring, presumably, to the
   period of expansion between the Civil War and World War I,
   when industrialization really took hold in America. What characteristics of the new era does his description of Grant anticipate?

4. Catton does not describe, in any detail, how Grant and Lee behaved as they worked out the terms of peace at Appomattox; but
   what does he *imply* about the conduct of the two generals? Why
   was their conduct important to "all succeeding generations" (par.
   16) of Americans?

5. Catton gives no specific reasons for the Confederacy's defeat. He
   says nothing, for example, about the Union's greater numbers or
   its superior communications system. What general explanation
   does he imply, however, when he associates Lee with a "static"
   society (par. 10) and Grant with a society of "restless burgeoning
   vitality" (par. 12)?

Strategies and Structure

1. Beginning with paragraph 3, Catton gets down to the particulars
   of his contrast between the two generals. Where does the contrast end? In which paragraph does he begin to list similarities
   between the two men?

2. Except for mentioning their strength, Catton says little about the unique physical appearance of either Grant or Lee. Is this a weakness in his essay or is there some justification for avoiding such details? Explain your answer.

3. Which sentence in paragraph 16 brings together the contrasts and the similarities of the preceding paragraphs? How does this final paragraph recall the opening paragraphs of the essay? Why might Catton end with an echo of his beginning?

4. Would you say that the historian's voice in this essay is primarily DESCRIPTIVE, NARRATIVE, or EXPOSITORY? Explain your answer.

Words and Figures of Speech

1. Catton describes the parlor where Grant and Lee met as the *scene* of a *dramatic* contrast (par. 2), and he says in paragraph 12 that the post–Civil War era was "ready to come on stage." Where do such METAPHORS come from, and what view of history do they suggest?

2. What is the Lost Cause of paragraph 6, and what does the phrase (in capital letters) CONNOTE?

3. Catton does not use the phrase *noblesse oblige*, but it could be applied to General Lee's beliefs as Catton defines them. What does the phrase mean?

4. What is the precise meaning of *obeisance* (par. 7), and why might Catton have chosen it instead of the more common *obedience* when describing General Grant?

5. Look up any of these words with which you are not on easy terms: *fugitive* (par. 2), *poignant* (2), *chivalry* (5), *sinewy* (7), *implicit* (8), *tenacity* (11), *diametrically* (12), *acute* (14), *profound* (14), and *indomitable* (14).

Comparing

1. Both Catton and Alex Haley in "My Furthest-Back Person—'The African'" (Chapter 1) are writing about the past from vantage points in the present. How do they differ in their approaches to history and to the historian's role?

2. Catton speaks often of the "conduct" and "deportment" of Grant and Lee. How does his idea of human behavior compare with

that of sociologist Desmond Morris in "Barrier Signals" (Chapter 5)?

Discussion and Writing Topics

1. Write an essay contrasting Thomas Jefferson and Alexander Hamilton (or John F. Kennedy and Richard Nixon) as men who represented the conflicting forces of their time.

2. "America," Catton writes, "was a land that was beginning all over again . . ." (par. 5). Discuss this idea as one way of formulating the "American dream."

3. Grant, we are told, saw the nation's "destiny" (par. 9) as coinciding with his own. What was the notion of "Manifest Destiny," and how did it help to shape American history?

4. Do you agree with Catton's assessment of General Lee as a man of the past and, therefore, a fitting emblem of the South? Why or why not?

5. Is history the story of forces acting through great personalities (as Catton assumes) or of great personalities who control forces? Or neither? Explain your answer.

Barry Curtis

Two Jews

Barry Curtis is an English major at the Ohio State University. He was born in Oklahoma City in 1953 and moved to Ohio in 1972. He is married to a former theology student whose plans for graduate school will probably take them east. While going to school, Curtis has worked as a janitor, garden nurseryman, and proofreader. He consumes The New Yorker *magazine and admires the work of James Thurber, E. B. White, and S. J. Perelman. "Two Jews" was written at the beginning of Curtis's junior year, as an assignment in English 301. His teacher suggested artists as a possible subject and brought to class a Chagall painting of a man looking at a horse.*

There is an old man who looks like he was once a sailor. He [1]
wears a brimmed cap. It is the kind you sometimes see on
immigrants in faded photographs. His long, loose-fitting coat
identifies him as a peasant. He sits dog-tired on a bench after
a hard day in the fields. His hands are on his knees; and he is
either giving his right eye a rest, or he is squinting. Close behind him is a large cottage with a pyramid roof and, past that,
a few small cottages with chimneys. The old man seems to
lean out of the center of the painting, but he is never able to
escape the village. Why do we feel that we are looking down
at him; is it because his feet bend toward the ground?

The old man's coat is gray, and he wears blue pants. His [2]
face and his left hand are white. His right hand is green. A
pinkish haze washes the front and roof of the first house, and
the opposite sides are stained a dark red. The colors blend
into a checkerboard of pink and red squares stretching to a

yellow horizon. Hung from the sky and resting across the town is a golden band with Hebrew letters. Yet the bearded man's back is turned to the wonderful spectacle that has transformed his tiny town. This is Chagall's *The Jew, in Pink, 1914–15.*[1]

The old man's green hand should point us to another work by   3 the same artist, *The Jew, in Green, 1914.* This Jew retains the somber face, one eye open and one closed, with the beard; he is still catching his breath. The difference is that the village has totally disappeared. The bench, too, is gone, and the man sits alone on what appear to be holy scrolls, perhaps the Torah.[2] The dark landscape behind him looks empty. But upon closer inspection, you can see the dim outline of the man's shadow—or is it the shadow of an angel?—in a field of black on black. The old man's beard is yellow now, and his battered face has turned green. He is even closer to us than the Jew in pink. The open eye is more prominent in this version. It is the eye of someone who has seen many generations; it stares you down.

I don't know what Marc Chagall had on his mind when he   4 painted these two pieces. Maybe he was thinking about his childhood; maybe he was thinking about the soul. What interests me about these two paintings, however, is how the contrasting colors tell contrasting stories. The first Jew dominates his pink cloud-world like a statue rising from a dream. Although his village pulls him back, the Jew in pink dreams of selling his home and escaping to America. The second Jew is almost engulfed by the darkness at his back. These shadows are a mirror of his doubt. The Jew in green cannot sleep; he is half blinded, half wakened by a light shining upon his face from a slight parting in the clouds. In both paintings, the faces of the bearded men reflect the same sorrowful resignation. I think they are the same man. There is only one bearded Jew; sometimes he lives in a pink land, and sometimes he lives in a green land. Perhaps the man is the artist's father.

[1] Marc Chagall, painter and illustrator, born in Russia in 1887, has lived mostly in France.

[2] Hebrew name for the first five books of the Old Testament; the word can refer broadly to all the teachings and sacred writings of Judaism.

QUESTIONS

Understanding

1. What is the basic difference between the "two Jews" that Curtis is comparing? What do they have in common?
2. What does Curtis mean when he says "there is only one bearded Jew" (par. 4)?
3. Curtis says that he does not know what Chagall meant to portray in the two paintings he compares. Should he have tried to find out by reading art history books? Why or why not?
4. How legitimate is it to apply the standards of one form of art to other forms—to "read" a painting as you would a story or to discuss a piece of music in the language of drama? Explain your answer.

Strategies and Structure

1. Curtis does not identify who or what he is comparing until the end of paragraph 2 (more than a third of the way through his essay). Why do you think he withholds this information? Do you find the delay an effective tactic? Why or why not?
2. Curtis says that what interests him in these paintings is their NARRATIVE quality. How is this interest anticipated in paragraph 1?
3. Curtis gives us only a few details of the stories that the two paintings tell him. Which are the most important ones? Should he have given more? Why or why not?
4. In paragraph 4, Curtis speculates that Chagall may have been thinking about the soul when he painted the two Jews. How has this remark been prepared for earlier?
5. What single earlier line prepares us for the last sentence of Curtis's essay, "Perhaps the man is the artist's father"?
6. How would you describe the TONE of Curtis's essay, with its short sentences and relatively simple vocabulary?
7. Curtis's essay in COMPARISON AND CONTRAST is also a descriptive essay. Point out several passages of DESCRIPTION. To what aspect of the paintings as paintings (rather than narratives) does he pay greatest attention?
8. How do the backgrounds of the two paintings as described by Curtis contribute to the stories he elicits from them?

Words and Figures of Speech

1. Why is "had on his mind" (par. 4) a better phrase, given the tone of Curtis's essay, than "had in mind"?
2. Curtis says that the first Jew rises like a statue from a dream (par. 4). How well does this SIMILE work? Explain your answer.

Comparing

1. How does the "I" in Curtis's essay resemble the doctor in "The Discus Thrower" (Chapter 8)? How does Curtis's "report" resemble the doctor's?

Discussion and Writing Topics

1. Compare and contrast two paintings or photographs on a similar theme by the same artist—for example, two of Claude Monet's haystacks or studies of Rouen Cathedral. An art history book can help here.
2. Compare and contrast two different artists' renditions of the same scene. For example: crucifixions by the Spaniard El Greco (1548?–1614?) and by the Flemish painter, Jan van Eyck (1370?–1440?), or mothers and children by the German Käthe Kollwitz (1867–1945) and the American Mary Cassatt (1845–1926).
3. Compare W. H. Auden's poem "Musée des Beaux Arts" with Pieter Brueghel's (1525?–1569) *The Fall of Icarus,* the painting described in the poem.

Jeff Greenfield

The Black and White Truth about Basketball

Jeff Greenfield is a political analyst and sportswriter. He was born in New York in 1943, the son of a lawyer; he attended the University of Wisconsin and Yale (LL.B., 1967). Once a speechwriter and legislative aide to Robert F. Kennedy and former Mayor Lindsay of New York, he is the co-author of The Advance Man *(1971) and* A Populist Manifesto *(1972). In 1973, pursuing other interests, Greenfield published* Where Have You Gone, Joe DiMaggio?; *he is currently working on a book about the Boston Celtics. "The Black and White Truth about Basketball," from* Esquire *magazine, contrasts two styles of play; it carries the subtitle, "A Skin-Deep Theory of Style." This is primarily an essay in comparison and contrast, but it also analyzes* CAUSE AND EFFECT.

The dominance of black athletes over professional basketball is beyond dispute. Two thirds of the players are black, and the number would be greater were it not for the continuing practice of picking white bench warmers for the sake of balance. The Most Valuable Player award of the National Basketball Association has gone to blacks for sixteen of the last twenty years, and in the newer American Basketball Association, blacks have won it all but once in the league's eight years. In the 1974–75 season, four of the top five All-Stars and seven of the top ten were black. The N.B.A. was the first pro sports league of any stature to hire a black coach (Bill Russell of the Celtics) and the first black general manager (Wayne Embry of the Bucks). What discrimination remains—lack of opportunity for lucrative benefits such as speaking engagements and product endorsements—has more to do with society than with basketball.

This dominance reflects a natural inheritance; basketball is a 2 pastime of the urban poor. The current generation of black athletes are heirs to a tradition half a century old: in a neighborhood without the money for bats, gloves, hockey sticks, tennis rackets, or shoulder pads, basketball is accessible. "Once it was the game of the Irish and Italian Catholics in Rockaway and the Jews on Fordham Road in the Bronx," writes David Wolf in his brilliant book, *Foul!* "It was recreation, status, and a way out." But now the ethnic names are changed; instead of Red Holzmans, Red Auerbachs, and McGuire brothers, there are Earl Monroes and Connie Hawkins and Nate Archibalds. And professional basketball is a sport with a national television contract and million-dollar salaries.

But the mark on basketball of today's players can be measured 3 by more than money or visibility. It is a question of style. For there is a clear difference between "black" and "white" styles of play that is as clear as the difference between 155th Street at Eighth Avenue and Crystal City, Missouri. Most simply (remembering we are talking about culture, not chromosomes), "black" basketball is the use of superb athletic skill to adapt to the limits of space imposed by the game. "White" ball is the pulverization of that space by sheer intensity.

It takes a conscious effort to realize how constricted the space 4 is on a basketball court. Place a regulation court (ninety-four by fifty feet) on a football field, and it will reach from the back of the end zone to the twenty-one-yard line; its width will cover less than a third of the field. On a baseball diamond, a basketball court will reach from home plate to just beyond first base. Compared to its principal indoor rival, ice hockey, basketball covers about one fourth the playing area. And during the normal flow of the game, most of the action takes place on about the third of the court nearest the basket. It is in this dollhouse space that ten men, each of them half a foot taller than the average man, come together to battle each other.

There is, thus, no room; basketball is a struggle for the edge: the 5 half step with which to cut around the defender for a lay-up, the half second of freedom with which to release a jump shot, the instant a head turns allowing a pass to a teammate breaking for the basket. It is an arena for the subtlest of skills: the head fake, the shoulder fake, the shift of body weight to the right and the sudden cut to the left. Deception is crucial to success; and to young men who have learned early and painfully that life is a battle for survival, basketball is one of the few games in which the weapon of deception is a legitimate rule and not the source of trouble.

If there is, then, the need to compete in a crowd, to battle for the edge, then the surest strategy is to develop the *unexpected*; to develop a shot that is simply and fundamentally different from the usual methods of putting the ball in the basket. Drive to the hoop, but go under it and come up the other side; hold the ball at waist level and shoot from there instead of bringing the ball up to eye level; leap into the air and fall away from the basket instead of toward it. All these tactics take maximum advantage of the crowding on a court; they also stamp uniqueness on young men who may feel it nowhere else.   6

"For many young men in the slums," David Wolf writes, "the school yard is the only place they can feel true pride in what they do, where they can move free of inhibitions and where they can, by being spectacular, rise for the moment against the drabness and anonymity of their lives. Thus, when a player develops extraordinary 'school yard' moves and shots . . . [they] become his measure as a man."   7

So the moves that begin as tactics for scoring soon become calling cards. You don't just lay the ball in for an uncontested basket; you take the ball in both hands, leap as high as you can, and slam the ball through the hoop. When you jump in the air, fake a shot, bring the ball back to your body, and throw up a shot, all without coming back down, you have proven your worth in uncontestable fashion.   8

This liquid grace is an integral part of "black" ball, almost exclusively the province of the playground player. Some white stars like Richie Guerin, Bob Cousy, and Billy Cunningham have it: the body control, the moves to the basket, the free-ranging mobility. They also have the surface ease that is integral to the "black" style; an incorporation of the ethic of mean streets—to "make it" is not just to have wealth, but to have it without strain. Whatever the muscles and organs are doing, the face of the "black" star almost never shows it. Bob McAdoo of the Buffalo Braves can drive to the basket with two men on him, pull up, turn around, and hit a basket without the least flicker of emotion. The   9

Knicks' Walt Frazier, flamboyant in dress, cars, and companions, displays nothing but a quickly raised fist after scoring a particularly important basket. (Interestingly, the black coaches in the N.B.A. exhibit far less emotion on the bench than their white counterparts; Washington's K. C. Jones and Seattle's Bill Russell are statuelike compared with Tommy Heinsohn, Jack Ramsey, or Dick Motta.)

If there is a single trait that characterizes "black" ball it is leaping agility. Bob Cousy, ex-Celtic great and former pro coach, says that "when coaches get together, one is sure to say, 'I've got the one black kid in the country who can't jump.' When coaches see a white boy who can jump or who moves with extraordinary quickness, they say, 'He should have been born black, he's that good.' "   10

Don Nelson of the Celtics recalls that in 1970, Dave Cowens, then a relatively unknown Florida State graduate, prepared for his rookie season by playing in the Rucker League, an outdoor Harlem competition that pits pros against playground stars and college kids. So ferocious was Cowens' leaping power, Nelson says, that "when the summer was over, everyone wanted to know who the white son of a bitch was who could jump so high." That's another way to overcome a crowd around the basket—just go over it.   11

Speed, mobility, quickness, acceleration, "the moves"—all of these are catch-phrases that surround the "black" playground style of play. So does the most racially tinged of attributes, "rhythm." Yet rhythm is what the black stars themselves talk about; feeling the flow of the game, finding the tempo of the dribble, the step, the shot. It is an instinctive quality, one that has led to difficulty between systematic coaches and free-form players. "Cats from the street have their own rhythm when they play," said college dropout Bill Spivey, onetime New York high-school star. "It's not a matter of somebody setting you up and you shooting. You *feel* the shot. When a coach holds you back, you lose the feel and it isn't fun anymore."   12

Connie Hawkins, the legendary Brooklyn playground star, said of Laker coach Bill Sharman's methodical style of teaching, "He's systematic to the point where it begins to be a little too much. It's such an action-reaction type of game that when you have to do everything the same way, I think you lose something."   13

There is another kind of basketball that has grown up in   14

America. It is not played on asphalt playgrounds with a crowd of kids competing for the court; it is played on macadam driveways by one boy with a ball and a backboard nailed over the garage; it is played in Midwestern gyms and on Southern dirt courts. It is a mechanical, precise development of skills (when Don Nelson was an Iowa farm boy his incentive to make his shots was that an errant rebound would land in the middle of chicken droppings), without frills, without flow, but with effectiveness. It is "white" basketball: jagged, sweaty, stumbling, intense. A "black" player overcomes an obstacle with finesse and body control; a "white" player reacts by outrunning or outpowering the obstacle.

By this definition, the Boston Celtics and the Chicago Bulls are [15] classically "white" teams. The Celtics almost never use a player with dazzling moves; that would probably make Red Auerbach swallow his cigar. Instead, the Celtics wear you down with execution, with constant running, with the same play run again and again. The rebound triggers the fast break, with everyone racing downcourt; the ball goes to John Havlicek, who pulls up and takes the jump shot, or who fakes the shot and passes off to the man following, the "trailer," who has the momentum to go inside for a relatively easy shot.

The Bulls wear you down with punishing intensity, hustling, [16] and defensive tactics which are either aggressive or illegal, depending on what side you're on. The Bulls—particularly Jerry Sloan and Norm Van Lier (one white, one black for the quota-minded)— seem to reject the concept of an out-of-bounds line. They are as likely to be found under the press table or wrapped around the ushers as on the court.

Perhaps the most classically "white" position is that of the quick [17] forward, one without great moves to the basket, without highly developed shots, without the height and mobility for rebounding effectiveness. What does he do? He runs. He runs from the opening jump to the last horn. He runs up and down the court, from base line to base line, back and forth under the basket, looking for the opening, for the pass, for the chance to take a quick step and the high-percentage shot. To watch Boston's Don Nelson, a player without speed or moves, is to wonder what this thirty-five-year-old is doing in the N.B.A.—until you see him swing free and throw up a shot that, without demanding any apparent skill, somehow goes in the basket more frequently than the shots of any of his team-mates. And to watch his teammate John Havlicek, also thirty-five, is to see "white" ball at its best.

Havlicek stands in dramatic contrast to Julius Erving of the New   18
York Nets. Erving has the capacity to make legends come true; leaping from the foul line and slam-dunking the ball on his way down; going up for a lay-up, pulling the ball to his body and throwing under and up the other side of the rim, defying gravity and probability with moves and jumps. Havlicek looks like the living embodiment of his small-town Ohio background. He brings the ball downcourt, weaving left, then right, looking for the path. He swings the ball to a teammate, cuts behind a pick, takes the pass and releases the shot in a flicker of time. It looks plain, unvarnished. But there are not half a dozen players in the league who can see such possibilities for a free shot, then get that shot off as quickly and efficiently as Havlicek.

To Jim McMillian of Buffalo, a black with "white" attributes,   19
himself a quick forward, "it's a matter of environment. Julius Erving grew up in a different environment from Havlicek—John came from a very small town in Ohio. There everything was done the easy way, the shortest distance between two points. It's nothing fancy, very few times will he go one-on-one; he hits the lay-up, hits the jump shot, makes the free throw, and after the game you look up and you say, 'How did he hurt us that much?'"

"White" ball, then, is the basketball of patience and method.   20
"Black" ball is the basketball of electric self-expression. One player has all the time in the world to perfect his skills, the other a need to prove himself. These are slippery categories, because a poor boy who is black can play "white" and a white boy of middle-class parents can play "black." K. C. Jones and Pete Maravich are athletes who seem to defy these categories. And what makes basketball the most intriguing of sports is how these styles do not necessarily clash; how the punishing intensity of "white" players and the dazzling moves of the "blacks" can fit together, a fusion of cultures that seems more and more difficult in the world beyond the out-of-bounds line.

QUESTIONS

Understanding

1. What are the most important aspects of "black" basketball as Greenfield defines it? Of "white" basketball?

2. Why is basketball basically a city game, according to this essay? In particular, what has space in the city to do with the "black" player's approach to space on the court?

3. Why are "black" players and coaches more poker-faced than their "white" counterparts? What strategy and what ethic contribute to this seeming unconcern?

4. What does Greenfield mean when he reminds us that "we are talking about culture, not chromosomes" (par. 3)? How does this statement fit in with the subtitle of his essay "A Skin-Deep Theory of Style"?

Strategies and Structure

1. Greenfield starts to compare the two styles of play in paragraph 3; which sentence signals this intention?

2. Greenfield's method of development is to concentrate on one style before going on to the other. Where does his explanation of the "black" style end? Where does his explanation of the "white" style begin? Which paragraph brings the two together in summation?

3. Paragraph 2 in this essay serves to explain the origin of basketball in general before the author goes on to define two different types. What is the purpose of paragraph 1, in which basketball is considered not so much a game as a social phenomenon?

4. Paragraph 4 (about the size of a basketball court in comparison to the playing areas of other sports) looks at first like a digression from the matter of style, introduced in paragraph 3. Is Greenfield really off the track here? Why or why not?

5. How effective do you find the example of Jim McMillian in paragraph 19? Why? Of Don Nelson in paragraph 14? Why?

6. Why do you think Greenfield ends his essay by referring to "the world beyond the out-of-bounds line" (par. 20)? What is he implying about the common ground of both "white" and "black" basketball?

Words and Figures of Speech

1. What is the pun in Greenfield's title? How effective is it? Why does Greenfield put "black" and "white" in quotation marks throughout his essay?

2. Why is Greenfield nervous about using the word *rhythm* in paragraph 12? How does he legitimize his use of the term?

3. What attribute is "only skin-deep" according to the proverb? In what sense does Greenfield reverse the meaning of the proverb when adapting it to a discussion of style?

4. What does Greenfield's use of the phrase, "for the quota-minded" (par. 16), imply about his own feelings about quotas?

5. If you are not sure of any of the following words, look them up in your dictionary: *lucrative* (par. 1), *inhibitions* (7), *anonymity* (7), *province* (9), *ethic* (9), *flamboyant* (9), *catch-phrases* (12), *finesse* (14). Why do you think a sports article might have relatively few unfamiliar words?

Comparing

1. Would you describe David Dubber's athletic style in "Crossing the Bar on a Fiberglas Pole" (Chapter 1) as essentially "black" or "white"? Why?

2. Greenfield points out that basketball (the city game) occupies much less space than does baseball (the country game). How is *time* treated in basketball in contrast to baseball's time, described by Roger Angell in "Time Out" ("Paragraphs for Analysis")?

3. In "Haircut" ("Paragraphs for Analysis"), William Allen defines style as form or arrangement (to be distinguished from content or substance). Apply Allen's definition to "black" style as defined by Greenfield? How well does it fit "white" style?

Discussion and Writing Topics

1. Compare and contrast the traditional role of a basketball forward with that of a guard or center.

2. What does it mean to be "cool"? What conditions encourage coolness, and what sports express that virtue?

3. What are the purposes of boundary lines in sports? Why might an athlete, a musician, or an artist welcome limits and boundaries in his or her field of endeavor?

4. Contrast the style of a typical professional tennis player, boxer, or golfer with the style of a typical amateur.

Eugene Raskin

Walls and Barriers

Eugene Raskin is an architect, playwright, and composer. Born in New York in 1909, he was educated at Columbia University and the University of Paris. He joined the Columbia faculty as a professor of architecture in 1942, became a Langley fellow of the American Institute of Architects in 1952, and in 1963 won first prize at the American Film Festival for the documentary, How to Look at a City. *Author of* Architecturally Speaking *(1954) and* The Post-Urban Society *(1969), Raskin has also written a number of plays, including* One's a Crowd *(1951);* Amata *(1952);* Last Island *(1954); and* Stranger in My Arms *(1971). Among his published songs was the international hit, "Those Were the Days." "Walls and Barriers" contrasts the modern notion of wall-as-window with the ancient conception of wall-as-barrier.*

My father's reaction to the bank building at 43rd Street and Fifth Avenue in New York City was immediate and definite: "You won't catch me putting my money in *there!*" he declared. "Not in that glass box!"

Of course, my father is a gentleman of the old school, a member of the generation to whom a good deal of modern architecture is unnerving; but I suspect—I more than suspect, I am convinced—that his negative response was not so much to the architecture as to a violation of his concept of the nature of money.

In his generation money was thought of as a tangible commodity—bullion, bank notes, coins—that could be hefted, carried, or stolen. Consequently, to attract the custom of a sensible man, a bank had to have heavy walls, barred windows, and bronze doors, to affirm the fact, however untrue, that money would be safe inside. If a building's design made it appear impregnable, the institution was necessarily sound, and the meaning of the heavy wall as an architectural symbol dwelt in the prevailing attitude toward money, rather than in any aesthetic theory.

But that attitude toward money has of course changed. Excepting pocket money, cash of any kind is now rarely used; money as a tangible commodity has largely been replaced by credit; a bookkeeping-banking matter. A deficit economy, accompanied by huge expansion, has led us to think of money as a product of the creative imagination. The banker no longer offers us a *safe*, he offers us a *service*—a service in which the most valuable elements are dash and a creative flair for the invention of large numbers. It is in no way surprising, in view of this change in attitude, that we are witnessing the disappearance of the heavy-walled bank. The Manufacturers Trust, which my father distrusted so heartily, is a great cubical cage of glass whose brilliantly lighted interior challenges even the brightness of a sunny day, while the door to the vault, far from being secluded and guarded, is set out as a window display.

Just as the older bank asserted its invulnerability, this bank *by its architecture* boasts of its imaginative powers. From this point of view it is hard to say where architecture ends and human assertion begins. In fact, there is no such division; the two are one and the same.

It is in the understanding of architecture as a medium for the expression of human attitudes, prejudices, taboos, and ideals that the new architectural criticism departs from classical aesthetics. The latter relied upon pure proportion, composition, etc., as bases for artistic judgment. In the age of sociology and psychology, walls are not simply walls but physical symbols of the barriers in men's minds.

In a primitive society, for example, men pictured the world as large, fearsome, hostile, and beyond human control. Therefore they built heavy walls of huge boulders, behind which they could feel themselves to be in a delimited space that was controllable and safe; these heavy walls expressed man's fear of the outer world and his need to find protection, however illusory. It might be argued that the undeveloped technology of the period precluded the construction of more delicate walls. This is of course true.

Still, it was not technology, but a fearful attitude toward the world, which made people want to build walls in the first place. The greater the fear, the heavier the wall, until in the tombs of ancient kings we find structures that are practically all wall, the fear of dissolution being the ultimate fear.

And then there is the question of privacy—for it *has* become 8 questionable. In some Mediterranean cultures it was not so much the world of nature that was feared, but the world of men. Men were dirty, prying, vile, and dangerous. One went about, if one could afford it, in guarded litters; women went about heavily veiled, if they went about at all. One's house was surrounded by a wall, and the rooms faced not out, but in, toward a patio, expressing the prevalent conviction that the beauties and values of life were to be found by looking inward, and by engaging in the intimate activities of a personal as against a public life. The rich intricacies of the decorative arts of the period, as well as its contemplative philosophies, are as illustrative of this attitude as the walls themselves.

We feel different today. For one thing, we place greater reliance 9 upon the control of human hostility, not so much by physical barriers, as by the conventions of law and social practice—as well as the availability of motorized police. We do not cherish privacy as much as did our ancestors. We are proud to have our women seen and admired, and the same goes for our homes. We do not seek solitude; in fact, if we find ourselves alone for once, we flick a switch and invite the whole world in through the television screen. Small wonder, then, that the heavy surrounding wall is obsolete, and we build, instead, membranes of thin sheet metal or glass.

The principal function of today's wall is to separate possibly 10 undesirable outside air from the controlled conditions of temperature and humidity which we have created inside. Glass may accomplish this function, though there are apparently a good many people who still have qualms about eating, sleeping, and dressing under conditions of high visibility; they demand walls that will at least give them a sense of adequate screening. But these shy ones are a vanishing breed. The Philip Johnson [1] house in Connecticut,

---

[1] American architect, born 1906; in 1949 he designed and constructed the Glass House for his residence in New Canaan, Connecticut.

which is much admired and widely imitated, has glass walls all
the way around, and the only real privacy is to be found in the
bathroom, the toilet taboo being still unbroken, at least in
Connecticut.

To repeat, it is not our advanced technology, but our changing   11
conceptions of ourselves in relation to the world that determine
how we shall build our walls. The glass wall expresses man's conviction that he can and does master nature and society. The "open
plan" and the unobstructed view are consistent with his faith in
the eventual solution of all problems through the expanding efforts
of science. This is perhaps why it is the most "advanced" and
"forward-looking" among us who live and work in glass houses.
Even the fear of the cast stone has been analyzed out of us.

QUESTIONS

Understanding

1. Raskin is contrasting ancient walls and modern walls. According
   to him, what was the function of walls in primitive society? What
   attitude toward nature is expressed by the glass walls of modern
   society?
2. Why has the function of walls changed, according to Raskin?
3. Raskin is also contrasting "classical" and "new" (par. 6) theories
   of architecture. Which stresses form? Which stresses function?
4. How, according to Raskin, has our culture's view of money
   changed since his father's day?

Strategies and Structure

1. Why do you think Raskin begins by quoting his father? Do you
   think this is an effective opening? Why or why not?
2. Is Raskin's father in any way a confusing example? He has an
   old-fashioned view of money; what is his view of architecture?
3. The "cast stone" (par. 11) of Raskin's last sentence echoes the
   proverb, "People who live in glass houses should not throw
   stones." How does this reference to traditional wisdom at the
   end resemble Raskin's reference to his father at the beginning?

4. Which phrase in his last paragraph (par. 11) signals that the author is summing up what he has to say?

5. Does the paragraph on Mediterranean houses (par. 8) continue or diverge from the preceding paragraph (par. 7) on walls in primitive culture?

Words and Figures of Speech

1. What is the meaning of the proverb about glass houses? Under what conditions might it be applied?

2. Which of the two key words in the title applies to primitive walls as Raskin describes them?

3. Paragraph 6 mentions "architectural criticism." What does *criticism* mean here and in phrases like "art criticism" or "literary criticism"?

4. In paragraph 4, Raskin says that the bright interior of the new bank "challenges" the daylight. How does that word apply to modern man's attitude toward nature as Raskin defines it?

5. Look up any of the following words that you do not already know: *tangible* (par. 3), *impregnable* (3), *aesthetic* (3), *deficit* (4), *taboos* (6), *composition* (6), *illusory* (7), *dissolution* (7), and *membrane* (9).

Comparing

1. How does Desmond Morris's explanation of the origin of barrier signals in Chapter 5 confirm what Raskin says about the original purpose of walls?

2. William Allen's "Haircut" (in "Paragraphs for Analysis") deals with a structure and the aesthetic theory that produced it. Is Allen's theory "classic" or modern by Raskin's standards? Explain your answer.

Discussion and Writing Topics

1. Raskin says we do not cherish privacy as much as our fathers did. Agree or disagree with this view by comparing and contrasting life in an old-fashioned single-family dwelling with life in a high-rise apartment or condominium.

2. What is the "international style" in modern architecture? Contrast it with what Raskin calls the "classical" style.

3. American architect Louis Sullivan (1856–1924) said that "form follows function" in architecture. By "follows" he meant "depends upon." Is his theory modern or classical by Raskin's standards?

4. Recall an old building in your hometown (a high school, library, or courthouse, for example) that has been replaced by a new building. Compare and contrast the two.

5. What is a proverb? How does it differ from a parable?

WRITING TOPICS for Chapter Six
Essays That Compare and Contrast

Write a comparison and contrast essay on one of the following topics:

1. Two different cities (for example, New York and Washington, D.C.)

2. The same city at different times of day or in different seasons

3. Two World War II generals (for example, Patton and Eisenhower)

4. Two teachers you have admired

5. Two neighborhoods you have lived in

6. The haves and the have-nots in your hometown

7. Two of your classmates from different geographical regions

8. Two roommates you have had

9. A job versus a profession

10. Modern versus old-fashioned families (or marriages)

11. Two churches or synagogues in your hometown

12. Life in a democracy versus life under some other form of government

13. Two styles of playing football, baseball, tennis, or golf

14. The styles of two political (or social) leaders on your campus

15. The styles of two national politicians

16. The work of two painters, singers, musicians, or writers

17. Two newspaper columns or magazines that you read

18. Two comic strips

7

Essays That Use
Metaphor and Analogy

METAPHORS [1] and ANALOGIES are FIGURES OF SPEECH or
"turns" of language that use words symbolically rather than
literally. The poet Carl Sandburg created a metaphor when
he wrote, "The woman named Tomorrow/sits with a hair-
pin in her teeth/and takes her time. . . ." His friend and
fellow poet, Robert Frost, was developing an analogy when
he told Sandburg that writing poetry without regular meter
and rhyme is like playing tennis with the net down. Metaphors and analogies (or "extended metaphors"), then, are
comparisons that reveal an object, event, or quality by iden-
tifying it with another object, event, or quality (usually one
more familiar than the first, as tennis is more familiar to
most of us than the rules of poetry).

The kinds of comparisons that metaphors and analogies
make, however, should not be confused with those discussed
in the last chapter ("Essays That Compare and Contrast").
When Bruce Catton compared Grant and Lee, he was as
much interested in one general as the other. COMPARISON
AND CONTRAST essays may not attend equally to the similarities and differences between their subjects, but they usually
give equal weight to the subjects themselves. Essays that use
metaphor and analogy, on the other hand, have a primary
subject, which the object of comparison is introduced to
explain. When Ernest Hemingway declared, for example,
that a fine English sentence has the clean grace of a mata-
dor's sweeping cape, he was talking about writing, not
bullfighting.

[1] Terms printed in all capitals are defined in the Glossary.

One common use of such comparisons is to advance an ARGU-MENT. If you were trying to convince a friend that the government should spend more money on the space program, you might argue that Americans have a pioneering spirit and that outer space is like the western frontier of a century ago; to advance across this new frontier is simply to fulfill our national destiny. Such a line of reasoning is an "argument by analogy." It assumes that, because two entities or ideas are alike in some ways, they are alike in other significant ways. An argument by analogy is the most vulnerable form of argument; it is only as strong as the analogy is close and complete. Your argument would collapse if your friend observed that spaceships are much more expensive than covered wagons and that the original frontier was conquered by exploiting the first Americans.

Another common function of analogies is to explain; the EXPOSITORY essays in the following pages are used for this purpose. "On Societies as Organisms" by Lewis Thomas, for example, teaches us something about humans in groups by comparing their social activity to the bustle of an insect colony. In finished essays, such analogies are primarily organizing devices; but when you are preparing an essay, they may actually aid you in finding something to say.

Suppose you were getting ready to write an essay on the expansion of the universe, and you were puzzled by the problem of locating the center of expansion. From our galaxy, all the other galaxies seem to be rushing out and away; yet astrophysicists tell us that we would experience the same sense of being left behind if we visited any other galaxy in the universe. To write your essay, you must resolve this apparent contradiction.

Now, suppose you hit upon the analogy of the balloon. (Your subject is the universe, remember, not balloons; an analogy illuminates a primary subject, it does not replace it with another.) You might begin to think of the many galaxies of our expanding universe as spots of dark paint dotting the surface of the inflating balloon. As the rubber surface expands, every dot draws apart from every other dot. Whichever dot you single out will appear to be the "center" of a surface that has no fixed middle point. Having used this analogy to grasp your subject, you may then turn around and use it to explain your complicated ideas to the reader.

Keep the following pointers in mind when developing an essay by analogy. Although an analogy will not "hold" if it compares objects that are too disparate, avoid obvious, trivial, or tired comparisons: life to a brief parade, a face without a smile to a day without sunshine. Analogies often liken the unfamiliar and the complicated to the common and the simple, but an analogy may also compare its primary subject with something exotic in order to discover the unexpected in the familiar. (This is Barry Lopez's strategy in "My Horse," an essay that is really about his Dodge van.) And, finally, try to compare your primary subject with something that is interesting and original in its own right. You are not likely to impress your reader if you explain the idea of blind choice by analogy with a stab in the dark or a number drawn from a hat.

Lewis Thomas

On Societies as Organisms

Lewis Thomas, M.D., a neurologist by training, is president and chief executive officer of the Memorial Sloan-Kettering Cancer Center in New York City. He was born in Flushing, New York, and attended Princeton University and Harvard Medical School (M.D., 1937). A member of the council of the Institute of Medicine, he has contributed many articles to scientific journals. In 1971, Thomas began writing "Notes of a Biology Watcher" for less specialized readers in the New England Journal of Medicine. His Lives of a Cell (1974), from which the following essay is taken, won the National Book Award for arts and letters in 1975. "On Societies as Organisms" begins by comparing ants to humans —not the other way around—and goes on to draw an extended analogy between all social groups and the activity of living beings.

Viewed from a suitable height, the aggregating clusters of medical scientists in the bright sunlight of the boardwalk at Atlantic City, swarmed there from everywhere for the annual meetings, have the look of assemblages of social insects. There is the same vibrating, ionic movement, interrupted by the darting back and forth of jerky individuals to touch antennae and exchange small bits of information; periodically, the mass casts out, like a trout-line, a long single file unerringly toward Childs's.[1] If the boards were not fastened down, it would not be a surprise to see them put together a nest of sorts.

It is permissible to say this sort of thing about humans. They do resemble, in their most compulsively social behavior,

[1] A local restaurant.

ants at a distance. It is, however, quite bad form in biological circles to put it the other way round, to imply that the operation of insect societies has any relation at all to human affairs. The writers of books on insect behavior generally take pains, in their prefaces, to caution that insects are like creatures from another planet, that their behavior is absolutely foreign, totally unhuman, unearthly, almost unbiological. They are more like perfectly tooled but crazy little machines, and we violate science when we try to read human meanings in their arrangements.

It is hard for a bystander not to do so. Ants are so much like   3
human beings as to be an embarrassment. They farm fungi, raise aphids as livestock, launch armies into wars, use chemical sprays to alarm and confuse enemies, capture slaves. The families of weaver ants engage in child labor, holding their larvae like shuttles to spin out the thread that sews the leaves together for their fungus gardens. They exchange information ceaselessly. They do everything but watch television.

What makes us most uncomfortable is that they, and the bees   4
and termites and social wasps, seem to live two kinds of lives: they are individuals, going about the day's business without much evidence of thought for tomorrow, and they are at the same time component parts, cellular elements, in the huge, writhing, ruminating organism of the Hill, the nest, the hive. It is because of this aspect, I think, that we most wish for them to be something foreign. We do not like the notion that there can be collective societies with the capacity to behave like organisms. If such things exist, they can have nothing to do with us.

Still, there it is. A solitary ant, afield, cannot be considered to   5
have much of anything on his mind; indeed, with only a few neurons strung together by fibers, he can't be imagined to have a mind at all, much less a thought. He is more like a ganglion on legs. Four ants together, or ten, encircling a dead moth on a path, begin to look more like an idea. They fumble and shove, gradually moving the food toward the Hill, but as though by blind chance. It is only when you watch the dense mass of thousands of ants, crowded together around the Hill, blackening the ground, that you begin to see the whole beast, and now you observe it thinking, planning, calculating. It is an intelligence, a kind of live computer, with crawling bits for its wits.

At a stage in the construction, twigs of a certain size are needed,   6 and all the members forage obsessively for twigs of just this size. Later, when outer walls are to be finished, thatched, the size must change, and as though given new orders by telephone, all the workers shift the search to the new twigs. If you disturb the arrangement of a part of the Hill, hundreds of ants will set it vibrating, shifting, until it is put right again. Distant sources of food are somehow sensed, and long lines, like tentacles, reach out over the ground, up over walls, behind boulders, to fetch it in.

Termites are even more extraordinary in the way they seem to 7 accumulate intelligence as they gather together. Two or three termites in a chamber will begin to pick up pellets and move them from place to place, but nothing comes of it; nothing is built. As more join in, they seem to reach a critical mass, a quorum, and the thinking begins. They place pellets atop pellets, then throw up columns and beautiful, curving, symmetrical arches, and the crystalline architecture of vaulted chambers is created. It is not known how they communicate with each other, how the chains of termites building one column know when to turn toward the crew on the adjacent column, or how, when the time comes, they manage the flawless joining of the arches. The stimuli that set them off at the outset, building collectively instead of shifting things about, may be pheromones [2] released when they reach committee size. They react as if alarmed. They become agitated, excited, and then they begin working, like artists.

Bees live lives of organisms, tissues, cells, organelles, all at the 8 same time. The single bee, out of the hive retrieving sugar (instructed by the dancer: "south-southeast for seven hundred meters, clover—mind you make corrections for the sundrift") is still as much a part of the hive as if attached by a filament. Building the hive, the workers have the look of embryonic cells organizing a developing tissue; from a distance they are like the viruses inside a cell, running off row after row of symmetrical polygons as though laying down crystals. When the time for swarming comes, and the old queen prepares to leave with her part of the population, it is as though the hive were involved in mitosis. There is an agitated moving of bees back and forth, like granules in cell sap. They distribute themselves in almost precisely equal parts, half to the departing queen, half to the new one. Thus, like an egg, the great,

---

[2] Hormones secreted by insects when communicating with other insects.

hairy, black and golden creature splits in two, each with an equal share of the family genome.

The phenomenon of separate animals joining up to form an organism is not unique in insects. Slime-mold cells do it all the time, of course, in each life cycle. At first they are single amebocytes swimming around, eating bacteria, aloof from each other, untouching, voting straight Republican. Then, a bell sounds, and acrasin [3] is released by special cells toward which the others converge in stellate ranks, touch, fuse together, and construct the slug, solid as a trout. A splendid stalk is raised, with a fruiting body on top, and out of this comes the next generation of amebocytes, ready to swim across the same moist ground, solitary and ambitious.

Herring and other fish in schools are at times so closely integrated, their actions so coordinated, that they seem to be functionally a great multi-fish organism. Flocking birds, especially the seabirds nesting on the slopes of offshore islands in Newfoundland, are similarly attached, connected, synchronized.

Although we are by all odds the most social of all social animals —more interdependent, more attached to each other, more inseparable in our behavior than bees—we do not often feel our conjoined intelligence. Perhaps, however, we are linked in circuits for the storage, processing, and retrieval of information, since this appears to be the most basic and universal of all human enterprises. It may be our biological function to build a certain kind of Hill. We have access to all the information of the biosphere, arriving as elementary units in the stream of solar photons. When we have learned how these are rearranged against randomness, to make, say, springtails, quantum mechanics, and the late quartets, we may have a clearer notion how to proceed. The circuitry seems to be there, even if the current is not always on.

The system of communications used in science should provide a neat, workable model for studying mechanisms of information-building in human society. Ziman, in a recent *Nature* essay, points out, "the invention of a mechanism for the systematic publication of *fragments* of scientific work may well have been the key event in the history of modern science." He continues:

[3] Chemical attractant named after the class (Acrasiae) to which these special slime molds belong.

A regular journal carries from one research worker to another the various . . . observations which are of common interest. . . . A typical scientific paper has never pretended to be more than another little piece in a larger jigsaw—not significant in itself but as an element in a grander scheme. *This technique, of soliciting many modest contributions to the store of human knowledge, has been the secret of Western science since the seventeenth century, for it achieves a corporate, collective power that is far greater than any one individual can exert* [italics mine].

With some alternation of terms, some toning down, the passage could describe the building of a termite nest.   13

It is fascinating that the word "explore" does not apply to the searching aspect of the activity, but has its origins in the sounds we make while engaged in it. We like to think of exploring in science as a lonely, meditative business, and so it is in the first stages, but always, sooner or later, before the enterprise reaches completion, as we explore, we call to each other, communicate, publish, send letters to the editor, present papers, cry out on finding.   14

QUESTIONS

Understanding

1. In paragraph 1, what is Thomas comparing to what? In paragraph 3? Which of the two paragraphs formulates the ANALOGY that Thomas will develop throughout his essay?

2. The title of Thomas's essay expresses his main analogy in its most general terms. Which term applies to individual human beings? Which applies to *groups* of insects, fish, birds, or humans?

3. What is an organism? How does it differ from a mechanism, one of the "crazy little machines" that Thomas refers to in paragraph 2?

4. Why, according to Thomas, are we reluctant to attribute human characteristics to insect colonies? How might people in Russia or Communist China be expected to react to such comparisons?

5. Thomas says that, like the ant's, mankind's biological function is "to build a certain kind of Hill" (par. 11). What, specifically, is

the basic enterprise of human society in Thomas's view? What kind of hill is the human community erecting?

Strategies and Structure

1. In the opening paragraph, Thomas looks down upon his fellow medical scientists from a "suitable height." Why do you suppose he establishes this perspective? Why does Thomas call himself a "bystander" in paragraph 3?

2. How might paragraph 5 be interpreted as a mini-version of Thomas's entire essay?

3. Thomas develops a single elaborate analogy by building upon a number of smaller analogies. To what specialized human beings does he compare the builder termites in paragraph 7? Why does an egg provide a fitting analogy for describing the swarming bee colony in paragraph 8? What analogy is suggested by "voting straight Republican" in paragraph 9?

4. Throughout most of this essay, the author is applying what he knows about human society to learn more about insect behavior. When does he begin to reverse this procedure? In what sense is Thomas's essay not about insects at all?

5. Thomas is writing here for a more general audience than a convention of medical specialists at Atlantic City, but he nevertheless speaks with the authority of a trained scientist. How is that authority conveyed to us?

6. Explain the analogy in paragraphs 12, 13, and 14. Does it make for a satisfying ending to Thomas's essay? Why or why not?

Words and Figures of Speech

1. Look up the root meaning of *explore* (par. 14). Applied to scientific investigation, how does the word in its original meaning support Thomas's analogy in paragraphs 12–14?

2. Look up *biology* in your dictionary. In which sense is Thomas using the word when he refers to insects as "unbiological" (par. 2) and to the "biological function" of humanity (par. 11)?

3. Why do you think Thomas applies such terms as *quorum* and *committee* (par. 7) to groups of insects that begin to act intelligently?

4. In paragraph 11, when Thomas says that "the current is not always on," to what circuit is he referring? Why is the METAPHOR amusing?

5. Consult your dictionary for definitions of the following words: *ionic* (par. 1), *ruminating* (1), *ganglion* (5), *critical mass* (7), *organelles* (8), *embryonic* (8), *mitosis* (8), *genome* (8), *amebocytes* (9), *stellate* (9), *biosphere* (11), *photons* (11), *springtails* (11), and *quantum mechanics* (11).

Comparing

1. If you compare Thomas's essay with Alexander Petrunkevitch's "The Spider and the Wasp" (Chapter 3), which reads more like a technical scientific report? Explain your answer.

2. In its use of analogy does Thomas's essay more closely resemble Petrunkevitch's or Virginia Woolf's "The Death of the Moth" (Chapter 8)? Explain your answer.

Discussion and Writing Topics

1. Describe some human social enterprise—a party, field trip, class session, convention, or bargain sale—by analogy with a collective gathering of insects.

2. Thomas suggests that human beings work collectively to gather information. Speculate on other motives for human social activity —companionship, for example.

3. If societies are organisms with a group mind or will, what becomes of the individual's responsibility for his or her behavior when he or she acts as part of a group? Is a lynch mob, say, an amoral thing like a cold virus?

Barry Lopez

My Horse

The son of a publisher, Barry Lopez is a full-time writer and free-lance photographer. He was born in Port Chester, New York, but now lives with his wife in Finn Rock, Oregon. He was educated at Notre Dame and the University of Oregon. A contributor to Harper's, the North American Review, and Audubon, among other magazines, he is the author of a collection of American Indian trickster tales, a book on wolves (illustrated with his own photographs), and Desert Notes: Reflections in the Eye of a Raven (1976). Lopez is now at work on "River Notes" and "Animal Notes." "My Horse," which originally appeared in the North American Review, draws an analogy between the author's Dodge Sportsman 300 van and Coke High, a quarter horse that Lopez rode as a wrangler in Wyoming.

It is curious that Indian warriors on the northern plains in the nineteenth century, who were almost entirely dependent on the horse for mobility and status, never gave their horses names. If you borrowed a man's horse and went off raiding for other horses, however, or if you lost your mount in battle and then jumped on mine and counted coup [1] on an enemy—well, those horses would have to be shared with the man whose horse you borrowed, and that coup would be mine, not yours. Because even if I gave him no name, he was my horse.

If you were a Crow warrior and I a young Teton Sioux out after a warrior's identity and we came over a small hill some-

[1] The custom among the Plains Indians of striking or touching an enemy as a sign of courage.

where in the Montana prairie and surprised each other, I could tell a lot about you by looking at your horse.

Your horse might have feathers tied in his mane, or in his tail, or a medicine bag tied around his neck. If I knew enough about the Crow, and had looked at you closely, I might make some sense of the decoration, even guess who you were if you were well-known. If you had painted your horse I could tell even more, because we both decorated our horses with signs that meant the same things. Your white handprints high on his flanks would tell me you had killed an enemy in a hand-to-hand fight. Small horizontal lines stacked on your horse's foreleg, or across his nose, would tell me how many times you had counted coup. Horse hoof marks on your horse's rump, or three-sided boxes, would tell me how many times you had stolen horses. If there was a bright red square on your horse's neck I would know you were leading a war party and that there were probably others out there in the coulees behind you.   3

You might be painted all over as blue as the sky and covered with white dots, with your horse painted the same way. Maybe hailstorms were your power—or if I chased you a hailstorm might come down and hide you. There might be lightning bolts on the horse's legs and flanks, and I would wonder if you had lightning power, or a slow horse. There might be white circles around your horse's eyes to help him see better.   4

Or you might be like Crazy Horse,[2] with no decoration, no marks on your horse to tell me anything, only a small lightning bolt on your cheek, a piece of turquoise tied behind your ear.   5

You might have scalps dangling from your rein.   6

I could tell something about you by your horse. All this would come to me in a few seconds. I might decide this was my moment and shout my war cry—*Hoka hey!* Or I might decide you were like the grizzly bear: I would raise my weapon to you in salute and go my way, to see you again when I was older.   7

I do not own a horse. I am attached to a truck, however, and I have come to think of it in a similar way. It has no name; it never occurred to me to give it a name. It has little decoration; neither   8

---

[2] (1849?–1877), a Sioux chief, born in Nebraska; he fought General Custer at the Little Big Horn.

of us is partial to decoration. I have a piece of turquoise in the truck because I had heard once that some of the southwestern tribes tied a small piece of turquoise in a horse's hock to keep him from stumbling. I like the idea. I also hang sage in the truck when I go on a long trip. But inside, the truck doesn't look much different from others that look just like it on the outside. I like it that way. Because I like my privacy.

For two years in Wyoming I worked on a ranch wrangling   9
horses. The horse I rode when I had to have a good horse was a quarter horse and his name was Coke High. This name came with him. At first I thought he'd been named for the soft drink. I'd known stranger names given to horses by whites. Years later I wondered if some deviant Wyoming cowboy wise to cocaine had not named him. Now I think he was probably named after a rancher, an historical figure of the region. I never asked the people who owned him for fear of spoiling the spirit of my inquiry.

We were running over a hundred horses on this ranch. They all   10
had names. After a few weeks I knew all the horses and the names too. You had to. No one knew how to talk about the animals or put them in order or tell the wranglers what to do unless they were using the names—Princess, Big Red, Shoshone, Clay.

My truck is named Dodge. The name came with it. I don't   11
know if it was named after the town or the verb or the man who invented it. I like it for a name. Perfectly anonymous, like Rex for a dog, or Old Paint. You can't tell anything with a name like that.

The truck is a van. I call it a truck because it's not a car and   12
because "van" is a suburban sort of consumer word, like "oxford loafer," and I don't like the sound of it. On the outside it looks like any other Dodge Sportsman 300. It's a dirty tan color. There are a few body dents, but it's never been in a wreck. I tore the antenna off against a tree on a pinched mountain road. A boy in Midland, Texas, rocked one of my rear view mirrors off. A logging truck in Oregon squeeze-fired a piece of debris off the road and shattered my windshield. The oil pan and gas tank are pug-faced from high-centering on bad roads. (I remember a horse I rode for a while named Targhee whose hocks were scarred from tangles in barbed wire when he was a colt and who spooked a lot in high grass, but these were not like "dents." They were more like bad tires.)

I like to travel. I go mostly in the winter and mostly on two- 13
lane roads. I've driven the truck from Key West to Vancouver,
British Columbia, and from Yuma to Long Island over the past
four years. I used to ride Coke High only about five miles every
morning when we were rounding up horses. Hard miles of twisting
and turning. About six hundred miles a year. Then I'd turn him
out and ride another horse for the rest of the day. That's what was
nice about having a remuda.[3] You could do all you had to do and
not take it all out on your best horse. Three car family.

My truck came with a lot of seats in it and I've never really 14
known what to do with them. Sometimes I put the seats in and go
somewhere with a lot of people, but most of the time I leave them
out. I like riding around with that empty cavern of space behind
my head. I know it's something with a history to it, that there's
truth in it, because I always rode a horse the same way—with
empty saddle bags. In case I found something. The possibility
of finding something is half the reason for being on the road.

The value of anything comes to me in its use. If I am not using 15
something it is of no value to me and I give it away. I wasn't
always that way. I used to keep everything I owned—just in case.
I feel good about the truck because it gets used. A lot. To haul
hay and firewood and lumber and rocks and garbage and animals.
Other people have used it to haul furniture and freezers and dirt
and recycled newspapers. And to move from one house to another.
When I lend it for things like that I don't look to get anything
back but some gas (if we're going to be friends). But if you go way
out in the country to a dump and pick up the things you can still
find out there (once a load of cedar shingles we sold for $175 to
an architect) I expect you to leave some of those things around
my place when you come back—if I need them.

When I think back, maybe the nicest thing I ever put in that 16
truck was timber wolves. It was a long night's drive from Oregon
up into British Columbia. We were all very quiet about it; it was
like moving clouds across the desert.

Sometimes something won't fit in the truck and I think about 17

---

[3] In the Southwest, a herd of horses from which ranch hands choose their
mounts.

improving it—building a different door system, for example. I am forever going to add better gauges on the dash and a pair of driving lamps and a sunroof, but I never get around to doing any of it. I remember I wanted to improve Coke High once too, especially the way he bolted like a greyhound through patches of cottonwood on a river flat. But all I could do with him was to try to rein him out of it. Or hug his back.

Sometimes, road-stoned in a blur of country like southwestern 18 Wyoming or North Dakota, I talk to the truck. It's like wandering on the high plains under a summer sun, on plains where, George Catlin [4] wrote, you were "out of sight of land." I say what I am thinking out loud, or point at things along the road. It's a crazy, sun-stroked sort of activity, a sure sign it's time to pull over, to go for a walk, to make a fire and have some tea, to lie in the shade of the truck.

I've always wanted to pat the truck. It's basic to the relation- 19 ship. But it never works.

I remember when I was on the ranch, just at sunrise, after I'd 20 saddled Coke High, I'd be huddled down in my jacket smoking a cigarette and looking down into the valley, along the river where the other horses had spent the night. I'd turn to Coke and run my hand down his neck and slap-pat him on the shoulder to say I was coming up. It made a bond, an agreement we started the day with.

I've thought about that a lot with the truck, because we've gone 21 out together at sunrise on so many mornings. I've even fumbled around trying to do it. But metal won't give.

The truck's personality is mostly an expression of two ideas: 22 "with-you" and "alone." When Coke High was "with-you" he and I were the same animal. We could have cut a rooster out of a flock of chickens, we were so in tune. It's the same with the truck: rolling through Kentucky on a hilly two-lane road, three in the morning under a full moon and no traffic. Picture it. You roll like water.

There are other times when you are with each other but there's 23 no connection at all. Coke got that way when he was bored and we'd fight each other about which way to go around a tree. When

[4] (1796–1872), American artist and writer who lived among the Indians.

the truck gets like that—"alone"—it's because it feels its Detroit fat-ass design dragging at its heart and making a fool out of it.

I can think back over more than a hundred nights I've slept in ²⁴ the truck, sat in it with a lamp burning, bundled up in a parka, reading a book. It was always comfortable. A good place to wait out a storm. Like sleeping inside a buffalo.

The truck will go past 100,000 miles soon. I'll rebuild the engine ²⁵ and put a different transmission in it. I can tell from magazine advertisements that I'll never get another one like it. Because every year they take more of the heart out of them. One thing that makes a farmer or a rancher go sour is a truck that isn't worth a shit. The reason you see so many old pickups in ranch country is because these are the only ones with any heart. You can count on them. The weekend rancher runs around in a new pickup with too much engine and not enough transmission and with the wrong sort of tires because he can afford anything, even the worst. A lot of them have names for their pickups too.

My truck has broken down, in out of the way places at the worst ²⁶ of times. I've walked away and screamed the foulness out of my system and gotten the tools out. I had to fix a water pump in a blizzard in the Panamint Mountains in California once. It took all day with the Coleman stove burning under the engine block to keep my hands from freezing. We drifted into Beatty, Nevada, that night with it jury-rigged together with—I swear—baling wire, and we were melting snow as we went and pouring it in to compensate for the leaks.

There is a dent next to the door on the driver's side I put there ²⁷ one sweltering night in Miami. I had gone to the airport to meet my wife, whom I hadn't seen in a month. My hands were so swollen with poison ivy blisters I had to drive with my wrists. I had shut the door and was locking it when the window fell off its runners and slid down inside the door. I couldn't leave the truck unlocked because I had too much inside I didn't want to lose. So I just kicked the truck a blow in the side and went to work on the window. I hate to admit kicking the truck. It's like kicking a dog, which I've never done.

Coke High and I had an accident once. We hit a badger hole ²⁸ at a full gallop. I landed on my back and blacked out. When I came to, Coke High was about a hundred yards away. He stayed a hundred yards away for six miles, all the way back to the ranch.

I want to tell you about carrying those wolves, because it was a 29 fine thing. There were ten of them. We had four in the truck with us in crates and six in a trailer. It was a five hundred mile trip. We went at night for the cool air and because there wouldn't be as much traffic. I could feel from the way the truck rolled along that its heart was in the trip. It liked the wolves inside it, the sweet odor that came from the crates. I could feel that same tireless wolf-lope developing in its wheels; it was like you might never have to stop for gas, ever again.

The truck gets very self-focused when it works like this; its 30 heart is strong and it's good to be around it. It's good to be *with* it. You get the same feeling when you pull someone out of a ditch. Coke High and I pulled a Volkswagen out of the mud once, but Coke didn't like doing it very much. Speed, not strength, was his center. When the guy who owned the car thanked us and tried to pat Coke, the horse snorted and swung away, trying to preserve his distance, which is something a horse spends a lot of time on.

So does the truck. 31

Being distant lets the truck get its heart up. The truck has been 32 cold and alone in Montana at 38 below zero. It's climbed horrible, eroded roads in Idaho. It's been burdened beyond overloading, and made it anyway. I've asked it to do these things because they build heart, and without heart all you have is a machine. You have nothing. I don't think people in Detroit know anything at all about heart. That's why everything they build dies so young.

One time in Arizona the truck and I came through one of the 33 worst storms I've ever been in, an outrageous, angry blizzard. But we went down the road, right through it. You couldn't explain our getting through by the sort of tires I had on the truck, or the fact that I had chains on, or was a good driver, or had a lot of weight over my drive wheels or a good engine, because it was more than this. It was a contest between the truck and the blizzard— and the truck wouldn't quit. I could have gone to sleep and the truck would have just torn a road down Interstate 40 on its own. It scared the hell out of me; but it gave me heart, too.

We came off the Mogollon Rim that night and out of the storm 34 and headed south for Phoenix. I pulled off the road to sleep for a few hours, but before I did I got out of the truck. It was raining. Warm rain. I tied a short piece of red avalanche cord into the grill. I left it there for a long time, like an eagle feather on a horse's tail. It flapped and spun in the wind. I could hear it ticking against the grill when I drove.

When I have to leave that truck I will just raise up my left   35 arm—*Hoka hey!*—and walk away.

QUESTIONS

Understanding

1. Which is the *primary* subject of Lopez's ANALOGY, his truck or his horse? Explain your answer.

2. What does Lopez mean by "heart" (par. 32)? How does his account of the drive through the blizzard (par. 33) help to define this virtue?

3. Why does Lopez admire Crazy Horse (par. 5)? How is his truck like Crazy Horse's mount?

4. How does Lopez resemble the young Teton Sioux at the beginning of his essay? How has he changed (almost) by the end? What accounts for the change?

5. Lopez says of riding in his empty truck that "it's something with a history to it, that there's truth in it" (par. 14). What does he mean by this statement? How has it been anticipated earlier?

6. What does Detroit come to signify in this essay?

7. When friends borrow Lopez's truck, they are expected to share what they find with it, even though he otherwise shuns possessions. Why? What tradition does this custom recall?

Strategies and Structure

1. Lopez's analogy between truck and horse is largely unstated; he does not often refer explicitly to the fact of resemblance. Instead, he proceeds by alternating between his two subjects until they blend and merge. Cite several examples of this technique.

2. Sometimes Lopez's analogy shifts unexpectedly from one subject

back to the other. Which examples do you find particularly surprising? How does Lopez use this technique to end his essay?

3. In what sense does the last line of paragraph 13 reverse Lopez's
basic analogy? Where else in his essay does this sort of reversal
occur?

4. Lopez's basic analogy is between his truck and a horse, but this
is not the only analogy in his essay. To what else, particularly
animals, does he compare his truck?

5. Lopez admits that his basic analogy breaks down in one respect.
How is his truck *not* like a horse? How does he turn this exception to advantage?

6. Lopez is drawing analogies here, but his essay also uses many of
the techniques of NARRATION. What are some of these techniques?
Point to specific examples.

Words and Figures of Speech

1. Names usually signify identity, but Lopez is glad that his truck
is named "Dodge" because it is thus *anonymous* (par. 11), like an
Indian pony. Look up the root meaning of this word. Why is it
appropriate here?

2. In a way, this is an essay about sign language. To whose language
does the word *van* (par. 12) belong, according to Lopez? What
does it signify or "sign"?

3. Some cultures assume that "signs" and the ideas they represent
are separate and distinct. Other cultures blur this distinction and
tend to *identify* a sign with what it refers to. Which is the case
with Lopez and his Indians? Explain your answer.

4. Is Coke High a METAPHOR for Lopez's truck or a SIMILE? Explain
your opinion.

5. If Lopez's horse stands for his truck, what does his truck stand
for?

Comparing

1. Describe how Barry Lopez's use of language resembles that of
Chief Seattle in his "Reply to the U.S. Government" (Chapter
10).

2. How does the sign language of Lopez's Indians resemble the

"secret language" that Desmond Morris defines in "Barrier Signals" (Chapter 5)?

3. Contrast Lopez's attitude toward new-fangled gadgets and ideas with that of Michael Rogers in "Portrait of the Newlyweds as a Young Hologram" (Chapter 5).

Discussion and Writing Topics

1. If you know someone who identifies with his or her car, motorcycle, or bike, develop an analogy between them.

2. Develop an analogy between someone you know and his or her pet.

3. Some tasks and responsibilities (raising a colt, harvesting a crop, maintaining a boat) have been considered as aids to growing up. Describe some such task as a metaphor for coming-of-age.

Annie Dillard

Transfiguration

Annie Dillard was born in Pittsburgh in 1945, attended Hollins College, and lived in Virginia's Roanoke Valley from 1965 to 1975, when she moved to an island in Puget Sound for a period of meditation. She has written a book of poems, Tickets for a Prayer Wheel (1974); her Pilgrim at Tinker Creek (1974), an account of mystical contact with the natural world, won the Pulitzer Prize. (One critic called that book a "psalm of terror and celebration.") "Transfiguration" (editor's title) is from Part One of her latest book, Holy the Firm (1977). The students mentioned in it studied with Dillard at Western Washington State College in Bellingham.

I live on northern Puget Sound, in Washington State, alone.   1
I have a gold cat, who sleeps on my legs, named Small. In the
morning I joke to her blank face, Do you remember last
night? Do you remember? I throw her out before breakfast,
so I can eat.

There is a spider, too, in the bathroom, with whom I keep   2
a sort of company. Her little outfit always reminds me of a
certain moth I helped to kill. The spider herself is of uncertain lineage, bulbous at the abdomen and drab. Her six-inch
mess of a web works, works somehow, works miraculously, to
keep her alive and me amazed. The web itself is in a corner
behind the toilet, connecting tile wall to tile wall and floor,
in a place where there is, I would have thought, scant traffic.
Yet under the web are sixteen or so corpses she has tossed
to the floor.

The corpses appear to be mostly sow bugs, those little   3 armadillo creatures who live to travel flat out in houses, and die round. There is also a new shred of earwig, three old spider skins crinkled and clenched, and two moth bodies, wingless and huge and empty, moth bodies I drop to my knees to see.

Today the earwig shines darkly and gleams, what there is of him: a dorsal curve of thorax and abdomen, and a smooth pair of cerci [1] by which I knew his name. Next week, if the other bodies are any indication, he will be shrunken and gray, webbed to the floor with dust. The sow bugs beside him are hollow and empty of color, fragile, a breath away from brittle fluff. The spider skins lie on their sides, translucent and ragged, their legs drying in knots. And the moths, the empty moths, stagger against each other, headless, in a confusion of arching strips of chitin like peeling varnish, like a jumble of buttresses for cathedral domes, like nothing resembling moths, so that I should hesitate to call them moths, except that I have had some experience with the figure Moth reduced to a nub.   4

Two summers ago I was camping alone in the Blue Ridge   5
Mountains in Virginia. I had hauled myself and gear up there to read, among other things, James Ramsey Ullman's *The Day on Fire*, a novel about Rimbaud that had made me want to be a writer when I was sixteen; [2] I was hoping it would do it again. So I read, lost, every day sitting under a tree by my tent, while warblers swung in the leaves overhead and bristle worms trailed their inches over the twiggy dirt at my feet; and I read every night by candlelight, while barred owls called in the forest and pale moths massed round my head in the clearing, where my light made a ring.

Moths kept flying into the candle. They would hiss and recoil,   6
lost upside down in the shadows among my cooking pans. Or they would singe their wings and fall, and their hot wings, as if melted, would stick to the first thing they touched—a pan, a lid, a spoon—so that the snagged moths could flutter only in tiny arcs, unable to struggle free. These I could release by a quick flip with a stick; in the morning I would find my cooking stuff gilded with torn flecks

[1] Plural of *cercus*, posterior "feeler" of an insect.
[2] French poet Arthur Rimbaud (1854–1891) himself began writing at age sixteen and produced his major work before he was twenty. Ullman's novel was published in 1958.

of moth wings, triangles of shiny dust here and there on the aluminum. So I read, and boiled water, and replenished candles, and read on.

One night a moth flew into the candle, was caught, burnt dry, and held. I must have been staring at the candle, or maybe I looked up when a shadow crossed my page; at any rate, I saw it all. A golden female moth, a biggish one with a two-inch wingspan, flapped into the fire, dropped her abdomen into the wet wax, stuck, flamed, frazzled and fried in a second. Her moving wings ignited like tissue paper, enlarging the circle of light in the clearing and creating out of the darkness the sudden blue sleeves of my sweater, the green leaves of jewelweed by my side, the ragged red trunk of a pine. At once the light contracted again and the moth's wings vanished in a fine, foul smoke. At the same time her six legs clawed, curled, blackened, and ceased, disappearing utterly. And her head jerked in spasms, making a spattering noise; her antennae crisped and burned away and her heaving mouth parts crackled like pistol fire. When it was all over, her head was, so far as I could determine, gone, gone the long way of her wings and legs. Had she been new, or old? Had she mated and laid her eggs, had she done her work? All that was left was the glowing horn shell of her abdomen and thorax—a fraying, partially collapsed gold tube jammed upright in the candle's round pool.

And then this moth-essence, this spectacular skeleton, began to act as a wick. She kept burning. The wax rose in the moth's body from her soaking abdomen to her thorax to the jagged hole where her head should be, and widened into flame, a saffron-yellow flame that robed her to the ground like any immolating monk. That candle had two wicks, two flames of identical height, side by side. The moth's head was fire. She burned for two hours, until I blew her out.

She burned for two hours without changing, without bending or leaning—only glowing within, like a building fire glimpsed through silhouetted walls, like a hollow saint, like a flame-faced virgin gone to God, while I read by her light, kindled, while Rimbaud in Paris burnt out his brains in a thousand poems, while night pooled wetly at my feet.

And that is why I believe those hollow crisps on the bathroom floor are moths. I think I know moths, and fragments of moths, and chips and tatters of utterly empty moths, in any state. How many of you, I asked the people in my class, which of you want to give your lives and be writers? I was trembling from coffee, or cigarettes, or the closeness of faces all around me. (Is this what we live for? I thought; is this the only final beauty: the color of any skin in any light, and living, human eyes?) All hands rose to the question. (You, Nick? Will you? Margaret? Randy? Why do I want them to mean it?) And then I tried to tell them what the choice must mean: you can't be anything else. You must go at your life with a broadax. . . . They had no idea what I was saying. (I have two hands, don't I? And all this energy, for as long as I can remember. I'll do it in the evenings, after skiing, or on the way home from the bank, or after the children are asleep. . . .) They thought I was raving again. It's just as well.

I have three candles here on the table which I disentangle from   11
the plants and light when visitors come. Small usually avoids them, although once she came too close and her tail caught fire; I rubbed it out before she noticed. The flames move light over everyone's skin, draw light to the surface of the faces of my friends. When the people leave I never blow the candles out, and after I'm asleep they flame and burn.

QUESTIONS

Understanding

1. What is the most important ANALOGY in Dillard's essay? What is she comparing to what?

2. What is Dillard referring to in paragraph 10 when she says, "I'll do it in the evening, after skiing, or on the way home from the bank . . ."?

3. At what cost does Dillard seem to think the writer does her (or his) work?

4. When Dillard draws an analogy between the moth and an "immolating monk" (par. 8) or a "flame-faced virgin" (par. 9), she gets beyond the realm of merely natural phenomena. Into what?

5. What is "miraculous" about the spider's web in paragraph 2? Of

all nature as Dillard sees it? What miracle does she celebrate throughout the essay?

6. Why does Dillard refer to the corpses of the moths beneath the spider web in her bathroom?

7. What kind of beauty does Dillard have in mind when she refers to "the color of any skin in any light, and living, human eyes" (par. 10)?

8. What is the significance of the book Dillard is reading when the moth burns?

Strategies and Structure

1. When did you first realize that Dillard's essay draws an extended analogy between the writer and the moth? How does she introduce the comparison without saying flatly, "The writer is like . . ."?

2. How does Dillard's main analogy help to explain the kind of beauty the writer seeks? Her (or his) dedication to her art?

3. How does Dillard's main analogy convey her own sense of awe and wonder at the sacredness of the writer's calling?

4. What analogy is Dillard drawing in the line, "You must go at your life with a broadax . . ." (par. 10)?

5. What is the effect of Dillard's calling the moth "she" instead of "it"? Of Dillard's wondering whether the moth has finished her earthly work (par. 7)?

6. How effective do you find the specific details of the DESCRIPTION in paragraph 3? Explain your answer.

7. How does Dillard give the impression of seeing her world intently, as if through a magnifying glass?

8. In paragraph 9, moth and candle seem almost to be holding the night at bay. How does Dillard create this impression? How does she get across to us the sudden flare of the moth as it first hits the flame?

9. Dillard's analogies are developed through a personal NARRATIVE of the sort exemplified in Chapter 1. Which parts of her narrative are set in the present (the time at which she writes)? Where is she located physically in the present time?

10. In what *two* places is the past action of Dillard's narrative located? When does she return to the present?

11. How does Dillard achieve a welcome comic relief in paragraph 11?

Words and Figures of Speech

1. What is the effect of Dillard's including "like a jumble of but-tresses for cathedral domes" in the list of SIMILES at the end of paragraph 4?

2. Look up *transfiguration* in your dictionary. What does it mean in religious terms? How does it apply to Dillard's essay?

3. Why do you think Dillard uses such technical terms as *thorax, cerci,* and *chitin* (par. 4)?

4. How effective do you find the phrase "scant traffic" in paragraph 2? What is the effect of the word *raving* in paragraph 10?

5. Why does Dillard capitalize *Moth* in paragraph 4?

6. Consult your dictionary as necessary for the following words: *lineage* (par. 2), *bulbous* (2), *dorsal* (4), *thorax* (4), *translucent* (4), *chitin* (4), *buttresses* (4), *gilded* (6), *replenished* (6), *essence* (8), *immolating* (8).

Comparing

1. Which of the insects described in Lewis Thomas's "On Societies as Organisms" (Chapter 7) most closely resembles Dillard's burn-ing moth?

2. In a sense, Dillard's account of the death of a moth and Virginia Woolf's account of the same phenomenon (in the next chapter) come to opposite conclusions. What are those conclusions? Ex-plain the contrast.

Discussion and Writing Topics

1. Draw an analogy between human life and a bird flying through a house.

2. Compare the artist's or the musician's task to that of a champion athlete.

3. Draw an analogy between a nun, priest, rabbi, or other religious figure and a bridge; between a church or synagogue and a ship or city.

1. Explain your inner self by analogy with a car, truck, motorcycle, boat, or other vehicle that you consider to be a means of self-expression.

2. Write an essay using the shrinking size of American automobiles as indexes to the country's economic condition.

3. Describe a house you have seen as an emblem of the people that you know or imagine to inhabit it.

4. Define several different kinds of human intelligence by associating each type with a game that exemplifies it.

5. Explain how to develop self-confidence by comparing the process of acquiring it to weaving a design, cultivating a garden, or building a fire.

6. Explain the kind of education your college or university offers by comparing it to a meal in a restaurant or cafeteria.

7. Describe a typical day in your life as if you were threading your way through a maze.

8. Compare the maneuvers and challenges of the dating game to the activities of a disco lounge or other night spot.

9. Recall formative events of your past life by associating them with objects in an attic or pictures in a photo album.

10. Explain the typical life cycle of a human being by likening it to that of an insect or animal.

Description

8

Essays That Appeal to the Senses

DESCRIPTION [1] is the MODE of writing that appeals most directly to the senses either by telling us the qualities of a person, place, or thing or by showing them. For example, here are two descriptions of cemeteries. The first, from Natural History magazine, is written in the language of detached observation:

An old and popular New England tradition for resident and visitor alike, is a relaxing walk through one of our historical cemeteries. . . .

Haphazard rows of slate tablets give way in time to simple marble tablets bearing urn and willow motifs. The latter in turn lose popularity to marble gravestones of a variety of sizes and shapes and often arranged in groups or family plots. The heyday of ornate marble memorials lasted into the 1920s, when measured rows of uniformly sized granite blocks replaced them.

Compare this passage with novelist John Updike's far-from-detached description of the cemetery in the town where he lives:

The stones are marble, modernly glossy and simple, though I suppose that time will eventually reveal them as another fashion, dated and quaint. Now, the sod is still raw, the sutures of turf are unhealed, the earth still humped, the wreaths scarcely withered. . . . I remember my grandfather's funeral, the hurried cross of sand the minister drew on the coffin lid, the whine of the lowering straps, the lengthening, cleanly cut sides of clay, the thought of air, the lack of air forever in the close dark space lined with pink satin. . . .

[1] Terms printed in all capitals are defined in the Glossary.

Our first example relies heavily upon adjectives: "historical," "haphazard," "simple," "ornate," "measured," "uniformly sized." Except when they identify minerals—slate tablets, marble memorials—these adjectives tend to be ABSTRACT. Indeed, the movement of the entire passage is away from the particular. No single grave is described in detail. Even the "urn and willow motifs" adorn a number of tombs. The authors seem interested in the whole sweep of the cemetery from the haphazard rows of the oldest section to the ordered ranks of modern headstones in the newest. It is the arrangement, or shift in arrangement, that most concerns them.

Arrangement is an abstract concept, and we should remember that description is not limited to people or things that can be perceived directly by the physical senses. Description may also convey ideas: the proportions of a building, the style of a baseball player, the infinitude of space. Our first description of cemeteries, in fact, moves from the concrete to the abstract because it was written to support ideas. It is part of a sociological study of cemeteries as they reveal changing American attitudes toward death, family, and society. The authors take their "relaxing walk" not because they want to examine individual tombstones but because they want to generalize from a multitude of physical evidence. As reporters, they stand between us and the actual objects they tell about.

By contrast, the movement of the Updike passage is from the general to the particular. Starting where the other leaves off—with a field of glossy modern slabs—it focuses quickly upon the new-dug graves and then narrows even more sharply to a single grave kept fresh in the author's memory. This time the adjectives are CONCRETE: "raw," "unhealed," "humped," "withered," "hurried," "close," "dark." The nouns are concrete too: "sod" and "earth" give way to the "space" lined with satin. Death is no abstraction for Updike; it is the suffocating loss of personal life. Updike makes us experience the finality of death by recreating his own sensations of claustrophobia at his grandfather's funeral.

Different as they are, these two passages illustrate a single peculiarity of description as a mode: it seldom stands alone. As in our first example, "scientific" description shades easily into exposition. As in our second, "evocative" description shades just as easily into narration. The authors of example number one describe the changes in a cemetery in order to explain (EXPOSITION) what those changes mean for American culture. After evoking his feelings about a past event, the author of example number two goes on in later lines to show what happened (NARRATION) when his reverie was interrupted by his son, who was learning to ride a bicycle in the peaceful cemetery. Which kind of description is better—telling or showing, scientific or evocative? Neither is inherently better or worse than the other. The kind of description that a writer chooses depends upon what he wants to do with it.

Updike's reference to the "sutures" of "unhealed" turf suggests how easily description also falls into METAPHOR, SIMILE, and ANALOGY. This is hardly surprising, for we often describe a thing in everyday speech by telling what it is like. A thump in your closet at night sounds like an owl hitting a haystack. A crowd stirs like a jellyfish. The seams of turf on new graves are like the stitches binding a human wound.

The ease with which description shifts into other MODES does not mean that a good description has no unity or order of its own, however. When writing description, keep in mind that every detail should contribute to a dominant impression, mood, or purpose. The dominant impression he wanted to convey when describing his grandfather's funeral, says Updike, was "the foreverness, the towering foreverness." Updike creates this impression by moving from the outside to the inside of the grave. Depending upon the object or place you are describing, you may want to move from the inside out, from left to right, top to bottom, or front to back. Whatever arrangement you choose, present the details of your description systematically; but do not call so much attention to your system of organization that it dominates the thing you are describing.

What impression, mood, or purpose is your description intended to serve? What specific objects can contribute to it? What do they look, feel, smell, taste, or sound like? Does your object or place suggest any natural order of presentation? These are the questions to ask when you begin a descriptive essay.

Peter Freuchen

The Eskimo House

Six-foot-six and red-bearded, Peter Freuchen (1886–1957), the
famous Danish explorer, left medical school at age twenty on an
expedition to the Arctic. Along with Knud Rasmussen, he
founded Thule, Greenland, in 1910. He managed a station there
in "the northernmost house in the world" until 1919. His Eskimo
wife, Navarana, died on an expedition in 1921; and, soon after,
Freuchen lost his left foot as a result of frostbite. "That," he
said, "turned me into a writer"; and Freuchen settled down on a
little island in Denmark. He later married an heiress, traveled in
Arctic Russia and West Greenland, and went to Hollywood to
act in a film based on his novel Eskimo (1931). He died in
Alaska. Freuchen's other novels include Sea Tyrant (1932) and
Ivalu (1935), his favorite. Arctic Adventures appeared in 1935
and It's All Adventure came out in 1938. "The Eskimo House"
(editor's title) is an excerpt from Peter Freuchen's Book of the
Eskimos (1961); it describes a structure that looks like a mansion
when compared with the more familiar igloo.

The familiar igloo is used by the Polar Eskimos only as a   1
temporary shelter during travels. Most of the winter they live
in permanent winter houses made of stones and peat. Permanent, that is, for the winter, for each spring they are left by
the inhabitants and automatically become public property the
next fall.

You enter the winter house through an entrance tunnel,   2
usually about fifteen feet long so as to provide both ventilation and protection against the outside cold. Since the house
usually faces the sea, it is on a hill which the horizontal tunnel cuts into. The floor of the tunnel is laid with flat stones,

the walls are piled up stones, and the ceiling is made of flat stones covered with peat or turf. It is low, so that you have to crawl in on your hands and knees.

In the tunnel, you will find a strange little instrument, a little   3
saber of wood or bone, called a *tilugtut*. When snow is falling or drifting outside, thousands of snow crystals will be lodged in the long hair of your skin clothes. If you enter the warm house like that, they will melt and make your clothes wet and heavy. Moreover, if you soon have to go out again, they will freeze. The tilugtut is used to beat the clothes free of snow while still in the entrance tunnel. During this procedure, it is a good idea to call out a few remarks, like: "Somebody comes visiting, as it happens!" so that the people inside are prepared to see you. It is true that an Eskimo home is open to visitors at almost any time of day or night, but there are strained relationships everywhere in the world, and it is neither wise—nor polite—to show up in the house without a word of warning!

The entrance tunnel ends up just inside the front wall of the   4
house itself, and you find yourself a couple of feet below the level of the floor, which you then step onto. Now you are in a room, rarely more than fifteen feet in diameter and roughly circular, inasmuch as the wide front wall, the converging side walls, and the narrower back wall of the house are curved evenly into each other. It is about nine feet high from floor to ceiling, but the roof slants toward the back wall. Besides, the whole back half of the room is filled from wall to wall by a big platform about three feet high. Since the house is sunk a little into the earth to give it extra protection against the gales, the platform usually represents the level of the ground outside. It is laid with flat stones which are extended along the front edge so as to create an overhang, under which there is storage space. On the sides, they extend into two side platforms that rest on stone supports, but also have storage space under them. What is left of the floor, which is also laid with flat stones, is then only a space about seven feet square in the front center part of the house. It serves well when game or frozen meat has to be brought in for the family meal.

The walls of the house are double, two layers of stones with   5
peat or earth filled in between them. The roof is made of flat stones, deftly built up and overlapping each other, at last reaching so far toward the center that a main stone slab can rest on them,

their outer ends being weighed down with boulders for stability. The size of a house largely depends upon how many large flat stone slabs can be found for this purpose. Only when an extra large house is wanted will the Eskimos solve the problem by building pillars up from the platform to support the ceiling.

Lumber in sizes sufficient to support a roof was rare before the white man came to Thule.[1] Sometimes the Eskimos could barter a few little pieces of wood from the whalers, precious objects that they guarded with their lives. Also, they would find a little driftwood on their shores, and some of them believed that it came from forests that covered the bottom of the ocean like those in the white man's country. Actually, the driftwood was supplied by the rivers of Siberia and had drifted across the Polar Basin. After several years in salt water, it had chipped and was hard and difficult to work with. But its presence caused the Eskimos never completely to forget the use of wood.

The platform in the house is the family's sleeping bunk. Here they sleep in a neat row with their feet toward the back wall. Against the back wall are usually piled extra clothes and skins so that it isn't too cold. The bunk is covered with a thick layer of dried grass, upon which skins of musk ox and caribou are spread. The family and its eventual guests sleep under blankets made of fox, hare, caribou, and eider duck skins. The natural colors of these animals' feathers and fur are used to make beautiful patterns.

Only when it is overcrowded are the side bunks used for sleeping, but they are less desirable because they are colder. Otherwise, the blubber lamps are placed on the side bunks. One of them may be used to place a piece of meat or game on for everybody to nibble on. Then there is a bucket or sealskin basin for ice to thaw in for drinking water. Whenever possible, the lady of the house gets this ice from one of the icebergs floating in the fjord by the beach. That water tastes fresh and sweet. A dipper is placed in the basin or bucket for everybody to use when drinking, and this dipper is usually passed around after each meal.

[1] Town in western Greenland named by Freuchen. Ancient geographers called the northernmost region of the world *ultima Thule,* a Latin term which came to refer to any remote goal or ideal.

On the other side bunk, there would then be knives, trays, and [9]
other household gear. The storage space under the bunks is used
for skins and other property. On the walls may be pegs of caribou
ribs or antler for hanging things on. Under the ceiling is suspended
a framework of wood or bones. As it is for drying clothes on, it is
directly above one of the blubber lamps. It is very important
especially for the kamiks and stockings. Every evening, when the
master of the house comes home from the day's hunting, his wife
takes his kamiks and stockings and hangs them up to dry overnight.
In the morning she chews them carefully till they are pliable and
soft enough for his feet, and she puts new dried grass in between
the soles.

For this purpose, the women go every fall up to the rocks to [10]
cut grass off, dry it in the sun, and carry it home. The best harvest
is naturally around the bird cliffs, and they have to get a whole
year's supply for their family before winter.

Both men and women are usually undressed around the house. [11]
The wife is only in her scant foxskin panties, and she sits placidly
on the main bunk most of the time. Her cooking pots are suspended from the ceiling over the blubber lamp; everything is
within her easy reach, and no bustling around is necessary. Since
she has to cut and sew the skin garments of the entire family, that
is what busies her most. Like a Turkish tailor, she sits with her legs
stretched out at right angles to the body, her favorite position,
with her work between her toes. Her most important tool is the
ulo, a curved knife with a handle in the middle of the blade. From
intuition, she cuts her skins in the proper pieces and sews them
together, rarely measuring anything. The furs of the blue and the
white fox are woven together in intricate patterns, and her work
puts the finest Paris furrier to shame. With small, hardly visible
stitches she weaves her narwhal sinew thread in and out until the
skin pieces look as if they had grown together.

No wonder the needle is one of the most important Eskimo [12]
tools. It can be fatal, during a trip, if a torn garment cannot be
repaired to protect against the cold, or new garments cannot be
sewn. It is perfectly truthful to say that the lack of needles has
caused the death of many travelers in the Arctic. For this reason,
the woman's ability to sew well is one of her chief attractions.

The husband also undresses in the house. He may keep his bear- [13]

skin trousers on, or he may be in the nude. When his clothes have dried, he ties them together in a bundle with a thong and hangs them up under the ceiling by a hook. That is in order to get as few lice in them as possible.

The house has one window, which is in the front wall above   14 the entrance. The windowpane is made out of the intestines of the big bearded seal, which are split and dried and sewn together, then framed with sealskin, and the whole thing is put in the wall opening and fastened to the sides. One cannot see through such a window, but it lets quite a good light through. At one side there is a little peephole to look out of. More important, the ventilation of the house is provided through another and larger opening in the upper corner of the windowpane. Fresh air comes in through the entrance tunnel and is often regulated by a skin covering the entrance hole. This skin, when weighed down with a couple of stones, will also keep the dogs out of the house when the family is asleep. The dogs are rarely allowed in the house, anyway, but in very rough weather they may be resting in the entrance tunnel.

The flow of air out through the hole in the windowpane is   15 regulated by a whisk of hay stuck in it. It is easy to see when the air is getting close because the flame in the blubber lamp starts to burn low. And although no draft is ever felt, the house is always well ventilated.

Although the blood and blubber from the killed game smeared   16 over the floor and side bunks ofter give the new observer the impression of an animal cave, he will soon realize that the stone house is ingeniously suited to the arctic conditions. And it is well heated and lighted by the blubber lamps.

The Eskimo lamp is cut out of soapstone. It has a deep depres-   17 sion in the middle, at one side of which a whisk of long-burning moss is placed. Lumps of blubber are put in the lamp, and as the moss burns, the blubber melts and is sucked up in the moss to be consumed. By placing the lamp on three stones or on a tripod, and slanting it at the right angle, one can regulate the flow of blubber to the side where the moss-wick is. A stick serves to open or close the wick, making it narrow or wide according to whether a large or a small flame is wanted. This demands great practice, and only Eskimo women know this art to perfection. The lamp is kept burning at all times; only when the house goes to sleep the flame is made very narrow, and the lamp is filled up with fresh blubber. If it is properly regulated it burns easily through the period of sleep.

There are two types of lamps. One is oval, with a slanting bottom to help the regular flow of the blubber; the other is kind of shell-shaped, with a row of little knobs along the long curved side. This latter is a prototype of the Thule Culture, and is the one used by the Polar Eskimos.   18

This is rather significant, for there are few household possessions that play as big a part in Eskimo domestic life as the lamp. The wife has to tend the lamp, and it belongs under her jurisdiction. The more lamps she can take care of the cleverer she is, and many lamps are a sign of wealth and prestige. Since there rarely is any permanent place called home, the lamps become the symbol of the home.   19

QUESTIONS

Understanding

1. What are the principal permanent features of the Eskimo stone house as described by Freuchen? What tools and furnishings does the family carry with it from house to house?

2. How does the polar climate influence the construction of the Eskimo house? What determines the maximum size of a typical structure?

3. Freuchen is not only describing *where* the Eskimos live but also *how* they live. What social customs are suggested by his DESCRIPTION of the entrance hall and *tilugtut* (par. 3), of the sleeping facilities for family and guests, and of the drying rack (par. 9)?

4. The typical Eskimo wife is characterized here by her tools and her tasks. What do they suggest about the woman's role in the household and her relationship with the "master" (par. 9)?

5. Why is the needle such an important tool in the Eskimo household? What is the symbolic importance of the lamp?

6. Why does the Eskimo stone house become public property every spring? What does Freuchen's description of the Eskimo way of life suggest about their economic system?

Strategies and Structure

1. A good description often proceeds systematically—from front to back, top to bottom, inside to outside of the object or place being described. What system does Freuchen follow?

2. In which paragraph does Freuchen shift attention from the structure of the house to its contents and inhabitants?

3. Freuchen keeps his description from becoming overly methodical by interrupting it with interesting digressions: for example, he explains in paragraph 10 where the Eskimo women get dried grass for the family's shoes. Point out other such brief diversions in paragraphs 6, 8, 9, 11, and 17.

4. By using such words as *usually* (par. 2) and phrases like "there would then be" (par. 9), Freuchen reminds us that he is describing a typical house rather than any one in particular. Cite other examples, especially in paragraphs 6, 8, 9, 11, and 17.

5. Why do you think Freuchen writes in the present rather than the past TENSE? Why do you think he uses the second PERSON pronoun *you* instead of the first person *I*?

6. How does Freuchen create the impression in paragraph 16 that we are being led on our tour by an experienced guide?

Words and Figures of Speech

1. Freuchen gives us the Eskimo names for only a few objects—for example, *tilugtut* (par. 3) and *ulo* (par. 11). Should he have introduced many more Eskimo words? Why or why not?

2. The observation in paragraph 3 that "there are strained relationships everywhere in the world" is an example of UNDERSTATEMENT. What does the use of this device in a "warning" to unannounced guests suggest about the hospitality of the Eskimos?

3. In what sense is *eventual* used in paragraph 7? Who are the eventual guests of Freuchen's Eskimos?

4. Why is *jurisdiction* an appropriate word in paragraph 19? What does it CONNOTE about male and female roles in the Eskimos' domestic affairs?

5. We need little help from the dictionary to read Freuchen's essay. Given his subject and purpose, why might he choose a familiar, even simple, vocabulary?

Comparing

1. Both Freuchen and Edward Abbey in "The Great Globe Arizona Wild Pig and Varmint Hunt" (Chapter 10) are introducing outsiders to strange territory. Yet the two essays differ widely in TONE. How might their varying purposes—descriptive versus PERSUASIVE—help account for this difference?

2. Judged by the criteria set forth in Eugene Raskin's "Walls and Barriers" (Chapter 6), is the Eskimo house a primitive or a modern structure? Explain your answer by referring especially to the function of the house.

Discussion and Writing Topics

1. Describe a house-trailer to an Eskimo who has never seen one.

2. Describe an ideal modern house or building that is perfectly suited to its inhabitants' needs.

3. Describe the division of labor in your family through the household's simple objects and routine duties.

4. Our equivalent of the Eskimo lamp is the fireplace or hearth. Why is this often considered an emblem of the home? Describe several other physical symbols of domestic life in its various phases.

Horace Miner

Body Ritual among the Nacirema

Horace Miner is professor of social anthropology at the University
of Michigan; he is an authority on African cultures. A native of
St. Paul, Minnesota, he studied at the University of Kentucky and
the University of Chicago (Ph.D., 1937). He joined the faculty
at Michigan in 1946 after teaching at Wayne State University
and serving in the wartime army. Miner is the author of The
Primitive City of Timbuctoo (1953); Oasis and Casbah (1960);
and The City in Modern Africa (1967). "Body Ritual among the
Nacirema" first appeared in The American Anthropologist; it
uses the methods and language of social anthropology to describe
a curious North American tribe.

The anthropologist has become so familiar with the diversity   1
of ways in which different peoples behave in similar situations
that he is not apt to be surprised by even the most exotic customs. In fact, if all of the logically possible combinations of
behavior have not been found somewhere in the world, he is
apt to suspect that they must be present in some yet unde-
scribed tribe. This point has, in fact, been expressed with
respect to clan organization by Murdock.[1] In this light, the
magical beliefs and practices of the Nacirema present such
unusual aspects that it seems desirable to describe them as an
example of the extremes to which human behavior can go.

Professor Linton first brought the ritual of the Nacirema   2
to the attention of anthropologists twenty years ago, but the

[1] American anthropologist George Peter Murdock (b. 1897), authority
on primitive cultures.

culture of this people is still very poorly understood. They are a North American group living in the territory between the Canadian Cree, the Yaqui and Tarahumare of Mexico, and the Carib and Arawak of the Antilles.[2] Little is known of their origin, although tradition states that they came from the east. . . .

Nacirema culture is characterized by a highly developed market economy which has evolved in a rich natural habitat. While much of the people's time is devoted to economic pursuits, a large part of the fruits of these labors and a considerable portion of the day are spent in ritual activity. The focus of this activity is the human body, the appearance and health of which loom as a dominant concern in the ethos of the people. While such a concern is certainly not unusual, its ceremonial aspects and associated philosophy are unique.   3

The fundamental belief underlying the whole system appears to be that the human body is ugly and that its natural tendency is to debility and disease. Incarcerated in such a body, man's only hope is to avert these characteristics through the use of the powerful influences of ritual and ceremony. Every household has one or more shrines devoted to this purpose. The more powerful individuals in the society have several shrines in their houses and, in fact, the opulence of a house is often referred to in terms of the number of such ritual centers it possesses. Most houses are of wattle and daub construction, but the shrine rooms of the more wealthy are walled with stone. Poorer families imitate the rich by applying pottery plaques to their shrine walls.   4

While each family has at least one such shrine, the rituals associated with it are not family ceremonies but are private and secret. The rites are normally only discussed with children, and then only during the period when they are being initiated into these mysteries. I was able, however, to establish sufficient rapport with the natives to examine these shrines and to have the rituals described to me.   5

The focal point of the shrine is a box or chest which is built into the wall. In this chest are kept the many charms and magical potions without which no native believes he could live. These preparations are secured from a variety of specialized practitioners.   6

---

[2] Native American tribes formerly inhabiting the Saskatchewan region of Canada, the Sonora region of Mexico, and the West Indies.

The most powerful of these are the medicine men, whose assistance must be rewarded with substantial gifts. However, the medicine men do not provide the curative potions for their clients, but decide what the ingredients should be and then write them down in an ancient and secret language. This writing is understood only by the medicine men and by the herbalists who, for another gift, provide the required charm.

The charm is not disposed of after it has served its purpose, but   7 is placed in the charm-box of the household shrine. As these magical materials are specific for certain ills, and the real or imagined maladies of the people are many, the charm-box is usually full to overflowing. The magical packets are so numerous that people forget what their purposes were and fear to use them again. While the natives are very vague on this point, we can only assume that the idea in retaining all the old magical materials is that their presence in the charm-box, before which the body rituals are conducted, will in some way protect the worshipper.

Beneath the charm-box is a small font. Each day every member   8 of the family, in succession, enters the shrine room, bows his head before the charm-box, mingles different sorts of holy water in the font, and proceeds with a brief rite of ablution. The holy waters are secured from the Water Temple of the community, where the priests conduct elaborate ceremonies to make the liquid ritually pure.

In the hierarchy of magical practitioners, and below the medi-   9 cine men in prestige, are specialists whose designation is best translated "holy-mouth-men." The Nacirema have an almost pathological horror of and fascination with the mouth, the condition of which is believed to have a supernatural influence on all social relationships. Were it not for the rituals of the mouth, they believe that their teeth would fall out, their gums bleed, their jaws shrink, their friends desert them, and their lovers reject them. They also believe that a strong relationship exists between oral and moral characteristics. For example, there is a ritual ablution of the mouth for children which is supposed to improve their moral fiber.

The daily body ritual performed by everyone includes a mouth-   10 rite. Despite the fact that these people are so punctilious about care of the mouth, this rite involves a practice which strikes the uninitiated stranger as revolting. It was reported to me that the ritual consists of inserting a small bundle of hog hairs into the mouth, along with certain magical powders, and then moving the bundle in a highly formalized series of gestures.

In addition to the private mouth-rite, the people seek out a [11] holy-mouth-man once or twice a year. These practitioners have an impressive set of paraphernalia, consisting of a variety of augers, awls, probes, and prods. The use of these objects in the exorcism of the evils of the mouth involves almost unbelievable ritual torture of the client. The holy-mouth-man opens the client's mouth and, using the above mentioned tools, enlarges any holes which decay may have created in the teeth. Magical materials are put into these holes. If there are not naturally occurring holes in the teeth, large sections of one or more teeth are gouged out so that the supernatural substance can be applied. In the client's view, the purpose of these ministrations is to arrest decay and to draw friends. The extremely sacred and traditional character of the rite is evident in the fact that the natives return to the holy-mouth-men year after year, despite the fact that their teeth continue to decay.

It is to be hoped that, when a thorough study of the Nacirema [12] is made, there will be careful inquiry into the personality structure of these people. One has but to watch the gleam in the eye of a holy-mouth-man, as he jabs an awl into an exposed nerve, to suspect that a certain amount of sadism is involved. If this can be established, a very interesting pattern emerges, for most of the population shows definite masochistic tendencies. It was to these that Professor Linton referred in discussing a distinctive part of the daily body ritual which is performed only by men. This part of the rite involves scraping and lacerating the surface of the face with a sharp instrument. Special women's rites are performed only four times during each lunar month, but what they lack in frequency is made up in barbarity. As part of this ceremony, women bake their heads in small ovens for about an hour. The theoretically interesting point is that what seems to be a preponderantly masochistic people have developed sadistic specialists.

The medicine men have an imposing temple, or *latipso*, in [13] every community of any size. The more elaborate ceremonies required to treat very sick patients can only be performed at this temple. These ceremonies involve not only the thaumaturge but a permanent group of vestal maidens who move sedately about the temple chambers in distinctive costume and headdress.

The *latipso* ceremonies are so harsh that it is phenomenal that   14 a fair proportion of the really sick natives who enter the temple ever recover. Small children whose indoctrination is still incomplete have been known to resist attempts to take them to the temple because "that is where you go to die." Despite this fact, sick adults are not only willing but eager to undergo the protracted ritual purification, if they can afford to do so. No matter how ill the supplicant or how grave the emergency, the guardians of many temples will not admit a client if he cannot give a rich gift to the custodian. Even after one has gained admission and survived the ceremonies, the guardians will not permit the neophyte to leave until he makes still another gift.

The supplicant entering the temple is first stripped of all his or   15 her clothes. In everyday life the Nacirema avoids exposure of his body and its natural functions. Bathing and excretory acts are performed only in the secrecy of the household shrine, where they are ritualized as part of the body-rites. Psychological shock results from the fact that body secrecy is suddenly lost upon entry into the *latipso*. A man, whose own wife has never seen him in an excretory act, suddenly finds himself naked and assisted by a vestal maiden while he performs his natural functions into a sacred vessel. This sort of ceremonial treatment is necessitated by the fact that the excreta are used by a diviner to ascertain the course and nature of the client's sickness. Female clients, on the other hand, find their naked bodies are subjected to the scrutiny, manipulation and prodding of the medicine men.

Few supplicants in the temple are well enough to do anything   16 but lie on their hard beds. The daily ceremonies, like the rites of the holy-mouth-men, involve discomfort and torture. With ritual precision, the vestals awaken their miserable charges each dawn and roll them about on their beds of pain while performing ablutions, in the formal movements of which the maidens are highly trained. At other times they insert magic wands in the supplicant's mouth or force him to eat substances which are supposed to be healing. From time to time the medicine men come to their clients and jab magically treated needles into their flesh. The fact that these temple ceremonies may not cure, and may even kill the neophyte, in no way decreases the people's faith in the medicine men.

There remains one other kind of practitioner, known as a [17] "listener." This witchdoctor has the power to exorcise the devils that lodge in the heads of people who have been bewitched. The Nacirema believe that parents bewitch their own children. Mothers are particularly suspected of putting a curse on children while teaching them the secret body rituals. The counter-magic of the witchdoctor is unusual in its lack of ritual. The patient simply tells the "listener" all his troubles and fears, beginning with the earliest difficulties he can remember. The memory displayed by the Nacirema in these exorcism sessions is truly remarkable. It is not uncommon for the patient to bemoan the rejection he felt upon being weaned as a babe, and a few individuals even see their troubles going back to the traumatic effects of their own birth.

In conclusion, mention must be made of certain practices which [18] have their base in native esthetics but which depend upon the pervasive aversion to the natural body and its functions. There are ritual fasts to make fat people thin and ceremonial feasts to make thin people fat. Still other rites are used to make women's breasts larger if they are small, and smaller if they are large. General dissatisfaction with breast shape is symbolized in the fact that the ideal form is virtually outside the range of human variation. A few women afflicted with almost inhuman hyper-mammary development are so idolized that they make a handsome living by simply going from village to village and permitting the natives to stare at them for a fee.

Reference has already been made to the fact that excretory [19] functions are ritualized, routinized, and relegated to secrecy. Natural reproductive functions are similarly distorted. Intercourse is taboo as a topic and scheduled as an act. Efforts are made to avoid pregnancy by the use of magical materials or by limiting intercourse to certain phases of the moon. Conception is actually very infrequent. When pregnant, women dress so as to hide their condition. Parturition takes place in secret, without friends or relatives to assist, and the majority of women do not nurse their infants.

Our review of the ritual life of the Nacirema has certainly [20] shown them to be a magic-ridden people. It is hard to understand how they have managed to exist so long under the burdens which they have imposed upon themselves. But even such exotic customs as these take on real meaning when they are viewed with the insight provided by Malinowski [3] when he wrote:

"Looking from far and above, from our high places of safety in   21
the developed civilization, it is easy to see all the crudity and irrelevance of magic. But without its power and guidance early man could not have mastered his practical difficulties as he has done, nor could man have advanced to the higher stages of civilization."

QUESTIONS

Understanding

1. Who are these strange people, the Nacirema? How did they get their name?
2. What are "shrine rooms" (par. 4) and "charm-boxes"(par. 7) used in the morning rituals of the Nacirema?
3. Why do the Nacirema put "hog hairs" (par. 10) in their mouths? What is the "ritual ablution of the mouth" (par. 9) believed to improve the moral fiber of children?
4. Who is the "listener" (par. 17), and why do the Nacirema think that "parents bewitch their own children" (par. 17)?
5. Having closely observed their private behavior, Miner concludes that the Nacirema base their body rituals on the belief that "the human body is ugly" (par. 4) in its natural state. Do you agree? Why or why not?
6. What is the "real meaning" (par. 20) of the Nacirema's exotic customs when viewed in the light of Malinowski's statement in paragraph 21?

Strategies and Structure

1. When did you first suspect that Miner is writing tongue-in-cheek? What specific details in his DESCRIPTION tipped you off?
2. From what perspective is Miner describing the Nacirema? How

[3] Bronislaw Kasper Malinowski (1884–1942), Polish-born anthropologist, who came to America in 1938.

do paragraphs 1, 3, and 21 help to establish his "cultural" and professional vantage point?

3. Descriptions often strive to make the strange seem familiar, but Miner's makes the familiar seem strange. Give several examples, and analyze how they reverse the usual procedure.

4. What is the serious purpose behind Miner's "joke"? Do you think a mock-scientific paper is an effective means of accomplishing that purpose? Why or why not?

5. A social anthropologist, Miner originally wrote his "study" for *The American Anthropologist*, a journal whose audience expected writing in their field to follow conventional forms. How does Miner give his essay the flavor of a scientific (as opposed to a "literary") article or report? Pay special attention to paragraphs 1–3 and 18–21.

6. How can Miner's essay be seen in any way to SATIRIZE the methods and language of social anthropology?

Words and Figures of Speech

1. Where did the Nacirema get the word *latipso* (par. 13) for their temples of the sick?

2. Miner's last paragraph could be considered a non-sequitur, or conclusion that does not logically follow from the evidence it is built upon. What is wrong, logically, with the quoted statement? Why might Miner choose to end his essay with this device?

3. What is a *thaumaturge* (par. 13)? Given his true subject, what is the effect of Miner's using that term and such related terms as *herbalist* (par. 6), *medicine men* (par. 6), *holy-mouth-men* (par. 9), and *diviner* (par. 15)?

4. For which one of these practitioners does Miner have to invent a name? What does the lack of a standard term for it in the language of anthropology suggest about this role in modern society?

5. Why do you think Miner uses such clinical terms as *excreta* (par. 15), *hyper-mammary* (par. 18), and *parturition* (par. 19)?

6. Consult your dictionary for any of the following words you do not already know: *ethos* (par. 3), *incarcerated* (4), *opulence* (4), *ablution* (8), *pathological* (9), *punctilious* (10), *paraphernalia* (11), *sadism* (12), *masochistic* (12), *supplicant* (14), *neophyte* (14), *scrutiny* (15), *aversion* (18), *taboo* (19), *parturition* (19).

Comparing

1. Both Miner and Peter Freuchen describe "alien" cultures. What techniques of observation and description do their essays have in common—for example, the inclusion of "native" words?

2. Miner's vocabulary is more learned than Freuchen's. How does this difference reflect a difference in purpose?

3. Miner's irony is similar to Jonathan Swift's in "A Modest Proposal" ("Essays For Further Reading"); when you read Swift, ask yourself how the speakers in the two essays resemble each other.

Discussion and Writing Topics

1. Describe other rituals of the Nacirema—for example, those associated with wearing clothes and with transportation—that bear out Miner's findings about the tribe's distaste for the human body.

2. Although Miner says that the Nacirema have a "highly developed market economy" (par. 3), he says little about it. Describe their "economic pursuits" (par. 3) in such a way as to "prove" that these people who find the body ugly nevertheless find treasure beautiful.

3. Describe a barber or beauty shop or an exercise salon as if you were seeing one for the first time and so did not know the names or purposes of anything. Make up descriptive names for people and objects and assign causes according to the surface appearance of events.

Richard Selzer

The Discus Thrower

Richard Selzer is a surgeon. From his native Troy, New York, he
attended Union College and Albany Medical College (M.D.,
1953). After postdoctoral study at Yale, he entered private prac-
tice in 1960. A fellow of Ezra Stiles College of Yale University,
he also teaches surgery at Yale Medical School. Selzer has con-
tributed stories and essays to Harper's, Esquire, Redbook, Made-
moiselle, and other popular magazines. His Rituals of Surgery, a
collection of short stories, appeared in 1974. Selzer is best known
for his essays of the doctor's life, some of which are collected in
Mortal Lessons (1977). He is now at work on more essays and
stories and on a mythological treatment of the Civil War. "The
Discus Thrower" was published in Harper's with the subtitle "Do
Not Go Gentle"; it describes a terminally ill patient in a bare
hospital room.

I spy on my patients. Ought not a doctor to observe his   1
patients by any means and from any stance, that he might the
more fully assemble evidence? So I stand in the doorways of
hospital rooms and gaze. Oh, it is not all that furtive an act.
Those in bed need only look up to discover me. But they
never do.

From the doorway of Room 542 the man in the bed seems   2
deeply tanned. Blue eyes and close-cropped white hair give
him the appearance of vigor and good health. But I know
that his skin is not brown from the sun. It is rusted, rather,
in the last stage of containing the vile repose within. And the
blue eyes are frosted, looking inward like the windows of a
snowbound cottage. This man is blind. This man is also leg-

less—the right leg missing from midthigh down, the left from just below the knee. It gives him the look of a bonsai, roots and branches pruned into the dwarfed facsimile of a great tree.

Propped on pillows, he cups his right thigh in both hands. Now and then he shakes his head as though acknowledging the intensity of his suffering. In all of this he makes no sound. Is he mute as well as blind?

The room in which he dwells is empty of all possessions—no get-well cards, small, private caches of food, day-old flowers, slippers, all the usual kickshaws of the sickroom. There is only the bed, a chair, a nightstand, and a tray on wheels that can be swung across his lap for meals.

"What time is it?" he asks.

"Three o'clock."

"Morning or afternoon?"

"Afternoon."

He is silent. There is nothing else he wants to know.

"How are you?" I say.

"Who is it?" he asks.

"It's the doctor. How do you feel?"

He does not answer right away.

"Feel?" he says.

"I hope you feel better," I say.

I press the button at the side of the bed.

"Down you go," I say.

"Yes, down," he says.

He falls back upon the bed awkwardly. His stumps, unweighted by legs and feet, rise in the air, presenting themselves. I unwrap the bandages from the stumps, and begin to cut away the black scabs and the dead, glazed fat with scissors and forceps. A shard of white bone comes loose. I pick it away. I wash the wounds with disinfectant and redress the stumps. All this while, he does not speak. What is he thinking behind those lids that do not blink? Is he remembering a time when he was whole? Does he dream of feet? Of when his body was not a rotting log?

He lies solid and inert. In spite of everything, he remains impressive, as though he were a sailor standing athwart a slanting deck.

"Anything more I can do for you?" I ask.

For a long moment he is silent.   22

"Yes," he says at last and without the least irony. "You can   23
bring me a pair of shoes."

In the corridor, the head nurse is waiting for me.   24

"We have to do something about him," she says. "Every morn-   25
ing he orders scrambled eggs for breakfast, and, instead of eating
them, he picks up the plate and throws it against the wall."

"Throws his plate?"   26

"Nasty. That's what he is. No wonder his family doesn't come   27
to visit. They probably can't stand him any more than we can."

She is waiting for me to do something.   28

"Well?"   29

"We'll see," I say.   30

The next morning I am waiting in the corridor when the   31
kitchen delivers his breakfast. I watch the aide place the tray on
the stand and swing it across his lap. She presses the button to
raise the head of the bed. Then she leaves.

In time the man reaches to find the rim of the tray, then on to 32
find the dome of the covered dish. He lifts off the cover and places
it on the stand. He fingers across the plate until he probes the
eggs. He lifts the plate in both hands, sets it on the palm of his
right hand, centers it, balances it. He hefts it up and down
slightly, getting the feel of it. Abruptly, he draws back his right
arm as far as he can.

There is the crack of the plate breaking against the wall at the 33
foot of his bed and the small wet sound of the scrambled eggs
dropping to the floor.

And then he laughs. It is a sound you have never heard. It is   34
something new under the sun. It could cure cancer.

Out in the corridor, the eyes of the head nurse narrow.   35

"Laughed, did he?"   36

She writes something down on her clipboard.   37

A second aide arrives, brings a second breakfast tray, puts it on 38
the nightstand, out of his reach. She looks over at me shaking her
head and making her mouth go. I see that we are to be accomplices.

"I've got to feed you," she says to the man.   39

"Oh, no you don't," the man says.   40

"Oh, yes I do," the aide says, "after the way you just did. Nurse 41
says so."

"Get me my shoes," the man says.   42

"Here's oatmeal," the aide says. "Open." And she touches the   43
spoon to his lower lip.

"I ordered scrambled eggs," says the man.   44

"That's right," the aide says.   45

I step forward.   46

"Is there anything I can do?" I say.   47

"Who are you?" the man asks.   48

In the evening I go once more to that ward to make my rounds.   49
The head nurse reports to me that Room 542 is deceased. She
has discovered this quite by accident, she says. No, there had been
no sound. Nothing. It's a blessing, she says.

I go into his room, a spy looking for secrets. He is still there in   50
his bed. His face is relaxed, grave, dignified. After a while, I turn
to leave. My gaze sweeps the wall at the foot of the bed, and I see
the place where it has been repeatedly washed, where the wall
looks very clean and very white.

QUESTIONS

Understanding

1. Why does Selzer's dying patient throw his breakfast against the
   wall?

2. What is the significance of the patient's repeatedly calling for
   shoes? Of his reminding the aide in paragraph 44 that he had
   ordered scrambled eggs?

3. Selzer says that the discus thrower is "impressive" (par. 19) despite his mutilation. Why is he impressive to the doctor?

4. What is the significance of the patient's question about time in
   paragraph 7?

5. What attitude is revealed by the doctor's questions to his patient?
   What is revealed by the dying patient's responses, "Who is it?"
   (par. 11) and "Who are you?" (par. 48)?

6. How might the doctor's response to the nurse (par. 30) be interpreted to carry the "mortal lesson" of Selzer's entire essay?

Strategies and Structure

1. The doctor's role throughout this essay is to DESCRIBE without interpreting. How is this role anticipated in paragraph 1? Why do you think Selzer adopts it?

2. How does the doctor's physical stance during much of the essay contribute to the POINT OF VIEW from which it is told?

3. Selzer's essay alternates between dialogue and description, with little commentary on the meaning of what he describes. Point out the few passages of actual commentary or interpretation. Would Selzer's essay have been more or less successful with more such commentary? Explain your answer.

4. Analyze the TONE of Selzer's description of dressing his patient's stumps in paragraph 19. How well does the tone comport with the doctor's role throughout the essay?

5. How does Selzer avoid sentimentality in his description of the dying man?

6. Describe the function of the head nurse in this essay.

7. What is the effect of Selzer's using the second PERSON "you" in paragraph 34?

8. Why does Selzer end his essay with a reference to the wall?

Words and Figures of Speech

1. An *epithet* is a descriptive title or name for a person, such as "giant-killer" for Jack in the fairy tale. What are the implications of Selzer's main epithet for this patient?

2. Why is the "rotting log" METAPHOR appropriate (par. 19)?

3. The second nurse's aide and the doctor are said to be "accomplices" (par. 38). What does this term CONNOTE? Why does Selzer use it? What similar term does he use in paragraph 1?

4. A *kickshaw* (par. 4) is a trinket or other little gift, often of food. What does Selzer's reference to kickshaws show about his patient? About the doctor?

5. HYPERBOLE is exaggeration. How effective is Selzer's use of this figure of speech in paragraph 34? Explain your answer.

6. Selzer's alternate title, or subtitle, for "The Discus Thrower" is "Do Not Go Gentle," an ALLUSION to the Dylan Thomas poem,

"Do Not Go Gentle into That Good Night." Find a copy of the poem in your school library and explain why Selzer refers to it.

Comparing

1. Both Selzer's essay and the next one (by Virginia Woolf), deal with death; but Woolf's essay, you will find, includes much more commentary on what it describes. What accounts for this difference, and how does it influence our response in each case?
2. What attitudes (both physical and intellectual) does the speaker in Selzer's essay share with the speaker in Lewis Thomas's "On Societies as Organisms" (Chapter 7)?

Discussion and Writing Topics

1. Write a description of a person in a place or situation that is characteristic of him or her. Use dialogue to support your description.
2. Describe the "kickshaws" of any sickroom or rooms with which you have been acquainted. Try to suggest the emotions that those objects represent or fail to represent.
3. Define and describe the role of the physician, as you see it, after his or her patient is beyond the help of medicine.

Virginia Woolf
The Death of the Moth

Virginia Woolf (1882–1941), the distinguished novelist, was the daughter of Leslie Stephen, a Victorian literary critic. She became the center of the "Bloomsbury Group" of writers and artists that flourished in London from about 1907 to 1930. Terrified by the return of her recurring mental depression, she drowned herself in the river Ouse near her home at Rodmell, England. The Voyage Out (1915), Mrs. Dalloway (1925), To the Lighthouse (1927), Orlando (1928), and The Waves (1931) are among the works with which she helped to alter the course of the English novel. Today she is recognized as a psychological novelist especially gifted at exploring the minds of her female characters. "The Death of the Moth" is the title essay of a collection published soon after her suicide; it describes "a tiny bead of pure life."

Moths that fly by day are not properly to be called moths; they do not excite that pleasant sense of dark autumn nights and ivy-blossom which the commonest yellow underwing asleep in the shadow of the curtain never fails to rouse in us. They are hybrid creatures, neither gay like butterflies nor sombre like their own species. Nevertheless the present specimen, with his narrow hay-coloured wings, fringed with a tassel of the same colour, seemed to be content with life. It was a pleasant morning, mid-September, mild, benignant, yet with a keener breath than that of the summer months. The plough was already scoring the field opposite the window, and where the share had been, the earth was pressed flat and gleamed with moisture. Such vigour came rolling in from the fields and the down beyond that it was difficult to keep the eyes strictly turned upon the book. The rooks too were keeping one of their annual festivities; soaring round the tree-tops until it looked as if a vast net with thousands of black knots in it has been cast up into the air; which, after a few moments sank slowly down upon the trees until every twig seemed to have a knot at the end of it. Then, suddenly, the net would be thrown into the air again in a wider circle this time, with the utmost clamour and vociferation, as though to be thrown into the air and settle slowly down upon the tree-tops were a tremendously exciting experience.

The same energy which inspired the rooks, the ploughmen, the horses, and even, it seemed, the lean bare-backed downs, sent the moth fluttering from side to side of his square of the window-pane. One could not help watching him. One was, indeed, conscious of a queer feeling of pity for him. The possibilities of pleasure seemed that morning so enormous and so various that to have only a moth's part in life, and a day moth's at that, appeared a hard fate, and his zest in enjoying his meagre opportunities to the full, pathetic. He flew vigorously to one corner of his compartment, and, after waiting there a second, flew across to the other. What remained for him but to fly to a third corner and then to a fourth? That was all he could do, in spite of the size of the downs, the width of the sky, the far-off smoke of houses, and the romantic voice, now and then, of a steamer out at sea. What he could do he did. Watching him, it seemed as if a fiber, very thin but pure, of the enormous energy of the world had been thrust into his frail and diminutive body. As often as he crossed the pane, I could fancy that a thread of vital light became visible. He was little or nothing but life.

Yet, because he was so small, and so simple a form of the energy that was rolling in at the open window and driving its way through so many narrow and intricate corridors in my own brain and in those of other human beings, there was something marvelous as well as pathetic about him. It was as if someone had taken a tiny bead of pure life and decking it as lightly as possible with down and feathers, had set it dancing and zigzagging to show us the true nature of life. Thus displayed one could not get over the strangeness of it. One is apt to forget all about life, seeing it humped and bossed and garnished and cumbered so that it has to move with the greatest circumspection and dignity. Again, the thought of all that life might have been had he been born in any other shape caused one to view his simple activities with a kind of pity.

After a time, tired by his dancing apparently, he settled on the window ledge in the sun, and the queer spectacle being at an end, I forgot about him. Then, looking up, my eye was caught by him. He was trying to resume his dancing, but seemed either so stiff or so awkward that he could only flutter to the bottom of the window-pane; and when he tried to fly across it he failed. Being intent on other matters I watched these futile attempts for a time without thinking, unconsciously waiting for him to resume his flight, as one waits for a machine, that has stopped momentarily, to start again without considering the reason for its failure. After perhaps a seventh attempt he slipped from the wooden ledge and fell, fluttering his wings, on to his back on the window-sill. The helplessness of his attitude roused me. It flashed upon me that he was in difficulties; he could no longer raise himself; his legs struggled vainly. But, as I stretched out a pencil, meaning to help him to right himself, it came over me that the failure and awkwardness were the approach of death. I laid the pencil down again.

The legs agitated themselves once more. I looked as if for the enemy against which he struggled. I looked out of doors. What had happened there? Presumably it was midday, and work in the fields had stopped. Stillness and quiet had replaced the previous animation. The birds had taken themselves off to feed in the brooks. The horses stood still. Yet the power was there all the same, massed outside indifferent, impersonal, not attending to anything in particular. Somehow it was opposed to the little hay-coloured moth. It was useless to try to do anything. One could only watch the extraordinary efforts made by those tiny legs against an oncoming doom which could, had it chosen, have submerged an entire city, not merely a city, but masses of human beings; nothing, I knew, had any chance against death. Nevertheless after a pause of exhaustion the legs fluttered again. It was superb this last protest, and so frantic that he succeeded at last in righting himself. One's sympathies, of course, were all on the side of life. Also, when there was nobody to care or to know, this gigantic effort on the part of an insignificant little moth, against a power of such magnitude, to retain what no one else valued or desired to keep, moved one strangely. Again, somehow, one saw life, a pure bead. I lifted the pencil again, useless though I knew it to be. But even as I did so, the unmistakable tokens of death showed themselves. The body relaxed, and instantly grew stiff. The struggle was over. The insignificant little creature now knew death. As I looked at the dead moth, this minute wayside triumph of so great a force over so mean an antagonist filled me with wonder. Just as life had been strange a few minutes before, so death was now as strange. The moth having righted himself now lay most decently and uncomplainingly composed. O yes, he seemed to say, death is stronger than I am.

QUESTIONS

Understanding

1. The author of this essay is describing much more than just an insect. What is the true object of her studied observation? What name does she give it in paragraph 3?

2. What does Woolf's tiny moth have in common with the rooks, ploughmen, horses, and fields? Why does the moth's dance seem "strange" (par. 3) to Woolf?

3. If "the true nature of life" (par. 3) is animation, or mere movement, what is the essence of death as Woolf describes it?

4. What role is the speaker in Woolf's essay vainly assuming when she starts to interpose a pencil between the moth and death? Why does she tell us so little about who or what set the moth dancing in the first place?

Strategies and Structure

1. Woolf's essay opens with a DESCRIPTION of moths in general. In which sentence does she begin to describe a particular moth? Through what specific details?

2. How does Woolf use the window to help organize her description?

3. Paragraphs 1 and 3 picture the same scene outside Woolf's window. How has the picture altered in the second version? How does she convey the change?

4. What is the observer in this essay doing when she is not watching the moth or looking out the window?

5. Approximately how much time elapses during the course of this essay? How does Woolf indicate the passage of time?

6. What time of year is Woolf describing here? How does she give us a sense of the season?

7. At first, the speaker in this essay feels pity for the limitations of the moth's life. When the moth struggles against death at the end, how has her attitude changed?

8. Woolf does not use the first PERSON until she says (almost half-way through her essay), "I could fancy that a thread of vital light became visible" (par. 2). What effect does she achieve with such phrases as "in us," "the eyes," "one was," and "one could" (pars. 1 and 2)?

Words and Figures of Speech

1. Paragraph 3 describes the moth's "down and feathers." Why does Woolf choose to "deck" her specimen in the lightest of garments? What property or quality is expressed by "humped," "bossed," "garnished," and "cumbered" (also in par. 3)?

2. Which of the following possible definitions of *vigor* (par. 1) best fits the content of Woolf's essay: 1) physical or mental strength; 2) healthy growth; 3) intensity or force; 4) validity? Explain your choice.

3. Why does Woolf use the METAPHOR of the dance to describe the moth's frantic movements? How does the moth's dance resemble the flight of the rooks?

Comparing

1. Which essay—Woolf's or Annie Dillard's in the preceding chapter—do you find more effective as a description of a physical phenomenon? Explain your preference.

2. Woolf equates the moth's life with movement; to what does Dillard compare the "moth-essence" in "Transfiguration"? Which of the two essays seems more "religious"? Why?

Discussion and Writing Topics

1. Describe a pond, a dance, a journey, or a mountain as an emblem of life or one of life's phases.

2. Have you ever been tempted to interfere with a natural process or to save some animal from a natural enemy? Describe what you did and how you felt.

WRITING TOPICS for Chapter Eight
Essays That Appeal to the Senses

Describe one of the following:

1. The oldest person you know

2. Your dream house

3. The place you associate most closely with family vacations

4. A ghost town or dying neighborhood you have visited

5. A shipyard, dock, or harbor you have seen

6. The worst storm you can remember and its aftermath

7. A room in a hospital or rest home

8. An old-fashioned general store, hardware store, or drugstore

9. A carnival or fair

10. A building, street, or town that has given you a glimpse of foreign culture

11. A statue that seems out of place to you

12. A tropical garden

13. The waiting room of a bus or train station

14. The main reading room of a public library

15. An expensive sporting goods store

16. A factory or plant you have worked in or visited

17. A well-run farm

18. A junkyard

Persuasion and Argumentation

9
Essays That Appeal to Reason

PERSUASION [1] is the strategic use of language to move an audience to action or belief. In persuasive writing, readers can be moved in three ways: (1) by appealing to their reason; (2) by appealing to their emotions; and (3) by appealing to their sense of ethics (their standards of what constitutes proper behavior). The first of these, often called ARGUMENTATION, is discussed in this chapter; the other two will be taken up in Chapter 10.

Argumentation, as the term is used here, refers both to logical thinking and to the expression of that thought in such a way as to convince others to accept it. Argumentation, in other words, analyzes a subject or problem in order to induce belief. It may or may not go on to urge a course of action. In "Capital Punishment," for example, you will find William F. Buckley, Jr., laying out the case for the death penalty "without wholeheartedly endorsing it." Buckley wants to convince us that there are valid reasons for the death penalty, but he is also aware of good arguments on the other side. So he analyzes the issues; he takes a position; but he does not tell us to get out and write our congressman. Like most persuasive arguments, however, Buckley's at least implies a course of action.

Whether they induce action or belief or both, persuasive arguments appeal through logic to our capacity to reason. There are two basic kinds of logical reasoning: INDUCTION and DEDUCTION. When we deduce something, we reason from general premises to particular conclusions. When we

[1] Terms printed in all capitals are defined in the Glossary.

reason by induction, we proceed the other way—from particulars to generalities.

In Edgar Allan Poe's "The Murders in the Rue Morgue," master detective Auguste Dupin is investigating two brutal killings. One victim has been jammed up a chimney further than the strength of a normal man could have shoved her; the other lies in the courtyard below. Dupin notices a lightning-rod extending from the courtyard past the victims' window, but it is too far for an escaping man to negotiate. Putting these and other particulars together, Dupin reasons inductively that the murderer is not a man but a giant ape. Yet how did the animal escape?—the two windows of the apartment are nailed shut and the doors are locked from the inside. Reasoning deductively now, Dupin begins with the premise that a "material" killer—not the supernatural agent the authorities half-suspect—must have "escaped materially." Thus the closed windows must have the power of closing themselves: Dupin examines one window and finds a hidden spring; but the nail fastening the window is still intact. Therefore, Dupin reasons, the ape "must have escaped through the other window" and "there must be found a difference between the nails." Dupin examines the nail in the second window and, sure enough, it is broken; outside, moveover, hangs a shutter on which the animal could have swung to the lightning-rod. Dupin advertises for the owner of a missing orangutang, and that very night, a sailor appears at his door.

Inductive reasoning, then, depends upon examples—like the minute clues that lead Poe's Dupin to suspect an orangutang—and in many cases the validity of an inductive argument increases as the sheer number of examples increases. We are more likely to believe that UFOs exist if they have been sighted by ten thousand witnesses than by one thousand. In a short essay we seldom have room for more than a few examples, however. (You will be surprised how often they are reduced to the "magic" number three.) So we must select the most telling and representative ones.

Deductive reasoning depends upon the "syllogism." Here is Aristotle's famous example of this basic pattern of logical thinking:

Major premise: All men are mortal.
Minor premise: Socrates is a man.
Conclusion: Therefore, Socrates is mortal.

If we grant Aristotle's major assumption that all men must die and his minor (or narrower) assumption that Socrates is a man, the conclusion follows inevitably that Socrates must die. (Since Socrates had died about fifteen years before Aristotle was born, Aristotle was reasonably confident that his example would not be seriously challenged.)

When a conclusion follows from the premises or (in inductive reasoning) from the examples, we say that the argument is "valid." An invalid argument is one that jumps to conclusions: the conclusion does not follow logically from the premises or examples. Inductive arguments (from particulars to generalizations) are often invalid because they use too few examples, because the examples are not representative, or because the examples depend upon faulty authorities or faulty comparisons of the sort the Duchess makes in Lewis Carroll's Alice in Wonderland. In your own reasoning, strive to think like Alice:

> "Very true," said the Duchess: "flamingoes and mustard both bite. And the moral of that is—'Birds of a feather flock together.' "
>
> "Only mustard isn't a bird," Alice remarked.
>
> "Right, as usual," said the Duchess: "what a clear way you have of putting things!"

A deductive argument may be valid without being true, of course. Consider this valid argument by satirist Ambrose Bierce:

> Major Premise: Sixty men can do a piece of work sixty times as quickly as one man.
> Minor Premise: One man can dig a posthole in sixty seconds; therefore—
> Conclusion: Sixty men can dig a posthole in one second.

As Bierce was aware, this argument is valid but untrue. It would get too crowded around that posthole for efficiency. The trouble here, and with all deductive arguments that are valid but untrue, is a faulty premise. Sixty men cannot do work sixty times as fast as one if they have no place to stand. We can see why Bierce's Devil's Dictionary defines the syllogism as a "logical formula consisting of a major and a minor assumption and an inconsequent." The syllogism provides a manner for thinking logically; but as Bierce's irony would warn us, it does not provide the matter of logical thought. We have to supply that ourselves.

In real-life persuasive arguments, we seldom use the formal syllogism. We are much more likely to assert, "If one man can dig a posthole in sixty seconds, sixty men can do it in one." Or: "You know he is an atheist because he doesn't go to church." We can meet such faulty arguments more effectively if we realize that they are abbreviated syllogisms with one premise left unsaid. Stated as a formal syllogism, our second example would look like this:

Major premise: All people who do not go to church are atheists.
Minor premise: He does not go to church.
Conclusion: Therefore, he is an atheist.

The implied premise here is the major premise: "All people who do not go to church are atheists." Usually the implied premise is the weak spot in your opponent's argument. If you can challenge it, your own position has won an excellent foothold.

Most extended debates in real life arise because the parties disagree over the truth or untruth of one or more primary assumptions. "The U.S. should stay out of South American affairs." "Inflation will drop sharply next year." "All women should work." Propositions like these cannot be assumed; they must be debated. But in your own persuasive writing, be sure of your logic first. If it can be shown that your conclusions do not follow from your premises, the debate will be over before the crucial issue of truth can be raised.

In a short essay, you should not depend rigidly upon logical forms, and you cannot hope to prove anything worth proving to an absolute certainty. But an argumentative essay does not have to prove, remember. It has only to convince. Be as convincing as you reasonably can by appealing to your audience's reason.

Thomas Jefferson

The Declaration of Independence

The third American president, Thomas Jefferson (1743–1826) was born in Virginia, attended William and Mary College, and practiced law for several years. He entered local politics in 1769, was elected to the Continental Congress, and drafted the Declaration of Independence in 1776. After serving as Virginia's governor during the revolution, he became American minister to France and later Washington's secretary of state. His conflict with Alexander Hamilton contributed to the formation of separate political parties in America. Jefferson became vice-president of the United States in 1796 and president in 1801. During the first (and more successful) of his two terms, he engineered the Louisiana Purchase. Retiring to his estate, Monticello, in 1809, he died there on the fifteenth anniversary of American independence, July 4, 1826. Jefferson preferred the role of the philosopher to that of the politician, and the Declaration of Independence, which announced the thirteen colonies' break with England, was as much an essay on human rights as a political document. It is based upon the natural-rights theory of government, derived from eighteenth-century rationalism. The Declaration, written by Jefferson, was revised by Benjamin Franklin, John Adams, and the Continental Congress at large. The fifty-six colonial representatives signed it on August 2, 1776.

When in the course of human events, it becomes necessary 1 for one people to dissolve the political bands which have connected them with another, and to assume among the Powers of the earth, the separate and equal station to which the Laws of Nature and of Nature's God entitle them, a decent respect to the opinions of mankind requires that they should declare the causes which impel them to the separation.

We hold these truths to be self-evident, that all men are created   2
equal, that they are endowed by their Creator with certain unalienable Rights, that among these are Life, Liberty and the pursuit of Happiness. That to secure these rights, Governments are
instituted among Men, deriving their just powers from the consent
of the governed. That whenever any Form of Government becomes destructive of these ends, it is the Right of the People to
alter or to abolish it, and to institute new Government, laying its
foundation on such principles and organizing its powers in such
form, as to them shall seem most likely to effect their Safety and
Happiness. Prudence, indeed, will dictate that Governments long
established should not be changed for light and transient causes;
and accordingly all experience hath shown, that mankind are more
disposed to suffer, while evils are sufferable, than to right themselves by abolishing the forms to which they are accustomed. But
when a long train of abuses and usurpations pursuing invariably
the same Object evinces a design to reduce them under absolute
Despotism, it is their right, it is their duty, to throw off such government, and to provide new Guards for their future security.
Such has been the patient sufferance of these Colonies; and such
is now the necessity which constrains them to alter their former
Systems of Government. The history of the present King of Great
Britain [1] is a history of repeated injuries and usurpations, all having in direct object the establishment of absolute Tyranny over
these States. To prove this, let Facts be submitted to a candid
world.

He has refused his Assent to Laws, the most wholesome and   3
necessary for the public good.

He has forbidden his Governors to pass Laws of immediate and   4
pressing importance, unless suspended in their operation till his
Assent should be obtained; and when so suspended, he has utterly
neglected to attend to them.

He has refused to pass other Laws for the accommodation of   5
large districts of people, unless those people would relinquish the
right of Representation in the Legislature, a right inestimable to
them and formidable to tyrants only.

[1] George III (ruled 1761–1820).

He has called together legislative bodies at places unusual, uncomfortable, and distant from the depository of their Public Records, for the sole purpose of fatiguing them into compliance with his measures. 6

He has dissolved Representative Houses repeatedly, for opposing with manly firmness his invasions on the rights of the people. 7

He has refused for a long time, after such dissolutions, to cause others to be elected; whereby the Legislative Powers, incapable of Annihilation, have returned to the People at large for their exercise; the State remaining in the mean time exposed to all the dangers of invasion from without, and convulsions within. 8

He has endeavoured to prevent the population of these States; for that purpose obstructing the Laws of Naturalization of Foreigners; refusing to pass others to encourage their migration hither, and raising the conditions of new Appropriations of Lands. 9

He has obstructed the Administration of Justice, by refusing his Assent to Laws for establishing Judiciary Powers. 10

He has made Judges dependent on his Will alone, for the tenure of their offices, and the amount and payment of their salaries. 11

He has erected a multitude of New Offices, and sent hither swarms of Officers to harass our People, and eat out their substance. 12

He has kept among us, in time of peace, Standing Armies without the Consent of our Legislature. 13

He has affected to render the Military independent of and superior to the Civil Power. 14

He has combined with others to subject us to jurisdictions foreign to our constitution, and unacknowledged by our laws; giving us Assent to their acts of pretended Legislation: 15

For quartering large bodies of armed troops among us: 16

For protecting them, by a mock Trial, from Punishment for any Murders which they should commit on the Inhabitants of these States: 17

For cutting off our Trade with all parts of the world: 18

For imposing Taxes on us without our Consent: 19

For depriving us in many cases, of the benefits of Trial by Jury: 20

For transporting us beyond Seas to be tried for pretended offenses: 21

For abolishing the free System of English Laws in a Neighbouring Province, establishing therein an Arbitrary government, and enlarging its boundaries so as to render it at once an example and 22 fit instrument for introducing the same absolute rule into these Colonies:

For taking away our Charters, abolishing our most valuable 23 Laws, and altering fundamentally the Forms of our Governments:

For suspending our own Legislatures, and declaring themselves 24 invested with Power to legislate for us in all cases whatsoever.

He has abdicated Government here, by declaring us out of his 25 Protection and waging War against us.

He has plundered our seas, ravaged our Coasts, burnt our towns 26 and destroyed the Lives of our people.

He is at this time transporting large Armies of foreign Mer- 27 cenaries to complete the works of death, desolation and tyranny, already begun with circumstances of Cruelty & perfidy scarcely paralleled in the most barbarous ages, and totally unworthy the Head of a civilized nation.

He has constrained our fellow Citizens taken Captive on the 28 high Seas to bear Arms against their Colony, to become the exe- cutioners of their friends and Brethren, or to fall themselves by their Hands.

He has excited domestic insurrections amongst us, and has en- 29 deavoured to bring on the inhabitants of our frontiers, the merci- less Indian Savages, whose known rule of warfare, is an undistin- guished destruction of all ages, sexes and conditions.

In every stage of these Oppressions We have Petitioned for 30 Redress in the most humble terms: Our repeated petitions have been answered only by repeated injury. A Prince, whose character is thus marked by every act which may define a Tyrant, is unfit to be the ruler of a free People.

Nor have We been wanting in attention to our British brethren. 31 We have warned them from time to time of attempts by their legislature to extend an unwarrantable jurisdiction over us. We have reminded them of the circumstances of our emigration and settlement here. We have appealed to their native justice and magnanimity and we have conjured them by the ties of our com- mon kindred to disavow these usurpations, which would inevitably interrupt our connections and correspondence. They too have been deaf to the voice of justice and of consanguinity. We must, there- fore acquiesce in the necessity, which denounces our Separation, and hold them, as we hold the rest of mankind, Enemies in War, in Peace Friends.

We, therefore, the Representatives of the United States of ³²
America, in General Congress, Assembled, appealing to the Supreme Judge of the world for the rectitude of our intentions, do,
in the Name, and by Authority of the good People of these Colonies, solemnly publish and declare, That these United Colonies
are, and of Right ought to be Free and Independent States; that
they are Absolved from all Allegiance to the British Crown, and
that all political connection between them and the State of Great
Britain, is and ought to be totally dissolved; and that as Free and
Independent States, they have full power to levy War, conclude
Peace, contract Alliances, establish Commerce, and to do all other
Acts and Things which Independent States may of right do. And
for the support of this Declaration, with a firm reliance on the
protection of Divine Providence, we mutually pledge to each other
our lives, our Fortunes and our sacred Honor.

Q U E S T I O N S

Understanding

1. What is the purpose of government, according to Thomas
   Jefferson?
2. Where, in Jefferson's view, does a ruler get his authority?
3. "We hold these truths to be self-evident . . ." (par. 2). Another
   name for a self-evident "truth" granted at the beginning of an
   ARGUMENT is a *premise*. Briefly summarize the initial premises on
   which Jefferson's entire argument is built.
4. Which of Jefferson's premises is most crucial to his logic?
5. What is the ultimate conclusion of Jefferson's argument? Where
   is it stated?
6. Which of the many "injuries and usurpations" (par. 2) attributed
   by Jefferson to the British king seem most intolerable to you?
   Why?

Strategies and Structure

1. Jefferson gives the impression that the colonies are breaking away
   with extreme reluctance and only because of forces beyond any

colonist's personal power to overlook them. How does he create this impression?

2. What is the function of paragraph 31, which seems to be a digression from Jefferson's main line of argument?

3. A *hypothesis* is a theory or supposition to be tested by further proof. What is the hypothesis, introduced in paragraph 2, that Jefferson's long list of "Facts" is adduced to test?

4. Where is Jefferson's hypothesis restated (indirectly) as an established conclusion? Is the process of arriving at this conclusion basically INDUCTION (from examples to generalizations) or DEDUCTION (from premises to particular conclusions)?

5. Jefferson's conclusion to this line of argument might be restated simply as, "King George is a tyrant." We can take this conclusion as the *minor premise* of the underlying argument of the entire Declaration. If the *major premise* is "Tyrannical governments may be abolished by the People," what is the *conclusion* of that underlying argument?

6. Which sentence in paragraph 2 states Jefferson's major premise in so many words?

7. Is this underlying argument of the Declaration basically inductive or deductive? Explain your answer.

8. The signers of the Declaration of Independence wanted to appear as men of right reason, and they approved the logical form that Jefferson gave that document. Many of the specific issues their reason addressed, however, were highly emotional. What traces of strong feelings can you detect in Jefferson's wording of individual charges against the king?

9. The eighteenth-century is said to have admired and imitated "classical" balance and symmetry (as in the facade of Jefferson's Monticello). Does the form of the Declaration confirm or deny this observation? Explain your answer.

Words and Figures of Speech

1. Look up *unalienable* (or *inalienable*) in your dictionary. Considering that the Declaration was addressed, in part, to a "foreign" tyrant, why might Jefferson have chosen this adjective (par. 2) instead of, say, *natural, God-given,* or *fundamental*?

2. A *proposition* is a premise that is waiting to be approved. What single word signals us each time that Jefferson introduces a new proposition in his argument?

3. What is *consanguinity* (par. 31)? How may it be said to have a "voice"?

4. Look up *metonymy* under FIGURES OF SPEECH in the Glossary. What example of this figure can you find in paragraph 32?

5. For any of the following words you are not quite sure of, consult your dictionary: *transient* (par. 2), *usurpations* (2), *evinces* (2), *despotism* (2), *constrains* (2), *candid* (2), *abdicated* (25), *perfidy* (27), *redress* (30), *magnanimity* (31), *conjured* (31), *acquiesce* (31), *rectitude* (32).

Comparing

1. Like the Declaration of Independence, Chief Seattle's "Reply" (Chapter 10) is addressed to a "superior" head of state. Unlike Jefferson's, however, Chief Seattle's nation was toppling instead of rising. How does this difference in circumstances change the way the two speakers address their adversaries?

Discussion and Writing Topics

1. Compose a reply to Jefferson's charges by King George in defense of his actions and policies toward the colonies.

2. Jefferson lists "the pursuit of Happiness" (par. 2) as one of our basic rights. Construct an argument urging that this promise was unwise, that happiness cannot be guaranteed, and, therefore, that Americans have been set up for inevitable disappointment by the founding fathers. Your argument will have to anticipate the objection that the Declaration protects the *pursuit* of happiness, not happiness itself.

3. Some "loyalists" remained true to England at the time of the American Revolution. How might they have justified their "patriotism"?

William F. Buckley, Jr.

Capital Punishment

William F. Buckley, Jr., is a columnist, debater, conservative
politician, novelist, and sailor. One of ten children of a father
with oil interests in seven countries, he was born in New York
City in 1925 and lived in England and France for a time. He
studied at the University of Mexico and Yale (B.A., 1950). The
founder of the National Review *in 1955, Buckley ran as Conserva-*
tive party candidate for mayor of New York City in 1965, and
began the weekly television show, Firing Line, *in 1966. He writes*
three syndicated newspaper columns a week and contributes to,
among others, Esquire, Saturday Review, Harper's, Motor Boat-
ing, *and* Atlantic. *His books include* God and Man at Yale
(1951); Up from Liberalism *(1959);* Rumbles Right and Left
(1963); The Unmaking of a Mayor *(1966);* Cruising Speed
(1971); The United Nations Journal *(1975); and* Saving the
Queen *(a novel, 1976). "Capital Punishment" is one essay in the*
collection Execution Eve, and Other Contemporary Ballads
(1975).

There is national suspense over whether capital punishment   1
is about to be abolished, and the assumption is that when it
comes it will come from the Supreme Court. Meanwhile, (a)
the prestigious State Supreme Court of California has interrupted executions, giving constitutional reasons for doing so;
(b) the death wings are overflowing with convicted prisoners;
(c) executions are a remote memory; and—for the first time
in years—(d) the opinion polls show that there is sentiment
for what amounts to the restoration of capital punishment.

The case for abolition is popularly known. The other case   2
less so, and (without wholeheartedly endorsing it) I give it as

it was given recently to the Committee of the Judiciary of the House of Representatives by Professor Ernest van den Haag, under whose thinking cap groweth no moss. Mr. van den Haag, a professor of social philosophy at New York University, ambushed the most popular arguments of the abolitionists, taking no prisoners.

(1) The business about the poor and the black suffering excessively from capital punishment is no argument against capital punishment. It is an argument against the *administration* of justice, not against the penalty. Any punishment can be unfairly or unjustly applied. Go ahead and reform the processes by which capital punishment is inflicted, if you wish; but don't confuse maladministration with the merits of capital punishment.

(2) The argument that the death penalty is "unusual" is circular.[1] Capital punishment continues on the books of a majority of states, the people continue to sanction the concept of capital punishment, and indeed capital sentences are routinely handed down. What has made capital punishment "unusual" is that the courts and, primarily, governors have intervened in the process so as to collaborate in the frustration of the execution of the law. To argue that capital punishment is unusual, when in fact it has been made unusual by extra-legislative authority, is an argument to expedite, not eliminate, executions.

(3) Capital punishment is cruel. That is a historical judgment. But the Constitution suggests that what must be proscribed as cruel is (a) a particularly painful way of inflicting death, or (b) a particularly undeserved death; and the death penalty, as such, offends neither of these criteria and cannot therefore be regarded as objectively "cruel."

Viewed the other way, the question is whether capital punishment can be regarded as useful, and the question of deterrence arises.

(4) Those who believe that the death penalty does not intensify the disinclination to commit certain crimes need to wrestle with statistics that, in fact, it can't be proved that *any* punishment does that to any particular crime. One would rationally suppose that two years in jail would cut the commission of a crime if not exactly by 100 percent more than a penalty of one year in jail, at least that

---

[1] The Eighth Amendment to the U.S. Constitution (part of the Bill of Rights) forbids "cruel and unusual" punishment.

it would further discourage crime to a certain extent. The proof is unavailing. On the other hand, the statistics, although ambiguous, do not show either (a) that capital punishment net discourages; or (b) that capital punishment fails net to discourage. "The absence of proof for the additional deterrent effect of the death penalty must not be confused with the presence of proof for the absence of this effect."

The argument that most capital crimes are crimes of passion 8
committed by irrational persons is no argument against the death penalty, because it does not reveal how many crimes might, but for the death penalty, have been committed by rational persons who are now deterred.

And the clincher. (5) Since we do not know for certain whether 9
or not the death penalty adds deterrence, we have in effect the choice of two risks.

Risk One: If we execute convicted murderers without thereby 10
deterring prospective murderers beyond the deterrence that could have been achieved by life imprisonment, we may have vainly sacrificed the life of the convicted murderer.

Risk Two: If we fail to execute a convicted murderer whose 11
execution might have deterred an indefinite number of prospective murderers, our failure sacrifices an indefinite number of victims of future murderers.

"If we had certainty, we would not have risks. We do not have 12
certainty. If we have risks—and we do—better to risk the life of the convicted man than risk the life of an indefinite number of innocent victims who might survive if he were executed."

QUESTIONS

Understanding

1. If you have trouble keeping Buckley's ARGUMENT straight, make a list that states each proposition as briefly and simply as possible. How many items will be on your list?

2. What is the conclusion that Buckley's (and van den Haag's) entire argument is intended to prove?

3. What is the gist of Buckley's complicated reasoning in paragraph 7?

4. Paragraph 5 says it is a historical judgment to say that capital punishment is cruel. What does Buckley mean by a "historical" judgment? What alternate standard does he put forth?

5. Paragraph 5 of this essay can be restated as a syllogism with the following minor premise: "The death penalty is neither painful nor undeserved." What would be the conclusion of this syllogism? What would be the major premise?

6. When Buckley argues (par. 5) that only a "particularly undeserved death" is cruel, he assumes that some deaths are "deserved." What do you think of this unstated assumption?

7. Granted that Buckley's argument is *logical*, how might your reaction to his assumption about "deserved" deaths influence whether or not you grant the *truth* of Buckley's entire argument?

Strategies and Structure

1. What do Buckley's numbers in parentheses refer to? Do you find them an effective organizing device? Why or why not? How have we been prepared for them by paragraph 1?

2. Why do you think Buckley mentions public opinion polls in the first paragraph even though he does not refer to them again in the essay?

3. Buckley gives the case against abolishing the death penalty "without wholeheartedly endorsing it" (par. 2). Is this a legitimate strategy? Why or why not?

4. Buckley is making the case against abolition; where does he first address the case *for* it? What do you make of the *length* of his treatment?

5. In paragraph 4 Buckley writes that the argument condemning the death penalty as unusual is "circular." What is a circular argument? What is logically wrong with one?

6. Where does Buckley begin the part of his argument dealing with deterrence? How does his fifth proposition (in pars. 9–12) bear upon this argument?

7. This essay ends abruptly—with a quotation from Professor van den Haag's testimony instead of a summarizing statement by the

author of the essay. Why might Buckley want to end with another writer's words (and conclusion)?

8. Buckley's argument is really a counterargument that proceeds by addressing propositions already raised by others. Is this a legitimate tactic of debate? Explain your answer.

9. The great eighteenth-century man of reason, Samuel Johnson, once observed: "It is always easy to be on the negative. If a man were now to deny that there is salt upon the table you could not reduce him to an absurdity." How might Dr. Johnson's observation about negative reasoning be applied to Buckley's argument concerning deterrence?

10. How might Buckley turn Dr. Johnson's observation back on those who argue that the statistics do not prove the deterrent value of capital punishment?

11. In that part of paragraph 7 where he deals with statistics, is Buckley's method of reasoning basically INDUCTIVE (from particulars to generalizations) or DEDUCTIVE (from premises to conclusions)? In paragraphs 9–12?

Words and Figures of Speech

1. Professor van den Haag, Buckley tells us, "ambushed the most popular arguments of the abolitionists, taking no prisoners." How does this METAPHOR, particularly the word *ambushed*, reflect Buckley's mixed feelings toward what he is reporting?

2. When he says that no moss "groweth" under van den Haag's thinking cap, Buckley is purposely concocting an absurdity. Why might he want to do so, especially this early in his essay?

3. The phrase "does not intensify the disinclination" seems wordy and stilted. How might it be justified in its touchy context, nevertheless?

4. Describe the effect of Buckley's use of the word *indefinite* when he explains "Risk Two" (par. 11). How *low* might the number conceivably be?

Comparing

1. The bulk of Jefferson's reasoning in the Declaration of Independence is inductive; what about Buckley's? Does he reason most of the time by induction or deduction? Explain your answer.

2. Buckley is often called a "conservative," and the term could be applied with equal justice to Johnson C. Montgomery's position in the next essay, "The Island of Plenty." Judging from these two essays, how would you define a "conservative"?

3. Buckley's primary weapon is logic. What does Jonathan Swift say about the limits of this method of thinking in "A Modest Proposal" ("Essays For Further Reading")?

Discussion and Writing Topics

1. From Buckley's counterarguments, reconstruct the positive case for, and argue in favor of, abolishing capital punishment.

2. Make up your own positive argument *against* abolishing the death penalty.

3. Should the U.S. Constitution and other laws ultimately determine what is a "deserved" death and a "cruel" punishment, or are such questions beyond the scope of the law? Give your opinion in the form of a coherent logical argument.

4. What is the difference between a social philosopher and a sociologist?

5. The field of the social philosopher (as of all philosophers) is one of the "humanities." Do you find it at all strange that a philosopher should argue in favor of capital punishment? How could van den Haag's argument be interpreted, in the long run, as a "humanistic" argument?

Johnson C. Montgomery

The Island of Plenty

Johnson C. Montgomery was a California attorney and an early member of the Zero Population Growth organization. Born in 1934, Montgomery attended Harvard University and the Stanford University Law School; he was admitted to the California bar in 1960. "The Island of Plenty," in his own words, is an "elitist" argument in favor of American social isolationism. Until we have enough food to feed ourselves, he says, we owe it to future generations not to share our material resources with other countries of the world.

The United States should remain an island of plenty in a sea   1
of hunger. The future of mankind is at stake. We are not responsible for the rest of humanity. We should not accept responsibility for all humanity. We owe more to the hundreds of billions of *Homo futurans* than we do to the hungry millions—soon to be billions—of our own generation.

Ample food and resources exist to nourish man and all   2
other creatures indefinitely into the future. This planet is indeed an Eden—to date our only Eden. Admittedly our Eden is plagued by pollution. Some of us have polluted the planet by reproducing too many of us. Too many people have made excessive demands on the long-range carrying capacity of our garden; and during the last 200 years there has been dramatic, ever-increasing destruction of the web of life on earth. If we try to save the starving millions today, we will simply destroy what's left of Eden.

The problem is not that there is too little food. The problem   3
is there are too many people—many too many. It is not that the
children should never have been born. It is simply that we have
mindlessly tried to cram too many of us into too short a time
span. Four billion humans are fine—but they should have been
spread over several hundred years.

But the billions are already here. What should we do about   4
them? Should we send food, knowing that each child saved in
Southeast Asia, India or Africa will probably live to reproduce and
thereby bring more people into the world to live even more miserably? Should we eat the last tuna fish, the last ear of corn and
utterly destroy the garden? That is what we have been doing for a
long time and all the misguided efforts have merely increased the
number who go to bed hungry each night. There have never been
more miserable, deprived people in the world than there are right
now.

It was obvious even in the late 1950s that the famine the world   5
now faces was coming unless people immediately began exercising
responsibility for reducing population levels. It was also obvious
that too many people contributed to the risk of nuclear war, global
pestilence, illiteracy and even to many problems that are usually
classified as purely economic. For example, unemployment is having too many people for the available jobs. Inflation is in part the
result of too much demand from too many people. But in the
1950s, population control was taboo and those who warned of
impending disasters received a cool reception.

By the time Zero Population Growth, Inc., was formed, those of   6
us who wanted to do something useful decided to concentrate our
initial efforts on our own families and friends and then on the
white American middle and upper classes. Our belief was that by
setting an example, we could later insist that others pay attention
to our proposals.

I think I was the first in the original ZPG group to have had a   7
vasectomy. Nancy and I had two children—each doing superbly
well and each getting all the advantages of the best nutrition,
education, attention, love and other resources available. I think
Paul Ehrlich [1] (one child) was the next. Now don't ask me to

---

[1] Biology professor at Stanford, founder and past-president of Zero Population
Growth.

cut my children back to the same number of calories that children from large families eat. In fact, don't ask me to cut my children back on anything. I won't do it without a fight; and in today's world, power is in knowledge, not numbers. Nancy and I made a conscious decision to limit the number of our children so each child could have a larger share of whatever we could make available. We intend to keep the best for them.

The future of mankind is indeed with the children. But it is with the nourished, educated and loved children. It is not with the starving, uneducated and ignored. This is of course a highly elitist point of view. But that doesn't make the view incorrect. As a matter of fact, the lowest reproductive rate in the nation is that of one of the most elite groups in the world—black, female Ph.D.'s. They had to be smart and effective to make it. Having made it, they are smart enough not to wreck it with too many kids.   8

We in the United States have made great progress in lowering our birth rates. But now, because we have been responsible, it seems to some that we have a great surplus. There is, indeed, waste that should be eliminated, but there is not as much fat in our system as most people think. Yet we are being asked to share our resources with the hungry peoples of the world. But why should we share? The nations having the greatest needs are those that have been the least responsible in cutting down on births. Famine is one of nature's ways of telling profligate peoples that they have been irresponsible in their breeding habits.   9

Naturally, we would like to help; and if we could, perhaps we should. But we can't be of any use in the long run—particularly if we weaken ourselves.   10

Until we have at least a couple of years' supply of food and other resources on hand to take care of our own people and until those asking for handouts are doing at least as well as we are at reducing existing excessive population-growth rates, we should not give away our resources—not so much as one bushel of wheat. Certainly we should not participate in any programs that will increase the burden that mankind is already placing on the earth. We should not deplete our own soils to save those who will only die equally miserably a decade or so down the line—and in many cases only after reproducing more children who are inevitably doomed to live and die in misery.   11

We know the world is finite. There is only so much pie. We
may be able to expand the pie, but at any point in time, the pie
is finite. How big a piece each person gets depends in part on how
many people there are. At least for the foreseeable future, the
fewer of us there are, the more there will be for each. That is
true on a family, community, state, national and global basis.

At the moment, the future of mankind seems to depend on our
maintaining the island of plenty in a sea of deprivation. If everyone shared equally, we would all be suffering from protein-defi-
ciency brain damage—and that would probably be true even if we
ate every last animal on earth.

As compassionate human beings, we grieve for the condition of
mankind. But our grief must not interfere with our perception of
reality and our planning for a better future for those who will
come after us. Someone must protect the material and intellectual
seed grain for the future. It seems to me that that someone is the
U.S. We owe it to our children—and to their children's children's
children's children.

These conclusions will be attacked, as they have been within
Zero Population Growth, as simplistic and inhumane. But truth
is often very simple and reality often inhumane.

QUESTIONS

Understanding

1. What is Montgomery's main proposition in this essay? In which
   two paragraphs is it stated most directly?
2. What other general propositions does he put forth in support of
   his main proposition?
3. In paragraph 4, what is the last sentence (about the number of
   miserable people in the world) intended to prove?
4. Montgomery warns us not to "ask me to cut my children back on
   anything" (par. 7). How is this position consistent with what he
   says about the planet's not having enough to go around?

Strategies and Structure

1. The logic of Montgomery's basic ARGUMENT can be represented by a syllogism. *Major premise:* To provide undamaged human stock for the future, some people must remain healthy. *Minor premise:* All will suffer if all share equally in the world's limited bounty. *Conclusion:* Some must not share what they have. How sound is this logic? Will you grant Montgomery's premises? Why or why not?

2. Montgomery's hard-headed realism would show us the "truth" (par. 15) of the human condition; but it would also move us to action. What would Montgomery have us do?

3. Logic is only part of Montgomery's persuasive arsenal. Which paragraphs in his essay appeal more to emotion and ethics than to logic?

4. Montgomery seems to be speaking from authority. Where does he get his authority, and how much weight should it carry?

5. Montgomery admits that his position is "elitist" (par. 8). How does he head off the charge that it is racist?

6. Is Montgomery's last paragraph necessary? Why or why not?

7. Are you persuaded by Montgomery's essay? Why or why not?

Words and Figures of Speech

1. How does the METAPHOR of the island contribute to Montgomery's argument? Is there any IRONY in his title?

2. For the sake of the future, says Montgomery, we must save some "material and intellectual seed grain" (par. 14). Explain this metaphor: What is being compared to what? Why is the metaphor appropriate?

3. How is Montgomery altering the traditional definition of Eden? Is he rejecting the traditional idea altogether? Explain your answer.

4. *Homo futurans* (par. 1), meaning "man of the future," is modeled after such scientific terms as *Homo erectus* ("upright man") and *Homo sapiens* ("thinking man"). Why might Montgomery choose to use the language of science at the beginning of his argument?

5. How does Montgomery's use of the word *mindlessly* (par. 3) fit in with his entire argument?

6. What is the meaning of *profligate* (par. 9)?

Comparing

1. By comparison with William F. Buckley's "Capital Punishment," does "The Island of Plenty" seem more concerned with analyzing a condition or with persuading the reader to act? Explain.

2. Opponents of Montgomery's argument might charge that he has written "a modest proposal." What would they mean by this? Would they be justified? (See Jonathan Swift's "A Modest Proposal" in "Essays For Further Reading.")

Discussion and Writing Topics

1. Attack Montgomery's position on the grounds that he is confusing compassion with weakness.

2. Defend Montgomery's assertion that "there is not as much fat in our system as most people think" (par. 9).

3. Write your own "modest proposal" (for feeding the world, curing inflation, regulating human breeding habits, or some other "simple" task).

WRITING TOPICS for Chapter Nine
Essays That Appeal to Reason

Write a logical argument defending one of the following propositions:

1. Buying a house, condominium, or trailer makes (does not make) better sense in the long run than renting one

2. Grading standards are (are not) slipping in American colleges and universities

3. College students are (are not) as bright now as they used to be

4. College graduates get (do not get) better jobs than those who do not go to college

5. Graduate or professional school is (is not) worth the expense these days

6. Smoking is (is not) hazardous to your health

7. America has (has not) developed into a "welfare state"

8. Farm-life is (is not) a dying institution in America

9. Cities are (are not) dying in America

10. Women's liberation has (has not) produced desirable results

11. The "revolution" in sexual morality is (is not) a myth

12. Religion is (is not) reviving in America

13. Pollution is (is not) avoidable

14. Our society has (has not) curtailed racism

10

Essays That Appeal to Emotion and Ethics

PERSUASION,[1] we have said, is the strategic use of language to move an audience to action or belief. It works by appealing to our reason through logical ARGUMENT (the MODE OF PERSUASION discussed in Chapter 9). It also works by appealing to our emotions and to our sense of ethics.

The APPEAL TO EMOTION is nicely exemplified in "Being Prepared in Suburbia," the first essay in this chapter. Writing about gun-control legislation, Roger Verhulst deliberately sets aside reason and logic. He could produce statistics to show how many deaths will soon be caused by privately owned firearms, says Verhulst; but he finds "no point in citing those statistics again; they may prove something, but they're not likely to prompt any concrete action. There is nothing moving about statistics."

Here is the essence of the emotional appeal. It assumes, in Verhulst's words, that "what is needed to produce results is passion"; it aims at "the gut." Even if his own passion has cooled in the process of writing it down—and what passion can flare through several rewritings?—the author of an emotional appeal must kindle his original feelings in the reader. He cannot do this, however, simply by being emotional.

It is a fallacy to think that you can appeal to an emotion in your reader by imitating it: hysteria by being hysterical, anger by raging. Often the best measure is to appear calm, detached, thoroughly in control of your feelings—now. However intensely felt, your testimony must be orderly, or at least coherent. You may want to recreate the circumstances or perception that first excited in you the emotions that you

[1] Terms printed in all capitals are defined in the Glossary.

want to excite in your readers, but here again your narrative must be controlled and directed toward its desired effect. Even your choice of individual words cannot be haphazard; you must pay close attention to their CONNOTATIONS. If you are addressing a labor union, for example, it will make a great difference whether you refer to the members as drones, workers, comrades, or just people.

The APPEAL TO ETHICS is an appeal to the reader's sense of how people ought to behave. This mode of persuasion convinces the reader that it is written by a person of good character whose judgment should be heeded. We are moved by the force of the speaker's personality.

Because the author's personality is so important in an appeal to ethics, great care must be taken to measure his or her tone of voice. TONE is an author's revealed attitude toward the material; it conveys his or her temper. A writer can be a decent human being and may have the reader's best interests at heart; but the reader may not trust the writer if the tone clashes with the message. Sincerity is the soul of the ethical appeal, and a writer must take pains to appear trustworthy as well as to be so.

To appear trustworthy, the writer must seem to be not only a person of good character and even temper but also a person who is well-informed. When noted attorney F. Lee Bailey tells us to "watch out for trial lawyers" because too many are competent only in the research library, we tend to believe him. Bailey's own expertise in the courtroom makes him an expert witness. The appeal of the expert witness, in fact, is one of the most common modern forms of the appeal to ethics. We are won over not by the moral uprightness of the expert but by his or her knowledge and intellectual integrity.

For study purposes, the appeals to emotion and to ethics have been separated here from the appeal to reason and from each other. (The first two essays in this chapter appeal to emotions; the last two appeal to ethics.) In practice you may want to combine all three modes of persuasion in the same essay (as we sometimes combine the four MODES OF DISCOURSE). The goal of persuasive writing is to bring others around to your way of thinking in a good cause. Any honest means to this end is sound RHETORIC.

Roger Verhulst

Being Prepared in Suburbia

Roger Verhulst lives with his wife and two sons in Grand Rapids,
Michigan, where he writes about books and games. A former sup-
porter of gun-control legislation, he recently became the co-leader
of a Cub Scout den and acquired his first gun, a Crossman 760,
because the scouts wanted target practice. "Being Prepared in
Suburbia" testifies to a conversion, of sorts, that followed. Verhulst
found, he says, that the owners of guns have an irrational attach-
ment to their weapons that is stronger than the rational arguments against owning deadly firearms. In an essay analyzing the
emotion it arouses, Verhulst would persuade us that gun control
is as dead as the victims of uncontrolled guns.

Gun legislation is dead for another year. As a result, if sta-   1
tistics are any guide, there's every likelihood that a lot of people now living will also be dead before the year is over.

There's no point in citing those statistics again; they may   2
prove something, but they're not likely to prompt any concrete action. There is nothing very moving about statistics.

What is needed to produce results is passion—and that's   3
where the antigun-control lobby has it all over the rest of
us. Those who favor stronger gun legislation—a solid majority
of Americans—can't hold a candle to the lovers of guns when
it comes to zeal.

I had a taste of that passion recently, and I begin to under-   4
stand something of what it is that fosters in gun libbers such
dedicated resolve. Thanks to a bunch of Cub Scouts and an
absurd little creature that went bump in the night, I've begun
to realize why cold, unemotional tabulations of gun deaths will

never lead to effective gun control. It's because of what can happen to people—even sane, rational, firearm-hating people like me—when they get their hands on a genuine, authentic, real-life gun.

Until last fall, I had never owned any weapon more lethal than   5
a water pistol. I opposed guns as esthetically repugnant, noisy, essentially churlish devices whose only practical purpose was to blast holes of various sizes in entities that would thereby be rendered less functional than they would otherwise have been. I didn't object merely to guns that killed people; I also objected to guns that killed animals, or shattered windows, or plinked away at discarded beer bottles. Whenever a gun was put to effective use, I insisted, something broke; and it seemed absurd to go through life breaking things.

With arguments such as these, bolstered by assorted threats, I   6
tried to instill holey terror also in my sons. Initially, I imposed an absolute ban on even toy guns. When that didn't work—their determination to possess such toys exceeding by scores of decibels my determination to ban them—I tried substituting lectures on the merits of nonviolence and universal love. Nice try.

Then, last fall, I became co-leader of a Cub Scout den here in   7
Grand Rapids, Mich., consisting of half a dozen 9-, 10- and 11-year-old boys. Sharing the leadership responsibilities with me was a kind and gentle man named Mickey Shea, who happens to be extremely fond of outdoor activities—including, of course, hunting.

It was in Mickey's basement, in full view of an imposing gun   8
rack, that I yielded to the pressure of pleading Cubbers and agreed to add target shooting to our scheduled activities. (Though I should make it clear that it wasn't Mickey who forced, or even strongly urged, that agreement; it was rather a wish to be accepted by the boys—to be regarded as appropriately adult and masculine —that prompted my decision. I've no one to blame but myself.)

So, for the sake of my kids and under the auspices of the Boy   9
Scouts of America, I bought a gun—a Crossman Power Master 760 BB Repeater pump gun, with bolt action, adjustable sight and a satisfying heft. It was capable of putting holes in all sorts of things.

A few nights later we got the Cubs together and spent an hour   10
or two aiming and firing at targets taped to paper-filled cardboard cartons. After which I unloaded the gun and locked it in my study, intending to leave it there until future target shoots came along

to justify bringing it out again. But a roving opossum that took up residence in our garage for a few cold nights in January undermined my good intentions.

We were entertained, at first. We called the kids down to see [11] our visitor perched on the edge of the trash barrel; we recorded the event on film. We regarded the presence of authentic wild animals in our corner of suburbia as delightfully diverting.

Almost at once, however, the rat-faced prowler began to make [12] himself obnoxious. There was the midnight clatter of falling objects, and the morning-after disarray of strewn garbage. The possum, we decided, would have to go.

But he proved to be not only an unwelcome but also a recal- [13] citrant guest. It was cold outside, and rather than waddling willingly back through the open garage door he took refuge behind a pile of scrap lumber; my vigorous thrusts with a broomstick were parried by obstinacy, and an occasional grunt.

I was cold, too, by now; and tired; and becoming frustrated. [14] Drastic action was indicated; I poured a handful of BB's into the Crossman 760, pumped it up, pointed the barrel blindly into the woodpile and pulled the trigger.

Nothing happened. The opossum did not move. Shivering, I [15] went back inside the house, still holding my weapon. I sat down with a drink and a cigarette to warm up.

With little else to do, I put the gun to my shoulder and aimed [16] it idly at the clock above the fireplace; I aimed it at a light fixture across the room, pressing gently against the trigger; I aimed it at a row of glasses behind the bar, imagining the snap and shatter of breaking glass; I aimed it at my own reflection in the TV set, thinking how absurdly easy it would be to eliminate television from my life.

The more imaginary targets I selected, the stronger became the [17] urge to shoot—something, anything. The gun extended my potential range of influence to everyone within sight; I could alter the world around me without even moving from the couch, simply by pulling the trigger. Gun in hand, I was bravely prepared to defend myself against any intruder, man or beast. I felt omnipotent as Zeus,[1] with lightning bolts at my fingertips.

No wonder, I thought, that people become hooked on guns. [18]

---

[1] Ruler of the Greek gods; lightning was his special weapon.

This is the feeling that explains their passion, their religious fervor, their refusal to yield. It's rooted in the gut, not in the head. And in the recurrent struggle over gun legislation it is no wonder that their stamina exceeds mine.

I can understand that passion because I've felt it in my own   19
gut. I've felt the gun in my hand punch psychic holes in my intellectual convictions. And having felt all that, I do not have much hope that private ownership of deadly weapons will be at all regulated or controlled in the foreseeable future.

QUESTIONS

Understanding

1. According to Verhulst, what is the appeal of guns to those who own them? In which paragraph does he explain that appeal most explicitly?

2. Verhulst thinks that gun-control legislation is doomed. Why? What is his main reason?

3. Verhulst says that he yielded to the scouts' demand for target practice because he wished "to be accepted by the boys—to be regarded as appropriately adult and masculine" (par. 8). How far does this motive go toward explaining why some men like guns? How "sane" is it?

4. Why do you think Verhulst takes pains to point out that he came into contact with guns through the Cub Scouts?

5. In paragraph 19, Verhulst says that his gun opened "psychic holes" in his resolve. Which earlier paragraphs of his essay does this statement hark back to? How? With what unexpected twist has Verhulst's original theory about guns been confirmed?

6. Why is Verhulst's subject especially suited to an appeal to emotion?

Strategies and Structure

1. Verhulst writes as a "convert," an opponent of free guns who has come reluctantly to understand the appeal of firearms. Would his prediction about the failure of gun control be more or less con-

vincing if he were speaking as a long-time gun enthusiast? Explain your answer.

2. By telling the story of the author's conversion, this essay uses NARRATION to help achieve its persuasive purpose. Where does the narration begin? Where does it end? How compelling do you find Verhulst's narrative? Why?

3. As a general rule, do you think narration is more likely to be found in an APPEAL TO REASON or an APPEAL TO EMOTION? Why?

4. What is the strategy of Verhulst's first and second paragraphs? How successful is it?

5. Verhulst says that his sons' demand for toy guns exceeded "by scores of decibels" (par. 6) his resistance. What is the TONE of this remark? Of "Nice try" in the same paragraph? Describe Verhulst's TONE throughout the essay.

6. Why does Verhulst make himself look foolish, even mean, in the encounter with the "possum"?

7. How do the length and rhythm of the single sentence in paragraph 16 capture the author's state of mind at that point in his essay?

8. Far from assuming that a writer stirs emotion simply by being emotional, Verhulst comes across as remarkably cool-headed. How does he create this impression?

9. Whom do you take to be Verhulst's audience? In which paragraph does he, in effect, define it? Why is his cool-headed approach a good one for this audience?

10. When do you think a writer is better advised to be emotional (not just to describe emotions and appeal to them in the reader)—when he is addressing an audience that essentially agrees with him or one that disagrees? Why?

Words and Figures of Speech

1. Why does Verhulst use the word *hooked* in paragraph 18? What are the CONNOTATIONS of the term?

2. "Holey terror" (par. 6) and "delightfully diverting" (par. 11) represent two different LEVELS OF DICTION. Define the two levels and point out other examples of each. Why do you think Verhulst mixes the two?

3. *Psychic* (par. 19) has two basic meanings. What are they? Which one is intended here?

4. Look up the following words in your dictionary: *churlish* (par. 5), *decibels* (6), *auspices* (9), *obnoxious* (12), *recalcitrant* (13), *obstinacy* (13), *frustrated* (14), *omnipotent* (17), *fervor* (18).

Comparing

1. Compare and contrast "Being Prepared in Suburbia" with William F. Buckley's "Capital Punishment" (Chapter 9) as representative examples of two different MODES OF PERSUASION: the appeal to reason and the appeal to emotion, respectively.

2. Discuss both Verhulst's essay and Reynolds Price's "Summer Games" (Chapter 5) as commentaries on human irrationality.

Discussion and Writing Topics

1. Write a persuasive essay in favor of gun-control legislation that appeals to emotion and that argues that guns are "esthetically repugnant, noisy, essentially churlish devices" (par. 5).

2. Construct a persuasive rational argument *against* gun-control legislation, the sort of argument, though on the opposite side, that Verhulst declines to make at the start of his essay.

3. If Verhulst's experience is at all typical, under what circumstances do our irrational impulses come forth? Are they any less real for being irrational? Why or why not?

Edward Abbey

The Great Globe Arizona
Wild Pig and Varmint Hunt

Born in Home, Pennsylvania, in 1927, Edward Abbey is a former forest ranger and fire lookout who now lives in Arizona. After serving in the army, he attended the University of New Mexico (M.A., 1956) and the University of Edinburgh, Scotland. From 1956 until 1971, he was a member of the National Park Service stationed in the Southwest. He has written Jonathan Troy *(1956);* The Brave Cowboy *(1958);* Fire on the Mountain *(1962);* Desert Solitaire *(1968);* Appalachia *(with Eliot Porter, 1970);* Black Sun *(1971); and* Slickrock *(with Philip Hyde, 1971). "The Great Globe Arizona Wild Pig and Varmint Hunt" is an essay from Abbey's latest book,* The Journey Home: Some Words in Defense of the American West *(1977). It is the gentle manifesto of a conservationist.*

I have lived half my life in a state called Arizona, which means "arid zone." It also means Mississippi of the West. A popular local slogan, often seen on bumper stickers, is Keep Arizona Medieval. Some members of the state legislature here once proposed to send a committee to New York to investigate the United Nations. Ours is the only state in the Union that sends Barry Goldwater to the U.S. Senate. Quaintness is a strong point. Despite the infernal summers, the kissing bugs and scorpions, the lung fungus, and the mushroom cities, Arizona is still a pretty good place to live. I like it here. Part of it, part of the time. At any rate we still have the flashiest sunsets in the Western world, when you can see them through the belts of smelter smog.

One of Arizona's most important smog producers is a mine and   2
mill town called Globe. Globe, population about 10,000, lies deep
in the rocky hills east of Phoenix, not far from the Superstition
Mountains. This is good desert country, of the lower Sonoran
zone,[1] rich in giant cactus, such as the saguaro, and unusual wildlife, such as the javelina. It is the javelina, together with certain
other small mammals—the coyote, the bobcat, and the fox—which
is innocently responsible for a controversy often swirling through
the pages of Arizona newspapers.

For fifteen years the Globe Chamber of Commerce has been   3
sponsoring an annual event called the Javelina Derby. Each year
prizes are awarded to the sportsmen who bring in the first dead
javelina and the heaviest dead javelina, with separate categories
of prizes for in-state and out-of-state hunters, for bow hunters and
gun hunters.

One of the questions raised by this affair is why anyone would   4
want to kill a javelina. The javelina, also known as peccary, is a
small piglike animal that never weighs over fifty pounds. Almost
half the bulk of this creature is taken up by the head, so that it
looks like a caricature of a pig, as a child might draw one. The
javelina subsists chiefly on the pads, fruit, and roots of prickly pear
and barrel cactus and in higher desert terrain on the acorns of
scrub oak. It does not compete, therefore, with cattle or deer.
Being mostly bone, bristle, gristle, and hoof, the javelina is not
generally considered desirable eating. The javelina comes with
teeth and tusks but is harmless to humans, unless you should
happen to corner one in a telephone booth. I have several times
strolled into herds of these delightful little animals; their only
reaction is to panic in all directions.

Why then should anyone wish to shoot a javelina? The only   5
answer seems to be, because it's there. Or was there. The javelina,
which used to roam the southwestern deserts in great number,
has now been reduced by hunting and loss of habitat to a few
small scattered bands in isolated or protected areas in southern
Arizona. Nevertheless, it is still classified as a game animal by the
Arizona Game and Fish Department.

---

[1] In Arizona and New Mexico, the plant and animal life zone below an alti-
tude of about 3,000 feet.

This is more protection than the mountain lion, bobcat or fox [6] gets in our state. All these predators must be considered rare in the Southwest and possibly in danger of extinction. All but the mountain lion are regarded as varmints, without protection. Although the mountain lion was recently given big-game status in Arizona, it may still be trapped or hunted at any time by any rancher who claims he is losing livestock to lions. On this basis alone twenty-four lions were trapped and killed in one county in Arizona in 1972. At that rate of loss, the lion will not last long as a species.

Perhaps because the javelina, like the carnivores, is becoming [7] hard to find, the Globe Chamber of Commerce decided to combine the annual Javelina Derby with a predator hunt, in that way giving sport hunters something extra to compete for. The competition is based on a point system: five points for a bobcat, three for coyote, and two for fox. (Zero for hunter.) To receive points for a predator kill the hunter must bring in both ears of the animal, held together by skin. There is no limit on the number of these predators a sportsman may kill. Nor any limitation on hunting methods: It is considered sporting, for example, to use "varmint callers" to lure an animal within easy shooting range.

Why does the Globe Chamber of Commerce desire to kill coy- [8] otes, bobcats and foxes? The justification offered by Mrs. Donna Anderson, manager of that organization, is that these animals prey on domestic livestock to such an extent that they inflict serious financial losses on local cattlemen. One rancher in the area, Mr. Jimmy Griffin, claims to have lost $10,000 worth of cattle to predators (including mountain lions) in 1972. The Arizona Cattle Growers' Association claims total losses of over $500,000 statewide in 1972. The biggest villain in the picture, to the stockman's way of thinking, is the coyote, which is supposed to have killed 1,636 sheep and 1,539 calves. The lion is second. Even the bobcat, an animal not much larger than a domestic housecat, weighing from fifteen to thirty-five pounds, is accused of killing seven calves. How is this possible? A bobcat, some ranchers say, will attack a newborn calf when the mother cow is still too weak to defend her young. What's the evidence? Bobcat tracks in the vicinity of a dead calf.

The evidence against the other predators is similar. A dead calf [9] is found, body mangled or half-devoured and the remains scattered about. On the ground nearby, inevitably, appear the tracks of the omnivorous coyote, sometimes the tracks of a cat or fox. Was the calf killed by a predator or did it die of disease, exhaustion, starvation, or weed poisoning? Even an expert pathologist would find it impossible to determine the answer with any certainty. In the Southwest, which has been severely overgrazed for a century, and in most areas is still being overgrazed, the most common cause of death to domestic livestock is malnutrition and the diseases attendant upon malnutrition. The dead or dying animal attracts whatever predatory animals, such as coyote or lion or bear, may be lurking in the vicinity.

This does not mean that predators are innocent of causing losses   10 to the livestock industry. When you find a cow with its skull bashed in and bear tracks over the carcass there can be little doubt who did it. Nor can there be doubt that coyotes and mountain lions (and loose dogs) actually do destroy some number of livestock each year. But how many? No one knows.

The predator hunt at Globe has caused trouble in this state be-   11 cause many wildlife defenders are upset at having bobcat and fox among the victims. The fox, which in Arizona means the gray fox, is an animal even smaller than the bobcat, with an average weight of ten to eighteen pounds. Like the coyote, the fox and bobcat feed mainly on hares, rabbits and rodents and could be considered beneficial to the livestock industry. How beneficial in dollars? No one knows.

Perhaps the economic aspect of the argument will never be   12 settled to the satisfaction of all contenders. But conservationists in Arizona raise a further point: Wildlife, if it is the property of anyone, belongs to all. Sportsmen and ranchers, both of whom depend chiefly on use of the public lands for their activity, are making private use of a natural resource—wildlife—which should be public property, to be enjoyed by the public.

The Globe Chamber of Commerce may have stirred up more   13 publicity by this combined Javelina Derby and Predator Hunt than it really wants—or needs. Even staunch defenders of sport hunting, like columnist Bill Quimby of the Tucson *Daily Citizen*, have attacked the Globe event on the grounds that hunting contests bring out the worst in sportsmen and give sport hunting a bad reputation. Such an affair attracts the attention of fanatics on both sides of the wildlife-and-predator controversy and adds further passions to an already adequate supply of misunderstanding. When I interviewed her in Globe, Mrs. Anderson showed me a sheaf of letters, one of them written in red ink (simulating blood?), all of them attacking her or the hunt or the Globe Chamber of Commerce. But she took comfort, she said, in the fact that at least nobody in Globe itself objected to the hunt. That was Monday.

On Wednesday, a group was formed in Globe calling itself [14] Christian Citizens for Humane Treatment of Animals. They are now distributing free bumper stickers with the slogan, Javelinas Need Love Too.

QUESTIONS

Understanding

1. What is the point of Abbey's ARGUMENT? What is he trying to convince his readers to believe and do?

2. What is the gist of Abbey's argument in paragraph 12? In paragraph 13? Which argument is more clearly an APPEAL TO EMOTION? Why do you think so?

3. Why does Abbey pay so much attention to the different weights of the "predators" in the Globe hunt?

4. What interests and values does the javelina represent in Abbey's essay? Why is it important to his argument that the javelina be harmless?

5. How does the example of the bear (par. 10) support Abbey's argument?

6. What is the only concrete answer that the Globe Chamber of Commerce and the ranchers give to Abbey's repeated questions? How does he combat their response?

7. Abbey's essay is an appeal for conservation, but it is also an appeal for *tolerance*. How does this aspect of his appeal come out in his opening description of Arizona? In the last paragraph of the essay?

Strategies and Structure

1. Why do you think Abbey begins his essay by saying, "I like it here" (par. 1)?

2. What is the effect of Abbey's repeated use of the phrase, "No one knows"? What connection do you see between this repeated answer and the answer to Abbey's repeated question about who wants to kill a javelina or a bobcat or a fox?

3. Which sentence in paragraph 5 provides a TRANSITION from the discussion of the javelina's harmlessness to the discussion of its extinction? Which sentence serves a similar function in paragraph 13? Point out several other transition sentences in Abbey's essay that strike you as particularly effective.

4. How does Abbey show that he can keep his sense of humor despite his strong feelings about the Globe hunt? Point to specific passages.

5. Why does Abbey refer to columnist Bill Quimby of the Tucson *Daily Citizen*? In what sense is Quimby an expert witness?

6. How does Abbey's conclusion suggest that this has been an appeal to emotion despite his earlier concern with logic and evidence? How does his conclusion recall the opening paragraph of the essay?

7. Not only Abbey's but a number of essays in this book end by harking back to their beginnings. Why is this a satisfying device?

8. In his appeal for tolerance, Abbey sets the example by appearing tolerant himself (although he never accepts the ranchers' argument for a moment). How does he create this appearance? Refer to specific passages and incidents.

9. In what ways can the author of any persuasive essay best show his or her tolerance and balance? Why does the impression of tolerance help make a writer seem trustworthy?

Words and Figures of Speech

1. What is a "varmint"? Why are varmints often "without protection" (par. 6) in ranching and farming states?

2. Abbey says that the wildlife controversy has been "swirling" (par. 2) through the Arizona newspapers. In what sense does a controversy "swirl"? Why might Abbey have used the word instead of *building, progressing,* or *flowing*?

3. How does Abbey use the actual name of Globe, Arizona, to help teach the citizens of the town a lesson?

4. A rhetorical question (see FIGURES OF SPEECH in the Glossary) is one that helps to make a positive statement instead of actually calling for an answer. At what point in his essay does Abbey's question, about why anyone would want to kill harmless animals, become a strictly rhetorical question? Explain your answer.

5. Abbey's essay does not use many unfamiliar words, but you may want to consult your dictionary for the following: *caricature* (par. 4), *habitat* (5), *carnivores* (7), *omnivorous* (9), *pathologist* (9).

Comparing

1. Compare Abbey's method of discrediting statistics with Roger Verhulst's method in the first essay in this chapter.

2. How does Abbey's attitude toward the land resemble Chief Seattle's in his "Reply to the U.S. Government"?

3. At first glance, Abbey seems to have much in common with Barry Lopez in "My Horse" (Chapter 7). What differences do you see in the two men's views and values as they come across in the two essays?

Discussion and Writing Topics

1. Make the case for hunting as a competitive sport. You might want to take the approach that "hunters need love too."

2. Construct a persuasive essay on a religious, political, or social topic that uses as its main "evidence" the sayings on bumper stickers.

3. By appealing to your readers' emotions, convince them that hunters (or sportscar drivers or motorcyclists) will never give up their sport because it fulfills a primitive instinct inherited from early man.

Chief Seattle

Reply to the U.S. Government

Chief Seattle (c. 1786–1866) was the leader of the Dwamish, Suquamish, and allied Native American tribes living in the region of the city that now bears his name. He welcomed white settlers from the time of their first arrival and loyally resisted uprisings against them. He later converted to Roman Catholicism and began holding morning and evening services among the tribe. He was not pleased when the village of Seattle, Washington, took his name because he believed that his spirit would be disturbed in the afterlife each time his name was spoken by mortals. Toward the end of his life, Seattle exacted compensation for his broken sleep by seeking gifts among citizens of the region. The "Reply" printed here was Chief Seattle's response to the U.S. government's offer to buy two million acres of Indian land. The offer was made in 1854 through Governor Isaac Stevens of the Washington Territory. For his formal answer, spoken in the Dwamish language, Seattle gathered the tribe around him and placed his hand on Governor Stevens's head. He stood a foot taller than the governor, and his voice could be heard for half a mile. Henry A. Smith translated the speech. Seattle considered the government's proposal (as he promises to do here), decided to accept it, and signed the treaty of Point Elliott on January 22, 1855.

Yonder sky that has wept tears of compassion upon my people for centuries untold, and which to us appears changeless and eternal, may change. Today is fair. Tomorrow may be overcast with clouds. My words are like the stars that never change. Whatever Seattle says the great chief at Washington can rely upon with as much certainty as he can upon the return of the sun or the seasons. The White Chief says that Big Chief at Washington sends us greetings of friendship and goodwill. That is kind of him for we know he has little need of our friendship in return. His people are many. They are like the grass that covers vast prairies. My people are few. They resemble the scattering trees of a storm-swept plain. The great, and—I presume—good, White Chief sends us word that he wishes to buy our lands but is willing to allow us enough to live comfortably. This indeed appears just, even generous, for the Red Man no longer has rights that he need respect, and the offer may be wise also, as we are no longer in need of an extensive country. . . . I will not dwell on, nor mourn over, our untimely decay, nor reproach our paleface brothers with hastening it, as we too may have been somewhat to blame.

Youth is impulsive. When our young men grow angry at some [2] real or imaginary wrong, and disfigure their faces with black paint, it denotes that their hearts are black, and then they are often cruel and relentless, and our old men and old women are unable to restrain them. Thus it has ever been. Thus it was when the white men first began to push our forefathers further westward. But let us hope that the hostilities between us may never return. We would have everything to lose and nothing to gain. Revenge by young men is considered gain, even at the cost of their own lives, but old men who stay at home in times of war, and mothers who have sons to lose, know better.

Our good father at Washington—for I presume he is now our [3] father as well as yours, since King George [1] has moved his boundaries further north—our great good father, I say, sends us word that if we do as he desires he will protect us. His brave warriors will be to us a bristling wall of strength, and his wonderful ships of war will fill our harbors so that our ancient enemies far to the northward—the Hydas and Tsimpsians—will cease to frighten our women, children, and old men. Then in reality will he be our father and we his children. But can that ever be? Your God is not our God! Your God loves your people and hates mine. He folds his strong and protecting arms lovingly about the paleface and leads him by the hand as a father leads his infant son—but He

[1] George IV, king of England from 1820 to 1830.

has forsaken His red children—if they really are his. Our God, the Great Spirit, seems also to have forsaken us. Your God makes your people wax strong every day. Soon they will fill the land. Our people are ebbing away like a rapidly receding tide that will never return. The white man's God cannot love our people or He would protect them. They seem to be orphans who can look nowhere for help. How then can we be brothers? How can your God become our God and renew our prosperity and awaken in us dreams of returning greatness? If we have a common heavenly father He must be partial—for He came to his paleface children. We never saw Him. He gave you laws but He had no word for His red children whose teeming multitudes once filled this vast continent as stars fill the firmament. No; we are two distinct races with separate origins and separate destinies. There is little in common between us.

To us the ashes of our ancestors are sacred and their resting   4
place is hallowed ground. You wander far from the graves of your ancestors and seemingly without regret. Your religion was written upon tables of stone by the iron finger of your God so that you could not forget. The Red Man could never comprehend nor remember it. Our religion is the traditions of our ancestors—the dreams of our old men, given them in solemn hours of night by the Great Spirit; and the visions of our sachems; and it is written in the hearts of our people.

Your dead cease to love you and the land of their nativity as   5
soon as they pass the portals of the tomb and wander way beyond the stars. They are soon forgotten and never return. Our dead never forget the beautiful world that gave them being.

Day and night cannot dwell together. The Red man has ever   6
fled the approach of the White Man, as the morning mist flees before the morning sun. However, your proposition seems fair and I think that my people will accept it and will retire to the reservation you offer them. Then we will dwell apart in peace, for the words of the Great White Chief seem to be the words of nature speaking to my people out of dense darkness.

It matters little where we pass the remnant of our days. They   7
will not be many. A few more moons; a few more winters—and not one of the descendants of the mighty hosts that once moved over this broad land or lived in happy homes, protected by the Great Spirit, will remain to mourn over the graves of a people

once more powerful and hopeful than yours. But why should I mourn at the untimely fate of my people? Tribe follows tribe, and nation follows nation, like the waves of the sea. It is the order of nature, and regret is useless. Your time of decay may be distant, but it will surely come, for even the White Man whose God walked and talked with him as friend with friend, cannot be exempt from the common destiny. We may be brothers after all. We will see.

We will ponder your proposition, and when we decide we will [8] let you know. But should we accept it, I here and now make this condition that we will not be denied the privilege without molestation of visiting at any time the tombs of our ancestors, friends and children. Every part of this soil is sacred in the estimation of my people. Every hillside, every valley, every plain and grove, has been hallowed by some sad or happy event in days long vanished. . . . The very dust upon which you now stand responds more lovingly to their footsteps than to yours, because it is rich with the blood of our ancestors and our bare feet are conscious of the sympathetic touch. . . . Even the little children who lived here and rejoiced here for a brief season will love these somber solitudes and at eventide they greet shadowy returning spirits. And when the last Red Man shall have perished, and the memory of my tribe shall have become a myth among the White Men, these shores will swarm with the invisible dead of my tribe, and when your children's children think themselves alone in the field, the store, the shop, upon the highway, or in the silence of the pathless woods, they will not be alone. . . . At night when the streets of your cities and villages are silent and you think them deserted, they will throng with the returning hosts that once filled and still love this beautiful land. The White Man will never be alone.

Let him be just and deal kindly with my people, for the dead [9] are not powerless. Dead, did I say? There is no death, only a change of worlds.

QUESTIONS

Understanding

1. For what is Chief Seattle appealing to the White Man? What slightly veiled threat does he make in the last two paragraphs of his speech?

2. Describe the single condition that Chief Seattle puts upon his probable acceptance of the government's offer to buy the tribe's land. Why does he make this condition? What does it show about the basis of his religion?

3. How does this belief help to explain why many Native Americans moved onto the reservation only with the greatest reluctance?

4. The last paragraph of Chief Seattle's speech sounds at first like a Christian denial of death and affirmation of heavenly life, but what does he mean by "a change of worlds" (par. 9)? What other differences does Chief Seattle mention between his religion and Christianity?

5. Why does the Dwamish chief doubt that the White Man and the Red Man will ever be brothers? In what grim sense may they prove "brothers after all" (par. 7)?

6. Why, according to Chief Seattle, did the young men of his tribe paint their faces and go to war? What was their motive, and what was the meaning of their war-paint?

7. Chief Seattle refuses to mourn the "untimely fate" (par. 7) of his people or to grant the eternal supremacy of his conquerors. Why? Explain the pervasive theme of his speech.

Strategies and Structure

1. Does Chief Seattle appear trustworthy to you? Why or why not?

2. How does he attempt to establish his authority and trustworthiness in paragraph 1? What equivalent devices might you find in a modern speech?

3. What personal qualities do you attribute to Chief Seattle after reading his entire speech? Point out specific statements and phrases that help to characterize him.

4. How does paragraph 2 show Chief Seattle's wisdom?

5. What distinction is Chief Seattle making when he refers to the "great, and—I presume—good, White Chief" (par. 1)? How does his being anxious to draw this distinction help to qualify the chief as a person worthy to make an APPEAL TO ETHICS?

6. The Dwamish chief shows his respect for the Big Chief at Washington by thanking him for "his greetings of friendship and good-will" (par. 1) and by addressing him as "our good father" (par. 3). How does he also show that he is not afraid of the Big Chief?

7. Seattle's voice is said to have rumbled like the iron engine of a train when he delivered his speech. How is this rumbling quality conveyed in the sentence patterns of paragraphs 1 and 7? Why is an "iron" pace appropriate to Seattle's message?

8. Seattle begins his appeal by acknowledging the justice (even the generosity) and the power of the government; but he declines to make up his mind at once, and ends by asserting that the Red Man retains a degree of power. Is the order significant here? How would Seattle's speech have been changed if the order had been reversed?

9. When arguing at a disadvantage (against a popular opinion, for example), should you admit that disadvantage early on, mention it in closing, or not acknowledge it at all? Explain your answer.

10. Chief Seattle's ethical appeal also makes use of the APPEAL TO EMOTION. Discuss where and how the two work together. What emotion or emotions does his oration speak to?

Words and Figures of Speech

1. The White Man, we are told, is like "the grass that covers vast prairies" (par. 1) and the Indian is like "scattering trees" (par. 1) or the "receding tide" (par. 3), though once he was like the "stars" (par. 3). How do these natural METAPHORS fit in with Chief Seattle's general references to decay and to the cycle of the seasons?

2. What are the implications of the metaphor, "Day and night cannot dwell together" (par. 6)?

3. In what sense is the translator using the word *sympathetic* when he reports Seattle as saying that "our bare feet are conscious of the sympathetic touch" (par. 8)?

4. What analogy does Chief Seattle draw when he describes the role of the ideal leader or chief in paragraph 3?

Comparing

1. A representative of the old, dying order, Seattle resembles General Lee as Bruce Catton portrays him in "Grant and Lee: A Study in Contrasts" (Chapter 6). Pursue the parallel between the two men and the cultures they represent.

2. Analyze and explain what Barry Lopez in "My Horse" (Chapter 7) has "learned" from Chief Seattle's braves.

3. Compare and contrast Seattle's view of nature with Annie Dillard's in "Transfiguration" (Chapter 7).

4. Apply Horace Miner's explanation of how superstition and magic work in a primitive society ("Body Ritual Among the Nacirema," Chapter 8) to the society of the Dwamish tribe as revealed by Chief Seattle.

Discussion and Writing Topics

1. Speaking on behalf of the government, compose an appropriate reply to Chief Seattle's speech.

2. Write a persuasive ethical appeal in which you contend that it is not possible to restore all their lands to the Native Americans but that some reparation for past injustices is due them.

3. Judging from Chief Seattle's speech, why do you think Indian literature is full of natural metaphors?

Steven Brill

When Lawyers
Help Villains

Steven Brill is a contributing editor of Esquire Fortnightly, for which he writes a regular column entitled, "The Law." He is a graduate of Yale and the Yale Law School and was once an assistant to former New York mayor John V. Lindsay. He has written articles on law, firearms, and presidential politics for Harper's, New York, and other magazines. Editor Clay Felker of New York magazine has called Brill "a fantastic reporter, a trained lawyer who is not afraid to look at a document for the facts." Brill's critics charge that his objectivity is sometimes overwhelmed by his liberal's zeal. "When Lawyers Help Villains" is one of his Esquire essays; it gives an expert witness's testimony about the moral tightrope that lawyers must walk in order to maintain our present judicial system.

Leroy "Nicky" Barnes is one-hundred-percent villain. Recently he was convicted in federal court in New York of masterminding one of the city's largest heroin-dealer networks. A millionaire who spent lavishly on cars, homes and furs with the profits he made from delivering heroin to the veins of the men, women and children of Harlem, Barnes had been called Mr. Untouchable because his lawyers had in the past gotten him off when he faced charges of murder, gun possession, heroin dealing and bribery.   1

Barnes's lawyer is a young former assistant district attorney   2
named David Breitbart. He has handled Barnes's court fights since 1973. Sources close to this most recent case claim that Barnes gave Breitbart a million dollars in cash to split between himself and lawyers working for Barnes's codefendants.

Armed with that tip and curious to meet the man who'd argued with a straight face that his client was an innocent man framed by the government, I went to see Breitbart soon after the trial.

Breitbart's office is in a run-down building at Broadway and Canal Street. There Breitbart adamantly denied the story of the million-dollar fee, saying only that "Barnes paid me well."

"*If* you believed Barnes really was a top heroin dealer," I asked, "and he was supplying, even helping to hook, children on the stuff, would you have any qualms about working for him?" "Not at all," Breitbart shot back. "I don't care what he's done. . . . A criminal lawyer is an advocate. . . . If a man's got the price, I'll try his case and do everything I can to get him off. And I do a great job of it. . . ." Would there ever be a case he wouldn't take? "Well, I suppose if they found a Nazi who'd killed millions of Jews and put him on trial here, I'd have problems taking his case. But, you know, most of us are whores, and I guess if they offered me enough money for it I'd take it. . . ."

What's great about Nicky Barnes and David Breitbart is that they sharpen an issue about lawyers and lawyering that otherwise tends to be much fuzzier. For several days after the interview with Breitbart, I talked about it with several lawyer friends who work at prestigious New York firms. All seemed to have the same reaction—that Breitbart is a detestable type, hardly a credit to the bar.

But Breitbart isn't really much different from other lawyers. Give him some nicely tailored wools to replace his double knits, a hundred-lawyer office in a classy skyscraper, an Ivy League diploma and some skill at editing what he says to reporters, and he could be any of my lawyer friends who snickered at him, or, for that matter, any of the nation's respected attorneys who, for the right price, will take on clients engaged in all kinds of antisocial activities.

For example, there's Thomas Sullivan, a longtime criminal lawyer and a partner in the Chicago firm of Jenner & Block. In early 1975, Sullivan was the lead lawyer defending several organized-crime figures charged with defrauding the Teamsters' $1.6 billion Central States Pension Fund. His clients were accused of using a Teamster pension-fund loan to take over a small manufacturer, then siphoning off the loaned money from the company until it went bankrupt.

The jury found them not guilty. One reason was that one of   8
two star witnesses was shotgunned to death several weeks before
the trial. (The F.B.I. later found that the title to a getaway car
used by the murderers was under a phony name but had been
notarized by a secretary who worked for Sullivan's client.) Another
reason for the verdict was Tom Sullivan. He was brilliant. Trial
rules didn't allow the prosecution to mention the past organized-
crime activities of any of the defendants, and Sullivan got the jury
to accept the proposition that these were innocent entrepreneurs
whose dream of manufacturing plastic pails had failed.

Today, Sullivan is the United States attorney for the Northern   9
District of Illinois, which includes Chicago. President Carter appointed him last year. No reservations were expressed by the Senate committee that voted on his nomination or by the press about
his role in the Teamster-Mafia case or in cases where he had
defended other alleged pension-fund embezzlers and corrupt government officials.

That's the way it should be. Sullivan has an unblemished repu-   10
tation as an honest lawyer and a decent guy who has been involved
in a number of bar-related civic activities. Carter's decision to
replace Sullivan's Republican-appointed predecessor, like his more
recent dismissal of the U.S. attorney in Philadelphia, was not
based on merit. But the choice of Sullivan as a replacement was.
He was a good lawyer willing to cut his income to about a fourth
of what it had been in order to enter public service.

Sullivan has resolved conflict-of-interest problems by removing   11
himself from involvement in any case concerning former clients of
his, or his old law firm. With this restriction invoked, his side
switching—common among prosecutors and defense lawyers—becomes a plus. Who's better qualified to win cases for the government than a man who has beaten it so many times in the past?

On the other hand, isn't there something we should dislike   12
about men like Thomas Sullivan or David Breitbart, whose ethical
compasses, or lack thereof, allow them to make lots of money defending mobsters or heroin dealers?

Few lawyers see it that way. In broad terms, the lawyers' Code   13
of Professional Responsibility entitles the impeccably evil Nicky
Barnes to the best lawyer he can buy. It allows—in fact, encour-
ages—lawyers to be vigorous advocates of their clients' cases re-

gardless of what they personally believe about their clients' guilt or goodness (as long as they don't knowingly present perjured evidence).

There's good logic in these standards. If lawyers refused to rep-   14 resent clients because they felt they were guilty, many defendants wouldn't be able to find good lawyers and we'd have replaced a jury-trial system that puts the burden of proof on the government with one in which an accused person's fate is decided by the first-impression judgments of lawyers. Also, if lawyers were scared away from defending unpopular clients or people involved in unpopular issues, unpopular *innocent* people (the targets of a Joe McCarthy-type witch-hunt,[1] for instance) would suffer.

Most lawyers aren't as free of qualms as Breitbart in taking   15 clients. Sullivan, for example, says he'd never defend a heroin dealer.

Still, these personal hesitations rarely interfere with the general   16 willingness of lawyers to take any clients with cases falling within the bounds of their practices. The reason Breitbart sharpens this issue so nicely is not just that he apparently has none of these hang-ups but also that his practice is in a particularly unseemly field. He forces us to consider the most troubling consequence of the principle that lawyers shouldn't allow distaste for a client or an issue to dissuade them from taking a case and that lawyers who do take such cases should not be identified negatively with their clients for doing so—namely, that this often allows people like Barnes to go free. But there just isn't a better way to preserve a rule of law that resolves most civil disputes peaceably and does much to make sure that the government can't cut corners to put one of us in jail.

But look where that leaves lawyers. It makes them amoral auto-   17 matons. At a time when so many other pillars of our social and economic establishment, spurred by the Watergate and the cor-porate-bribery disclosures, are reassessing the ethical consequences of their conduct, lawyers have immunity from the new morality. They're in the unique, if not enviable, position of holding them-

[1] Persecution based on rumor: In the early 1950s, with little evidence, Joseph Raymond McCarthy, U.S. senator from Wisconsin (1946–1957), led an investigation of "un-American" activities in the army that extended to private citizens.

selves out as hired guns, allowed by their own code to be above the moral implications of their work because, as Breitbart puts it, "it's our tough advocacy that keeps the system honest."

Faced with the Breitbart lawyer-amorality question, one Wall [18] Street lawyer suggested that if we give lawyers a free pass on worrying about the moral consequences of what they do for a particular client, then maybe we should try to take something in return by asking them to do a set amount of noncompensated work for charitable or public-interest groups. Requiring such *pro bono* [2] work, or even defining what qualifies as such, has obvious practical pitfalls. Even so, many lawyers already do some charitable work. But if lawyers are going to lessen the growing public distrust and resentment of their profession, it would seem that they'd want to do something in a concrete, organized way to show that they're more than the "whores" Breitbart thinks they are.

QUESTIONS

Understanding

1. Brill says that heroin dealer "Nicky" Barnes and his attorney, David Breitbart, nicely "sharpen an issue about lawyers and lawyering" (par. 5). What is the issue and what makes their case such a clear-cut example?

2. How, according to Breitbart, do lawyers usually answer the charge that they should not defend men they know to be guilty?

3. Brill himself obviously has mixed feelings about this issue. Describe those mixed feelings and explain where he comes out—with or against the lawyers?

4. What additional issue does Brill introduce in paragraphs 17 and 18?

5. What are "conflict-of-interest problems" (par. 11)? Under what circumstances do they arise in business and politics?

6. To what extent do you agree with Brill's assertion that Breitbart "isn't really much different from other lawyers" (par. 6)? How important are the differences he mentions?

---

[2] *Pro bono publico*, "for the public good."

Strategies and Structure

1. Brill's essay is an APPEAL TO ETHICS in two senses: (1) it appeals to the ethical standards of its audience; (2) it is an appeal made by an ethical person. How does Brill create the impression that he has a highly developed sense of ethics?

2. In general, how are these two aspects of the appeal to ethics related? Why might an essay that adopts one of these strategies also be expected to adopt the other?

3. The first twelve paragraphs of Brill's essay contribute to an IN-DUCTIVE argument that ends, after a break, in paragraph 16. What is the conclusion of this argument? In which lines is it stated?

4. The word *logic* in paragraph 14 should alert us to look for a DEDUCTIVE argument. Analyze the reasoning in this paragraph.

5. Brill's inductive and deductive arguments come together in paragraph 16. Which sentence in that paragraph states the conclusion of his *deductive* line of reasoning?

6. How many examples does Brill use for the *inductive* part of his argument? How (and in which paragraph) does he justify so few? Is this a legitimate tactic in persuasive writing?

7. Explain why paragraphs 17 and 18 carry Brill's essay beyond logical argumentation and into the realm of ethical appeal. To whom are these final paragraphs directed? What do they urge that audience to do?

8. How effective do you find Brill's use of several different MODES OF PERSUASION in the same essay? Is this sort of combining a good idea as a general strategy of persuasive writing? Explain your answer.

Words and Figures of Speech

1. Brill says that the legal system puts lawyers in the position of being *automatons* (par. 17). What is an automaton and what qualities does the METAPHOR ascribe to lawyers?

2. *Villain* is a term often used in the theater and in sentimental literature. Why does Brill use it here?

3. Why do you think Brill uses the informal *fuzzier* in paragraph 5?

4. How effective do you find the "hired guns" ANALOGY in paragraph 17? Is it fair to lawyers?

5. In the last sentence, Brill turns attorney Breitbart's analogy against him and against the legal profession. How effective is this tactic? Why does attorney Breitbart draw the analogy in the first place?

Comparing

1. In "What You See Is the Real You" (Chapter 5), Willard Gaylin argues that morality is gauged by behavior. How well does this principle hold up in Brill's examination of legal ethics? Explain your answer.
2. Can Brill's charge that attorneys are "amoral automatons" (par. 17) be applied with any justice to attorney Johnson C. Montgomery's position in "Island of Plenty" (Chapter 9)? Why or why not?

Discussion and Writing Topics

1. Brill asserts that "side switching" (par. 11) is a "plus" when the lawyer moves from the side of the criminals to the side of the government. What about the morality of switching the other way, a common enough occurrence? Construct a persuasive argument in which you attack the ethics of this practice.
2. Defend the proposition that even "a Nazi who'd killed millions of Jews" (par. 4) is entitled to his day in court.
3. It was "trial rules" (par. 8), according to Brill, that kept out of court the information that attorney Sullivan's clients had ties with organized crime. How serious a stumbling block to justice do you consider rules of evidence, plea bargaining, and other "technical" aspects of our legal system? Write an appeal to ethics on this issue.
4. How important is the right to a speedy trial? Advance your opinion in a persuasive essay.

Essays That Appeal to Emotion and Ethics

Write an emotional or ethical appeal on one of the following subjects:

1. Marriage is (is not) a wretched institution

2. Doctors are (are not) technicians rather than healers

3. Lawyers are (are not) a dishonest breed

4. College athletics should (should not) be abolished

5. ROTC should (should not) be abolished on college campuses

6. Universities should (should not) allow radicals to speak in their facilities

7. Teachers should (should not) pass judgment on their students' work

8. Public schools are (are not) more responsive to the whole person than are private schools

9. Most college requirements are (are not) worthwhile

10. Seeking psychiatric help is (is not) a sign of weakness

11. The drug laws should (should not) be tightened up

12. Exercise: Analyze the appeal of several newspaper or magazine advertisements: For what audience are they intended? How do they attract that audience? What unstated assumptions do they make?

Essays for
Further Reading

Jonathan Swift
A Modest Proposal

The great satirist, Jonathan Swift (1667–1745), was born in Dublin, Ireland, and educated at Trinity College, Dublin, where he
was censured for breaking the rules of discipline and graduated
only by "special grace." He was ordained an Anglican clergyman
in 1694 and became Dean of St. Patrick's, Dublin in 1713. His
satires in prose and verse addressed three main issues: political
relations between England and Ireland; Irish social questions; and
matters of church doctrine. He is most famous for The Battle of
the Books (1704); A Tale of a Tub (1704); and Gulliver's Travels
(1726). His best-known essay was published in 1729 under the full
title, "A Modest Proposal for Preventing the Children of Poor
People from Being a Burden to Their Parents or the Country."
Assuming a mask, or persona, Swift poured into the essay his con-
tempt for human materialism and for logic without compassion.

It is a melancholy object to those who walk through this great   [1]
town [1] or travel in the country, when they see the streets, the
roads, and cabin doors, crowded with beggars of the female sex,
followed by three, four, or six children, all in rags and impor-
tuning every passenger for an alms. These mothers, instead of
being able to work for their honest livelihood, are forced to
employ all their time in strolling to beg sustenance for their
helpless infants, who, as they grow up, either turn thieves for
want of work, or leave their dear native country to fight for
the Pretender in Spain, or sell themselves to the Barbadoes.[2]

[1] Dublin, capital city of Ireland.
[2] The pretender to the throne of England was James Stuart (1688–1766),
son of the deposed James II. Barbados is an island in the West Indies.

I think it is agreed by all parties that this prodigious number of   2
children in the arms, or on the backs, or at the heels of their
mothers, and frequently of their fathers, is in the present deplor-
able state of the kingdom a very great additional grievance; and
therefore whoever could find out a fair, cheap, and easy method
of making these children sound, useful members of the common-
wealth would deserve so well of the public as to have his statue
set up for a preserver of the nation.

But my intention is very far from being confined to provide only   3
for the children of professed beggars; it is of a much greater extent,
and shall take in the whole number of infants at a certain age who
are born of parents in effect as little able to support them as those
who demand our charity in the streets.

As to my own part, having turned my thoughts for many years   4
upon this important subject, and maturely weighed the several
schemes of other projectors,[3] I have always found them grossly
mistaken in their computation. It is true, a child just dropped
from its dam may be supported by her milk for a solar year, with
little other nourishment; at most not above the value of two shillings,[4] which the mother may certainly get, or the value in scraps,
by her lawful occupation of begging; and it is exactly at one year
old that I propose to provide for them in such a manner as instead
of being a charge upon their parents or the parish, or wanting
food and raiment for the rest of their lives, they shall on the contrary contribute to the feeding, and partly to the clothing, of many
thousands.

There is likewise another great advantage in my scheme, that it   5
will prevent those voluntary abortions, and that horrid practice of
women murdering their bastard children, alas, too frequent among
us, sacrificing the poor innocent babes, I doubt, more to avoid the
expense than the shame, which would move tears and pity in the
most savage and inhuman breast.

The number of souls in this kingdom being usually reckoned   6
one million and a half, of these I calculate there may be about
two hundred thousand couple whose wives are breeders; from
which number I subtract thirty thousand couples who are able to

---

[3] Men whose heads were full of foolish schemes or projects.
[4] The British pound sterling was made up of twenty shillings; five shillings
made a crown.

maintain their own children, although I apprehend there cannot be so many under the present distress of the kingdom; but this being granted, there will remain an hundred and seventy thousand breeders. I again subtract fifty thousand for those women who miscarry, or whose children die by accident or disease within the year. There only remain an hundred and twenty thousand children of poor parents annually born. The question therefore is, how this number shall be reared and provided for, which, as I have already said, under the present situation of affairs, is utterly impossible by all the methods hitherto proposed. For we can neither employ them in handicraft or agriculture; we neither build houses (I mean in the country) nor cultivate land. They can very seldom pick up a livelihood by stealing till they arrive at six years old, except where they are of towardly parts;[5] although I confess they learn the rudiments much earlier, during which time they can however be looked upon only as probationers, as I have been informed by a principal gentleman in the county of Cavan, who protested to me that he never knew above one or two instances under the age of six, even in a part of the kingdom so renowned for the quickest proficiency in that art.

I am assured by our merchants that a boy or a girl before twelve years old is no salable commodity; and even when they come to this age they will not yield above three pounds, or three pounds and half a crown at most on the Exchange; which cannot turn to account either to the parents or the kingdom, the charge of nutriment and rags having been at least four times that value.

I shall now therefore humbly propose my own thoughts, which I hope will not be liable to the least objection.

I have been assured by a very knowing American of my acquaintance in London, that a young healthy child well nursed is at a year old a most delicious, nourishing, and wholesome food, whether stewed, roasted, baked, or boiled; and I make no doubt that it will equally serve in a fricassee or a ragout.

I do therefore humbly offer it to public consideration that of the hundred and twenty thousand children, already computed, twenty thousand may be reserved for breed, whereof only one fourth part to be males, which is more than we allow to sheep, black cattle, or swine; and my reason is that these children are

---

[5] Having natural ability.

seldom the fruits of marriage, a circumstance not much regarded by our savages, therefore one male will be sufficient to serve four females. That the remaining hundred thousand may at a year old be offered in sale to the persons of quality and fortune through the kingdom, always advising the mother to let them suck plentifully in the last month, so as to render them plump and fat for a good table. A child will make two dishes at an entertainment for friends; and when the family dines alone, the fore or hind quarter will make a reasonable dish, and seasoned with a little pepper or salt will be very good boiled on the fourth day, especially in winter.

I have reckoned upon a medium that a child just born will weigh twelve pounds, and in a solar year if tolerably nursed increaseth to twenty-eight pounds. 11

I grant this food will be somewhat dear, and therefore very proper for landlords, who, as they have already devoured most of the parents, seem to have the best title to the children. 12

Infant's flesh will be in season throughout the year, but more plentiful in March, and a little before and after. For we are told by a grave author, an eminent French physician,[6] that fish being a prolific diet, there are more children born in Roman Catholic countries about nine months after Lent than at any other season; therefore, reckoning a year after Lent, the markets will be more glutted than usual, because the number of popish infants is at least three to one in this kingdom; and therefore it will have one other collateral advantage, by lessening the number of Papists among us. 13

I have already computed the charge of nursing a beggar's child (in which list I reckon all cottagers, laborers, and four fifths of the farmers) to be about two shillings per annum, rags included; and I believe no gentleman would repine to give ten shillings for the carcass of a good fat child, which, as I have said, will make four dishes of excellent nutritive meat, when he hath only some particular friend or his own family to dine with him. Thus the squire will learn to be a good landlord, and grow popular among the tenants; the mother will have eight shillings net profit, and be fit for work till she produces another child. 14

Those who are more thrifty (as I must confess the times re- 15

[6] François Rabelais (1494?–1553), French satirist.

quire) may flay the carcass; the skin of which artificially [7] dressed will make admirable gloves for ladies, and summer boots for fine gentlemen.

As to our city of Dublin, shambles [8] may be appointed for this [16] purpose in the most convenient parts of it, and butchers we may be assured will not be wanting; although I rather recommend buying the children alive, and dressing them hot from the knife as we do roasting pigs.

A very worthy person, a true lover of his country, and whose [17] virtues I highly esteem, was lately pleased in discoursing on this matter to offer a refinement upon my scheme. He said that many gentlemen of this kingdom, having of late destroyed their deer, he conceived that the want of venison might be well supplied by the bodies of young lads and maidens, not exceeding fourteen years of age nor under twelve, so great a number of both sexes in every country being now ready to starve for want of work and service; and these to be disposed of by their parents, if alive, or otherwise by their nearest relations. But with due deference to so excellent a friend and so deserving a patriot, I cannot be altogether in his sentiments; for as to the males, my American acquaintance assured me from frequent experience that their flesh was generally tough and lean, like that of our schoolboys, by continual exercise, and their taste disagreeable; and to fatten them would not answer the charge. Then as to the females, it would, I think with humble submission, be a loss to the public, because they soon would become breeders themselves: and besides, it is not improbable that some scrupulous people might be apt to censure such a practice (although indeed very unjustly) as a little bordering upon cruelty; which, I confess, hath always been with me the strongest objection against any project, how well soever intended.

But in order to justify my friend, he confessed that this ex- [18] pedient was put into his head by the famous Psalmanazar,[9] a native of the island Formosa, who came from thence to London above twenty years ago, and in conversation told my friend that in his country when any young person happened to be put to death, the executioner sold the carcass to persons of quality as a prime

[7] Skillfully, artfully.
[8] Slaughterhouses.
[9] George Psalmanazar (1679?–1763), a Frenchman, fooled English society for several years by masquerading as a pagan Formosan.

dainty; and that in his time the body of a plump girl of fifteen, who was crucified for an attempt to poison the emperor, was sold to his Imperial Majesty's prime minister of state, and other great mandarins of the court, in joints from the gibbet, at four hundred crowns. Neither indeed can I deny that if the same use were made of several plump young girls in this town, who without one single groat to their fortunes cannot stir abroad without a chair, and appear at the playhouse and assemblies in foreign fineries which they never will pay for, the kingdom would not be the worse.

Some persons of a desponding spirit are in great concern about   19
that vast number of poor people who are aged, diseased, or maimed, and I have been desired to employ my thoughts what course may be taken to ease the nation of so grievous an encumbrance. But I am not in the least pain upon that matter, because it is very well known that they are every day dying and rotting by cold and famine, and filth and vermin, as fast as can be reasonably expected. And as to the younger laborers, they are now in almost as hopeful a condition. They cannot get work, and consequently pine away for want of nourishment to a degree that if at any time they are accidentally hired to common labor, they have not strength to perform it; and thus the country and themselves are happily delivered from the evils to come.

I have too long digressed, and therefore shall return to my sub-   20
ject. I think the advantages by the proposal which I have made are obvious and many, as well as of the highest importance.

For first, as I have already observed, it would greatly lessen the   21
number of Papists, with whom we are yearly overrun, being the principal breeders of the nation as well as our most dangerous enemies; and who stay at home on purpose to deliver the kingdom to the Pretender, hoping to take their advantage by the absence of so many good Protestants, who have chosen rather to leave their country than stay at home and pay tithes against their conscience to an Episcopal curate.[1]

Secondly, the poorer tenants will have something valuable of   22
their own, which by law may be made liable to distress, and help

---

[1] Swift blamed much of Ireland's poverty upon large landowners who avoided church tithes by living (and spending their money) abroad.

to pay their landlord's rent, their corn and cattle being already seized and money a thing unknown.

Thirdly, whereas the maintenance of an hundred thousand children, from two years old and upward, cannot be computed at less than ten shillings a piece per annum, the nation's stock will be thereby increased fifty thousand pounds per annum, besides the profit of a new dish introduced to the tables of all gentlemen of fortune in the kingdom who have any refinement in taste. And the money will circulate among ourselves, the goods being entirely of our own growth and manufacture.

Fourthly, the constant breeders, besides the gain of eight shillings sterling per annum by the sale of their children, will be rid of the charge of maintaining them after the first year.

Fifthly, this food would likewise bring great custom to taverns, where the vintners will certainly be so prudent as to procure the best receipts for dressing it to perfection, and consequently have their houses frequented by all the fine gentlemen, who justly value themselves upon their knowledge in good eating; and a skillful cook, who understands how to oblige his guests, will contrive to make it as expensive as they please.

Sixthly, this would be a great inducement to marriage, which all wise nations have either encouraged by rewards or enforced by laws and penalties. It would increase the care and tenderness of mothers toward their children, when they were sure of a settlement for life to the poor babes, provided in some sort by the public, to their annual profit instead of expense. We should see an honest emulation among the married women, which of them could bring the fattest child to the market. Men would become as fond of their wifes during the time of their pregnancy as they are now of their mares in foal, their cows in calf, or sows when they are ready to farrow; nor offer to beat or kick them (as is too frequent a practice) for fear of a miscarriage.

Many other advantages might be enumerated. For instance, the addition of some thousand carcasses in our exportation of barreled beef, the propagation of swine's flesh, and improvement in the art of making good bacon, so much wanted among us by the great destruction of pigs, too frequent at our tables, which are no way comparable in taste or magnificence to a well-grown, fat, yearling child, which roasted whole will make a considerable figure at a lord mayor's feast or any other public entertainment. But this and many others I omit, being studious of brevity.

Supposing that one thousand families in this city would be constant customers for infants' flesh, besides others who might have it at merry meetings, particularly weddings and christenings, I compute that Dublin would take off annually about twenty thousand carcasses, and the rest of the kingdom (where probably they will be sold somewhat cheaper) the remaining eighty thousand. 28

I can think of no one objection that will possibly be raised against this proposal, unless it should be urged that the number of people will be thereby much lessened in the kingdom. This I freely own, and it was indeed one principal design in offering it to the world. I desire the reader will observe, that I calculate my remedy for this one individual kingdom of Ireland and for no other that ever was, is, or I think ever can be upon earth. Therefore let no man talk to me of other expedients [2]: of taxing our absentees at five shillings a pound: of using neither clothes nor household furniture except what is of our own growth and manufacture: of utterly rejecting the materials and instruments that promote foreign luxury: of curing the expensiveness of pride, vanity, idleness, and gaming in our women: of introducing a vein of parsimony, prudence, and temperance: of learning to love our country, in the want of which we differ even from Laplanders and the inhabitants of Topinamboo [3]: of quitting our animosities and factions, nor acting any longer like the Jews, who were murdering one another at the very moment their city [4] was taken: of being a little cautious not to sell our country and conscience for nothing: of teaching landlords to have at least one degree of mercy toward their tenants: lastly, of putting a spirit of honesty, industry, and skill into our shopkeepers; who, if a resolution could now be taken to buy only our native goods, would immediately unite to cheat and exact upon us in the price, the measure, and the goodness, nor could ever yet be brought to make one fair proposal of just dealing, though often and earnestly invited to it. 29

Therefore I repeat, let no man talk to me of these and the like 30

[2] The following are all measures that Swift himself proposed in various pamphlets.
[3] In Brazil.
[4] Jerusalem, sacked by the Romans in A.D. 70.

expedients, till he hath at least some glimpse of hope that there will ever be some hearty and sincere attempt to put them in practice.

But as to myself, having been wearied out for many years with offering vain, idle, visionary thoughts, and at length utterly despairing of success, I fortunately fell upon this proposal, which, as it is wholly new, so it hath something solid and real, of no expense and little trouble, full in our own power, and whereby we can incur no danger in disobliging England. For this kind of commodity will not bear exportation, the flesh being of too tender a consistence to admit a long continuance in salt, although perhaps I could name a country [5] which would be glad to eat up our whole nation without it.

After all, I am not so violently bent upon my own opinion as to reject any offer proposed by wise men, which shall be found equally innocent, cheap, easy, and effectual. But before something of that kind shall be advanced in contradiction to my scheme, and offering a better, I desire the author or authors will be pleased maturely to consider two points. First, as things now stand, how they will be able to find food and raiment for an hundred thousand useless mouths and backs. And secondly, there being a round million of creatures in human figure throughout this kingdom, whose sole subsistence put into a common stock would leave them in debt two millions of pounds sterling, adding those who are beggars by profession to the bulk of farmers, cottagers, and laborers, with their wives and children who are beggars in effect; I desire those politicians who dislike my overture, and may perhaps be so bold to attempt an answer, that they will first ask the parents of these mortals whether they would not at this day think it a great happiness to have been sold for food at a year old in the manner I prescribe, and thereby have avoided such a perpetual scene of misfortunes as they have since gone through by the oppression of landlords, the impossibility of paying rent without money or trade, the want of common sustenance, with neither house nor clothes to cover them from the inclemencies of the weather, and the most inevitable prospect of entailing the like or greater miseries upon their breed forever.

[5] England.

I profess, in the sincerity of my heart, that I have not the least   33
personal interest in endeavoring to promote this necessary work,
having no other motive than the public good of my country, by
advancing our trade, providing for infants, relieving the poor, and
giving some pleasure to the rich. I have no children by which I
can propose to get a single penny; the youngest being nine years
old, and my wife past childbearing.

C. G. Jung

Freud and Jung: Contrasts

Carl Gustav Jung (1875–1961) was a renowned Swiss psychiatrist and the founder of analytic psychology. He studied medicine at the University of Basel, Switzerland, and in Paris. In 1907 he met and became a disciple of Sigmund Freud, but the two parted company in 1912 when Jung advanced theories rejecting Freud's idea that neuroses are sexually based. Jung then set up his own school of analytic psychology in Zürich. Later he became professor of psychology at universities in Zürich and Basel. Jung's works in English translation include The Theory of Psychoanalysis *(1912);* Psychology of the Unconscious *(1916);* Psychological Types *(1923);* Modern Man in Search of a Soul *(1933);* Psychology and Religion *(1938); and* Integration of the Personality *(1939). The essay presented here, "Freud and Jung: Contrasts," was written in 1929. It is Jung's estimate of his former colleague and sets forth the differences in their theories as Jung saw them.*

The difference between Freud's views and my own ought really to be dealt with by someone who stands outside the orbit of those ideas which go under our respective names. Can I be credited with sufficient impartiality to rise above my own ideas? Can any man do this? I doubt it. If I were told that someone had rivalled Baron Munchausen [1] by accomplishing such a feat, I should feel sure that his ideas were borrowed ones.

It is true that widely accepted ideas are never the personal property of their so-called author; on the contrary, he is the

[1] (1720–1790), German soldier, tall-tale hero of the *Marvelous Travels* published by Erich Raspe in 1785.

bondservant of his ideas. Impressive ideas which are hailed as truths have something peculiar about them. Although they come into being at a definite time, they are and have always been time-less; they arise from that realm of creative psychic life out of which the ephemeral mind of the single human being grows like a plant that blossoms, bears fruit and seed, and then withers and dies. Ideas spring from something greater than the personal human being. Man does not make his ideas; we could say that man's ideas make him.

Ideas are, inevitably, a fatal confession, for they bring to light 3 not only the best in us, but our worst insufficiencies and personal shortcomings as well. This is especially the case with ideas about psychology. Where should they come from except from our most subjective side? Can our experience of the objective world ever save us from our subjective bias? Is not every experience, even in the best of circumstances, at least fifty-per-cent subjective interpre-tation? On the other hand, the subject is also an objective fact, a piece of the world; and what comes from him comes, ultimately, from the stuff of the world itself, just as the rarest and strangest organism is none the less supported and nourished by the earth which is common to all. It is precisely the most subjective ideas which, being closest to nature and to our own essence, deserve to be called the truest. But: "What is truth?"

For the purposes of psychology, I think it best to abandon the 4 notion that we are today in anything like a position to make state-ments about the nature of the psyche that are "true" or "correct." The best that we can achieve is true expression. By true expression I mean an open avowal and detailed presentation of everything that is subjectively observed. One person will stress the *forms* into which he can work this material, and will therefore believe that he is the creator of what he finds within himself. Another will lay most weight on *what* is observed; he will therefore speak of it as a phenomenon, while remaining conscious of his own receptive attitude. The truth probably lies between the two: true expression consists in giving form to what is observed.

The modern psychologist, however ambitious, can hardly claim 5 to have achieved more than this. Our psychology is the more or less successfully formulated confession of a few individuals, and so far as each of them conforms more or less to a type, his confes-sion can be accepted as a fairly valid description of a large number of people. And since those who conform to other types none the less belong to the human species, we may conclude that this description applies, though less fully, to them too. What Freud has to say about sexuality, infantile pleasure, and their conflict with the "reality principle," as well as what he says about incest and the like, can be taken as the truest expression of his personal psychology. It is the successful formulation of what he himself subjectively observed. I am no opponent of Freud's; I am merely presented in that light by his own short-sightedness and that of his pupils. No experienced psychiatrist can deny having met with dozens of cases whose psychology answers in all essentials to that of Freud. By his own subjective confession, Freud has assisted at the birth of a great truth about man. He has devoted his life and strength to the construction of a psychology which is a formulation of his own being.

Our way of looking at things is conditioned by what we are. 6 And since other people have a different psychology, they see things differently and express themselves differently. Adler,[2] one of Freud's earliest pupils, is a case in point. Working with the same empirical material as Freud, he approached it from a totally different standpoint. His way of looking at things is at least as convincing as Freud's, because he too represents a psychology of a well-known type. I know that the followers of both schools flatly assert that I am in the wrong, but I may hope that history and all fair-minded persons will bear me out. Both schools, to my way of thinking, deserve reproach for overemphasizing the pathological aspect of life and for interpreting man too exclusively in the light of his defects. A convincing example of this in Freud's case is his inability to understand religious experience, as is clearly shown in his book *The Future of an Illusion*.

For my part, I prefer to look at man in the light of what in him 7 is healthy and sound, and to free the sick man from just that kind of psychology which colours every page Freud has written. I cannot see how Freud can ever get beyond his own psychology and relieve the patient of a suffering from which the doctor still suffers. It is the psychology of neurotic states of mind, definitely one-sided, and its validity is really confined to those states. Within these limits it is true and valid even when it is in error, for error

[2] Alfred Adler (1870–1937), Austrian psychiatrist.

also belongs to the picture and carries the truth of a confession. But it is not a psychology of the healthy mind, and—this is a symptom of its morbidity—it is based on an uncriticized, even an unconscious, view of the world which is apt to narrow the horizon of experience and limit one's vision. It was a great mistake on Freud's part to turn his back on philosophy. Not once does he criticize his assumptions or even his personal psychic premises. Yet to do so was necessary, as may be inferred from what I have said above; for had he critically examined his own foundations he would never have been able to put his peculiar psychology so naïvely on view as he did in *The Interpretation of Dreams*. At all events, he would have had a taste of the difficulties I have met with. I have never refused the bitter-sweet drink of philosophical criticism, but have taken it with caution, a little at a time. All too little, my opponents will say; almost too much, my own feeling tells me. All too easily does self-criticism poison one's naïveté, that priceless possession, or rather gift, which no creative person can do without. At any rate, philosophical criticism has helped me to see that every psychology—my own included—has the character of a subjective confession. And yet I must prevent my critical powers from destroying my creativeness. I know well enough that every word I utter carries with it something of myself—of my special and unique self with its particular history and its own particular world. Even when I deal with empirical data I am necessarily speaking about myself. But it is only by accepting this as inevitable that I can serve the cause of man's knowledge of man—the cause which Freud also wished to serve and which, in spite of everything, he has served. Knowledge rests not upon truth alone, but upon error also.

It is perhaps here, where the question arises of recognizing that   8
every psychology which is the work of one man is subjectively coloured, that the line between Freud and myself is most sharply drawn.

A further difference seems to me to consist in this, that I try to   9
free myself from all unconscious and therefore uncriticized assumptions about the world in general. I say "I try," for who can be sure that he has freed himself from all of his unconscious assumptions? I try to save myself from at least the crassest prejudices, and am therefore disposed to recognize all manner of gods provided only that they are active in the human psyche. I do not doubt that

the natural instincts or drives are forces of propulsion in psychic life, whether we call them sexuality or the will to power; but neither do I doubt that these instincts come into collision with the spirit, for they are continually colliding with something, and why should not this something be called "spirit"? I am far from knowing what spirit is in itself, and equally far from knowing what instincts are. The one is as mysterious to me as the other; nor can I explain the one as a misunderstanding of the other. There are no misunderstandings in nature, any more than the fact that the earth has only one moon is a misunderstanding; misunderstandings are found only in the realm of what we call "understanding." Certainly instinct and spirit are beyond my understanding. They are terms which we posit for powerful forces whose nature we do not know.

My attitude to all religions is therefore a positive one. In their   10 symbolism I recognize those figures which I have met with in the dreams and fantasies of my patients. In their moral teaching I see efforts that are the same as or similar to those made by my patients when, guided by their own insight or inspiration, they seek the right way to deal with the forces of psychic life. Ceremonial ritual, initiation rites, and ascetic practices, in all their forms and variations, interest me profoundly as so many techniques for bringing about a proper relation to these forces. My attitude to biology is equally positive, and to the empiricism of natural science in general, in which I see a herculean attempt to understand the psyche by approaching it from the outside world, just as religious gnosis is a prodigious attempt of the human mind to derive knowledge of the cosmos from within. In my picture of the world there is a vast outer realm and an equally vast inner realm; between these two stands man, facing now one and now the other, and, according to temperament and disposition, taking the one for the absolute truth by denying or sacrificing the other.

This picture is hypothetical, of course, but it offers a hypothesis   11 which is so valuable that I will not give it up. I consider it heuristically and empirically justified and, moreover, it is confirmed by the *consensus gentium*.[3] This hypothesis certainly came to me from an inner source, though I might imagine that empirical findings had led to its discovery. Out of it has grown my theory of

[3] Common consent of mankind.

types, and also my reconciliation with views as different from my own as those of Freud.

I see in all that happens the play of opposites, and derive from   12
this conception my idea of psychic energy. I hold that psychic
energy involves the play of opposites in much the same way as
physical energy involves a difference of potential, that is to say the
existence of opposites such as warm and cold, high and low, etc.
Freud began by taking sexuality as the only psychic driving force,
and only after my break with him did he take other factors into
account. For my part, I have summed up the various psychic
drives or forces—all constructed more or less *ad hoc*—under the
concept of energy, in order to eliminate the almost unavoidable
arbitrariness of a psychology that deals purely with power-drives.
I therefore speak not of separate drives or forces but of "value
intensities." By this I do not mean to deny the importance of
sexuality in psychic life, though Freud stubbornly maintains that
I do deny it. What I seek is to set bounds to the rampant termi-
nology of sex which vitiates all discussion of the human psyche,
and to put sexuality itself in its proper place.

Common-sense will always return to the fact that sexuality   13
is only one of the biological instincts, only one of the psycho-
physiological functions, though one that is without doubt very
far-reaching and important. But—what happens when we can no
longer satisfy our hunger? There is, quite obviously, a marked disturbance today in the psychic sphere of sex, just as, when a tooth
really hurts, the whole psyche seems to consist of nothing but
toothache. The kind of sexuality described by Freud is that unmistakable sexual obsession which shows itself whenever a patient
has reached the point where he needs to be forced or tempted out
of a wrong attitude or situation. It is an over-emphasized sexuality
piled up behind a dam, and it shrinks at once to normal proportions as soon as the way to development is opened. Generally it
is being caught in the old resentments against parents and relations and in the boring emotional tangles of the "family romance"
that brings about the damming up of life's energies, and this
stoppage unfailingly manifests itself in the form of sexuality called
"infantile." It is not sexuality proper, but an unnatural discharge
of tensions that really belong to quite another province of life.
That being so, what is the use of paddling about in this flooded
country? Surely straight thinking will grant that it is more impor-

tant to open up drainage canals, that is, to find a new attitude or way of life which will offer a suitable gradient for the pent-up energy. Otherwise a vicious circle is set up, and this is in fact what Freudian psychology appears to do. It points no way that leads beyond the inexorable cycle of biological events. In despair we would have to cry out with St. Paul: "Wretched man that I am, who will deliver me from the body of this death?" And the spiritual man in us comes forward, shaking his head, and says in Faust's words: "Thou art conscious only of the single urge," [4] namely of the fleshly bond leading back to father and mother or forward to the children that have sprung from our flesh—"incest" with the past and "incest" with the future, the original sin of perpetuation of the "family romance." There is nothing that can free us from this bond except that opposite urge of life, the spirit. It is not the children of the flesh, but the "children of God," who know freedom. In Ernst Barlach's [5] tragedy *The Dead Day*, the mother-daemon says at the end: "The strange thing is that man will not learn that God is his father." That is what Freud would never learn, and what all those who share his outlook forbid themselves to learn. At least, they never find the key to this knowledge. Theology does not help those who are looking for the key, because theology demands faith, and faith cannot be made: it is in the truest sense a gift of grace. We moderns are faced with the necessity of rediscovering the life of the spirit: we must experience it anew for ourselves. It is the only way in which to break the spell that binds us to the cycle of biological events.

My position on this question is the third point of difference [14] between Freud's views and my own. Because of it I am accused of mysticism. I do not, however, hold myself responsible for the fact that man has, always and everywhere, spontaneously developed a religious function, and that the human psyche from time immemorial has been shot through with religious feelings and ideas. Whoever cannot see this aspect of the human psyche is blind, and whoever chooses to explain it away, or to "enlighten" it away, has no sense of reality. Or should we see in the father-

---

[4] In Act I of *Faust* by the German poet Johann Wolfgang von Goethe (1748–1832), the hero of the play is speaking to a student who recognizes only physical delights. Faust, however, is also conscious of humanity's spiritual needs.

[5] (1870–1938), German writer and artist, best known for his sculpture.

complex which shows itself in all members of the Freudian school, and in its founder as well, evidence of a notable release from the fatalities of the family situation? This father-complex, defended with such stubbornness and oversensitivity, is a religious function misunderstood, a piece of mysticism expressed in terms of biological and family relationships. As for Freud's concept of the "super-ego," it is a furtive attempt to smuggle the time-honoured image of Jehovah in the dress of psychological theory. For my part, I prefer to call things by the names under which they have always been known.

The wheel of history must not be turned back, and man's advance toward a spiritual life, which began with the primitive rites of initiation, must not be denied. It is permissible for science to divide up its field of inquiry and to operate with limited hypotheses, for science must work in that way: but the human psyche may not be so parcelled out. It is a whole which embraces consciousness, and it is the mother of consciousness. Scientific thought, being only one of the psyche's functions, can never exhaust all its potentialities. The psychotherapist must not allow his vision to be coloured by pathology: he must never allow himself to forget that the ailing mind is a human mind and that, for all its ailments, it unconsciously shares the whole psychic life of man. He must even be able to admit that the ego is sick for the very reason that it is cut off from the whole, and has lost its connection not only with mankind but with the spirit. The ego is indeed the "place of fears," as Freud says in *The Ego and the Id*, but only so long as it has not returned to its "father" and "mother." Freud founders on the question of Nicodemus: "How can a man be born when he is old? Can he enter the second time into his mother's womb, and be born?" (John 3:4). History repeats itself, for—to compare small things with great—the question reappears today in the domestic quarrel of modern psychology.   15

For thousands of years, rites of initiation have been teaching rebirth from the spirit; yet, strangely enough, man forgets again and again the meaning of divine procreation. Though this may be poor testimony to the strength of the spirit, the penalty for misunderstanding is neurotic decay, embitterment, atrophy, and sterility. It is easy enough to drive the spirit out of the door, but when we have done so the meal has lost its savour—the salt of the earth. Fortunately, we have proof that the spirit always renews its   16 strength in the fact that the essential teaching of the initiations is handed on from generation to generation. Ever and again there are human beings who understand what it means that God is their father. The equal balance of the flesh and the spirit is not lost to the world.

The contrast between Freud and myself goes back to essential [17] differences in our basic assumptions. Assumptions are unavoidable, and this being so it is wrong to pretend that we have no assumptions. That is why I have dealt with fundamental questions; with these as a starting-point, the manifold and detailed differences between Freud's views and my own can best be understood.

James Thurber

University Days

James Thurber (1894–1961) was one of America's leading humorists, essayists, and cartoonists. He grew up in Columbus, Ohio, and attended the Ohio State University. In 1925 he joined the Staff of The New Yorker, where E. B. White (see the next essay) helped him to perfect his prose style. Aware that the humorist's imagination is "set in motion by the damp hand of melancholy," Thurber once defined humor as "a kind of emotional chaos told about calmly and quietly in retrospect." Among Thurber's books of stories, essays, and the drawings that Dorothy Parker called "unbaked cookies" are: Is Sex Necessary? (1929 with E. B. White); The Owl in the Attic (1931); The Middle-Aged Man on the Flying Trapeze (1935); Let Your Mind Alone! (1937); My World—and Welcome to It (1942); The Thurber Carnival (1945); Alarms and Diversions (1957); The Years with Ross (1959); Lanterns and Lances (1961) and Credos and Curios (1962). "University Days" appears in one of Thurber's most successful books, My Life and Hard Times (1933).

I passed all the other courses that I took at my University, but I could never pass botany. This was because all botany students had to spend several hours a week in a laboratory looking through a microscope at plant cells, and I could never see through a microscope. I never once saw a cell through a microscope. This used to enrage my instructor. He would wander around the laboratory pleased with the progress all the students were making in drawing the involved and, so I am told, interesting structure of flower cells, until he came to me. I would just be standing there. "I can't see anything," I would say. He would begin patiently enough, explaining how anybody can see through a microscope, but he would always end up in a fury; claiming that I could *too* see through a microscope but just pretended that I couldn't. "It takes away from the beauty of flowers anyway," I used to tell him. "We are not concerned with beauty in this course," he would say. "We are concerned solely with what I may call the *mechanics* of flars." "Well," I'd say. "I can't see anything." "Try it just once again," he'd say, and I would put my eye to the microscope and see nothing at all, except now and again a nebulous milky substance—a phenomenon of maladjustment. You were supposed to see a vivid, restless clockwork of sharply defined plant cells. "I see what looks like a lot of milk," I would tell him. This, he claimed, was the result of my not having adjused the microscope properly, so he would readjust it for me, or rather, for himself. And I would look again and see milk.

I finally took a deferred pass, as they called it, and waited a year and tried again. (You had to pass one of the biological sciences or you couldn't graduate.) The professor had come back from vacation brown as a berry, bright-eyed, and eager to explain cell-structure again to his classes. "Well," he said to me, cheerily, when we met in the first laboratory hour of the semester, "we're going to see cells this time, aren't we?" "Yes, sir," I said. Students to the right of me and left of me and in front of me were seeing cells; what's more, they were quietly drawing pictures of them in their notebooks. Of course, I didn't see anything. 2

"We'll try it," the professor said to me, grimly, "with every adjustment of the microscope known to man. As God is my witness, I'll arrange this glass so that you see cells through it or I'll give up teaching. In twenty-two years of botony, I—" He cut off abruptly for he was beginning to quiver all over, like Lionel Barrymore,[1] and he genuinely wished to hold onto his temper; his scenes with me had taken a great deal out of him. 3

So we tried it with every adjustment of the microscope known to man. With only one of them did I see anything but blackness or the familiar lacteal opacity, and that time I saw, to my pleasure and amazement, a variegated constellation of flecks, specks, and dots. These I hastily drew. The instructor, noting my activity, 4

[1] (1878–1954), American actor.

came from an adjoining desk, a smile on his lips and his eyebrows high in hope. He looked at my cell drawing. "What's that?" he demanded, with a hint of squeal in his voice. "That's what I saw," I said. "You didn't, you didn't, you *did*n't!" he screamed, losing control of his temper instantly, and he bent over and squinted into the microscope. His head snapped up. "That's your eye!" he shouted. "You've fixed the lens so that it reflects! You've drawn your eye!"

Another course that I didn't like, but somehow managed to pass, was economics. I went to that class straight from the botany class, which didn't help me any in understanding either subject. I used to get them mixed up. But not as mixed up as another student in my economics class who came there direct from a physics laboratory. He was a tackle on the football team, named Bolenciecwcz. At that time Ohio State University had one of the best football teams in the country, and Bolenciecwcz was one of its outstanding stars. In order to be eligible to play it was necessary for him to keep up in his studies, a very difficult matter, for while he was not dumber than an ox he was not any smarter. Most of his professors were lenient and helped him along. None gave him more hints, in answering questions, or asked him simpler ones than the economics professor, a thin, timid man named Bassum. One day when we were on the subject of transportation and distribution, it came Bolenciecwcz's turn to answer a question. "Name one means of transportation," the professor said to him. No light came into the big tackle's eyes. "Just any means of transportation," said the professor. Bolenciecwcz sat staring at him. "That is," pursued the professor, "any medium, agency, or method of going from one place to another." Bolenciecwcz had the look of a man who is being led into a trap. "You may choose among steam, horse-drawn, or electrically propelled vehicles," said the instructor. "I might suggest the one which we commonly take in making long journeys across land." There was a profound silence in which everybody stirred uneasily, including Bolenciecwcz and Mr. Bassum. Mr. Bassum abruptly broke this silence in an amazing manner. "Choo-choo-choo," he said, in a low voice, and turned instantly scarlet. He glanced appealingly around the room. All of us, of course, shared Mr. Bassum's desire that Bolenciecwcz should stay abreast of the class in economics, for the Illinois game, one

5

of the hardest and most important of the season, was only a week off. "Toot, toot, too-toooooooot!" some student with a deep voice moaned, and we all looked encouragingly at Bolenciecwcz. Somebody else gave a fine imitation of a locomotive letting off steam. Mr. Bassum himself rounded off the little show. "Ding, dong, ding, dong," he said, hopefully. Bolenciecwcz was staring at the floor now, trying to think, his great brow furrowed, his huge hands rubbing together, his face red.

"How did you come to college this year, Mr. Bolenciecwcz?" 6 asked the professor. "*Chuffa* chuffa, *chuffa* chuffa."

"M'father sent me," said the football player. 7

"What on?" asked Bassum. 8

"I git an 'lowance," said the tackle, in a low, husky voice, 9 obviously embarrassed.

"No, no," said Bassum. "Name a means of transportation. 10 What did you *ride* here on?"

"Train," said Bolenciecwcz. 11

"Quite right," said the professor. "Now, Mr. Nugent, will you 12 tell us—"

If I went through anguish in botany and economics—for dif- 13 ferent reasons—gymnasium work was even worse. I don't even like to think about it. They wouldn't let you play games or join in the exercises with your glasses on and I couldn't see with mine off. I bumped into professors, horizontal bars, agricultural students, and swinging iron rings. Not being able to see, I could take it but I couldn't dish it out. Also, in order to pass gymnasium (and you had to pass it to graduate) you had to learn to swim if you didn't know how. I didn't like the swimming pool, I didn't like swimming, and I didn't like the swimming instructor, and after all these years I still don't. I never swam but I passed my gym work anyway, by having another student give my gymnasium number (978) and swim across the pool in my place. He was a quiet, amiable blonde youth, number 473, and he would have seen through a microscope for me if we could have got away with it, but we couldn't get away with it. Another thing I didn't like about gymnasium work was that they made you strip the day you registered. It is impossible for me to be happy when I am stripped and being asked a lot of questions. Still, I did better than a lanky agricultural student who was cross-examined just before I was. They asked each student what college he was in—that is, whether Arts, Engineering, Commerce, or Agriculture. "What college are you in?" the instructor snapped at the youth in front of me. "Ohio State University," he said promptly.

It wasn't that agricultural student but it was another a whole   14
lot like him who decided to take up journalism, possibly on the ground that when farming went to hell he could fall back on newspaper work. He didn't realize, of course, that that would be very much like falling back full-length on a kit of carpenter's tools. Haskins didn't seem cut out for journalism, being too embarassed to talk to anybody and unable to use a typewriter, but the editor of the college paper assigned him to the cow barns, the sheep house, the horse pavilion, and the animal husbandry department generally. This was a genuinely big "beat," for it took up five times as much ground and got ten times as great a legislative appropriation as the College of Liberal Arts. The agricultural student knew animals, but nevertheless his stories were dull and colorlessly written. He took all afternoon on each one of them, on account of having to hunt for each letter on the typewriter. Once in a while he had to ask somebody to help him hunt. "C" and "L," in particular, were hard letters for him to find. His editor finally got pretty much annoyed at the farmer-journalist because his pieces were so uninteresting. "See here, Haskins," he snapped at him one day, "why is it we never have anything hot from you on the horse pavilion? Here we have two hundred head of horses on this campus—more than any other university in the Western Conference except Purdue—and yet you never get any real low down on them. Now shoot over to the horse barns and dig up something lively." Haskins shambled out and came back in about an hour; he said he had something. "Well, start it off snappily," said the editor. "Something people will read." Haskins set to work and in a couple of hours brought a sheet of typewritten paper to the desk; it was a two-hundred word story about some disease that had broken out among the horses. Its opening sentence was simple but arresting. It read: "Who has noticed the sores on the tops of the horses in the animal husbandry building?"

Ohio State was a land grant university and therefore two years   15
of military drill was compulsory. We drilled with old Springfield rifles and studied the tactics of the Civil War even though the

World War was going on at the time.[2] At 11 o'clock each morning thousands of freshmen and sophomores used to deploy over
the campus, moodily creeping up on the old chemistry building.
It was good training for the kind of warfare that was waged at
Shiloh but it had no connection with what was going on in Europe. Some people used to think there was German money behind
it, but they didn't dare say so or they would have been thrown
in jail as German spies. It was a period of muddy thought and
marked, I believe, the decline of higher education in the Middle
West.

As a soldier I was never any good at all. Most of the cadets were   16
glumly indifferent soldiers, but I was no good at all. Once General
Littlefield, who was commandant of the cadet corps, popped up
in front of me during regimental drill and snapped, "You are the
main trouble with this university!" I think he meant that my type
was the main trouble with the university but he may have meant
me individually. I was mediocre at drill, certainly—that is, until
my senior year. By that time I had drilled longer than anybody
else in the Western Conference, having failed at military at the
end of each preceding year so that I had to do it all over again. I
was the only senior still in uniform. The uniform which, when
new, had made me look like an interurban railway conductor,
now that it had become faded and too tight made me look like
Bert Williams in his bellboy act. This had a definitely bad effect
on my morale. Even so, I had become by sheer practice little short
of wonderful at squad manoeuvres.

One day General Littlefield picked our company out of the   17
whole regiment and tried to get it mixed up by putting it through
one movement after another as fast as we could execute them:
squads right, squads left, squads on right into line, squads right
about, squads left front into line etc. In about three minutes one
hundred and nine men were marching in one direction and I was
marching away from them at an angle of forty degrees, all alone.
"Company, halt!" shouted General Littlefield, "That man is the
only man who has it right!" I was made a corporal for my achievement.

2 The World War I armistice was signed November 11, 1918, two days before Thurber landed in Paris as a code clerk for the state department.

The next day General Littlefield summoned me to his office.   18
He was swatting flies when I went in. I was silent and he was
silent too, for a long time. I don't think he remembered me or why
he had sent for me, but he didn't want to admit it. He swatted
some more flies, keeping his eyes on them narrowly before he let
go with the swatter. "Button up your coat!" he snapped. Looking
back on it now I can see that he meant me although he was looking at a fly, but I just stood there. Another fly came to rest on a
paper in front of the general and began rubbing its hind legs
together. The general lifted the swatter cautiously. I moved rest-
lessly and the fly flew away. "You startled him!" barked General
Littlefield, looking at me severely. I said I was sorry. "That won't
help the situation!" snapped the General, with cold military logic.
I didn't see what I could do except offer to chase some more flies
toward his desk, but I didn't say anything. He stared out the window at the faraway figures of co-eds crossing the campus toward
the library. Finally, he told me I could go. So I went. He either
didn't know which cadet I was or else he forgot what he wanted
to see me about. It may have been that he wished to apologize
for having called me the main trouble with the university; or
maybe he had decided to compliment me on my brilliant drilling
of the day before and then at the last minute decided not to. I
don't know. I don't think about it much any more.

E. B. White

Once More to the Lake

*Elwyn Brooks White, the dean of American essayists, a story-
teller and a poet, was born in Mount Vernon, New York, in 1899.
After studying at Cornell University, he joined the staff of The
New Yorker in 1926. A gifted reporter of urban life, White was
to find the city too "seductive," and he gradually spent more and
more time on his farm in Maine, where he moved more or less
permanently in 1957. Widely praised for his prose style, White
wrote a regular column, "One Man's Meat" for Harper's and
many editorials for The New Yorker. He has published nineteen
books, including Charlotte's Web (1952, for children); The
Second Tree from the Corner (1954); The Elements of Style
(1959, an enlargement of William Strunk's handbook for writers);
The Points of My Compass (1962); and The Letters of E. B.
White (1976). "Once More to the Lake," a narrative about the
generations, is reprinted from Essays of E. B. White (1977); written in August 1941, it originally appeared in Harper's and later
in One Man's Meat (1942).*

One summer, along about 1904, my father rented a camp   1
on a lake in Maine and took us all there for the month of
August. We all got ringworm from some kittens and had to
rub Pond's Extract on our arms and legs night and morning,
and my father rolled over in a canoe with all his clothes on;
but outside of that the vacation was a success and from then
on none of us ever thought there was any place in the world
like that lake in Maine. We returned summer after summer—
always on August 1 for one month. I have since become a
salt-water man, but sometimes in summer there are days

when the restlessness of the tides and the fearful cold of the sea water and the incessant wind that blows across the afternoon and into the evening make me wish for the placidity of a lake in the woods. A few weeks ago this feeling got so strong I bought myself a couple of bass hooks and a spinner and returned to the lake where we used to go, for a week's fishing and to revisit old haunts.

I took along my son, who had never had any fresh water up his   2
nose and who had seen lily pads only from train windows. On the journey over to the lake I began to wonder what it would be like. I wondered how the time would have marred this unique, this holy spot—the coves and streams, the hills that the sun set behind, the camps and the paths behind the camps. I was sure that the tarred road would have found it out, and I wondered in what other ways it would be desolated. It is strange how much you can remember about places like that once you allow your mind to return into the grooves that lead back. You remember one thing, and that suddenly reminds you of another thing. I guess I remembered clearest of all the early mornings, when the lake was cool and motionless, remembered how the bedroom smelled of the lumber it was made of and of the wet woods whose scent entered through the screen. The partitions in the camp were thin and did not extend clear to the top of the rooms, and as I was always the first up I would dress softly so as not to wake the others, and sneak out into the sweet outdoors and start out in the canoe, keeping close along the shore in the long shadows of the pines. I remembered being very careful never to rub my paddle against the gunwale for fear of disturbing the stillness of the cathedral.

The lake had never been what you would call a wild lake. There   3
were cottages sprinkled around the shores, and it was in farming country although the shores of the lake were quite heavily wooded. Some of the cottages were owned by nearby farmers, and you would live at the shore and eat your meals at the farmhouse. That's what our family did. But although it wasn't wild, it was a fairly large and undisturbed lake and there were places in it that, to a child at least, seemed infinitely remote and primeval.

I was right about the tar: it led to within half a mile of the   4
shore. But when I got back there, with my boy, and we settled into a camp near a farmhouse and into the kind of summertime I had known, I could tell that it was going to be pretty much the same as it had been before—I knew it, lying in bed the first morn

ing, smelling the bedroom and hearing the boy sneak quietly out and go off along the shore in a boat. I began to sustain the illusion that he was I, and therefore, by simple transposition, that I was my father. This sensation persisted, kept cropping up all the time we were there. It was not an entirely new feeling, but in this setting, it grew much stronger. I seemed to be living a dual existence. I would be in the middle of some simple act, I would be picking up a bait box or laying down a table fork, or I would be saying something, and suddenly it would be not I but my father who was saying the words or making the gesture. It gave me a creepy sensation.

We went fishing the first morning. I felt the same damp moss 5 covering the worms in the bait can, and saw the dragonfly alight on the tip of my rod as it hovered a few inches from the surface of the water. It was the arrival of this fly that convinced me beyond any doubt that everything was as it always had been, that the years were a mirage and that there had been no years. The small waves were the same, chucking the rowboat under the chin as we fished at anchor, and the boat was the same boat, the same color green and the ribs broken in the same places, and under the floorboards the same fresh-water leavings and débris—the dead helgramite, the wisps of moss, the rusty discarded fishhook, the dried blood from yesterday's catch. We stared silently at the tips of our rods, at the dragonflies that came and went. I lowered the tip of mine into the water, tentatively, pensively dislodging the fly, which darted two feet away, poised, darted two feet back, and came to rest again a little farther up the rod. There had been no years between the ducking of this dragonfly and the other one— the one that was part of memory. I looked at the boy, who was silently watching his fly, and it was my hands that held his rod, my eyes watching. I felt dizzy and didn't know which rod I was at the end of.

We caught two bass, hauling them in briskly as though they 6 were mackerel, pulling them over the side of the boat in a businesslike manner without any landing net, and stunning them with a blow on the back of the head. When we got back for a swim before lunch, the lake was exactly where we had left it, the same number of inches from the dock, and there was only the merest suggestion of a breeze. This seemed an utterly enchanted sea, this lake you could leave to its own devices for a few hours and come back to, and find that it had not stirred, this constant and trust-worthy body of water. In the shallows, the dark, water-soaked sticks and twigs, smooth and old, were undulating in clusters on the bottom against the clean ribbed sand, and the track of the mussel was plain. A school of minnows swam by, each minnow with its small individual shadow, doubling the attendance, so clear and sharp in the sunlight. Some of the other campers were in swimming, along the shore, one of them with a cake of soap, and the water felt thin and clear and unsubstantial. Over the years there had been this person with the cake of soap, this cultist, and here he was. There had been no years.

Up to the farmhouse to dinner through the teeming, dusty field, the road under our sneakers was only a two-track road. The middle track was missing, the one with the marks of the hooves and the splotches of dried, flaky manure. There had always been three tracks to choose from in choosing which track to walk in; now the choice was narrowed down to two. For a moment I missed ter-ribly the middle alternative. But the way led past the tennis court, and something about the way it lay there in the sun reassured me; the tape had loosened along the backline, the alleys were green with plantains and other weeds, and the net (installed in June and removed in September) sagged in the dry noon, and the whole place steamed with midday heat and hunger and emptiness. There was a choice of pie for dessert, and one was blueberry and one was apple, and the waitresses were the same country girls, there having been no passage of time, only the illusion of it as in a dropped cur-tain—the waitresses were still fifteen; their hair had been washed, that was the only difference—they had been to the movies and seen the pretty girls with the clean hair. 7

Summertime, oh, summertime, pattern of life indelible, the fade-proof lake, the woods unshatterable, the pasture with the sweetfern and the juniper forever and ever, summer without end; this was the background, and the life along the shore was the design, the cottages with their innocent and tranquil design, their tiny docks with the flagpole and the American flag floating against the white clouds in the blue sky, the little paths over the roots of the trees leading from camp to camp and the paths leading back to the outhouses and the can of lime for sprinkling, and at the souvenir counters at the store the miniature birch-bark canoes and the postcards that showed things looking a little better than 8 they looked. This was the American family at play, escaping the city heat, wondering whether the newcomers in the camp at the head of the cove were "common" or "nice," wondering whether it was true that the people who drove up for Sunday dinner at the farmhouse were turned away because there wasn't enough chicken.

It seemed to me, as I kept remembering all this, that those 9 times and those summers had been infinitely precious and worth saving. There had been jollity and peace and goodness. The arriving (at the beginning of August) had been so big a business in itself, at the railway station the farm wagon drawn up, the first smell of the pine-laden air, the first glimpse of the smiling farmer, and the great importance of the trunks and your father's enormous authority in such matters, and the feel of the wagon under you for the long ten-mile haul, and at the top of the last long hill catching the first view of the lake after eleven months of not seeing this cherished body of water. The shouts and cries of the other campers when they saw you, and the trunks to be unpacked, to give up their rich burden. (Arriving was less exciting nowadays, when you sneaked up in your car and parked it under a tree near the camp and took out the bags and in five minutes it was all over, no fuss, no loud wonderful fuss about trunks.)

Peace and goodness and jollity. The only thing that was wrong 10 now, really, was the sound of the place, an unfamiliar nervous sound of the outboard motors. This was the note that jarred, the one thing that would sometimes break the illusion and set the years moving. In those other summertimes all motors were inboard; and when they were at a little distance, the noise they made was a sedative, an ingredient of summer sleep. They were one-cylinder and two-cylinder engines, and some were make-and-break and some were jump-spark, but they all made a sleepy sound across the lake. The one-lungers throbbed and fluttered, and the twin-cylinder ones purred and purred, and that was a quiet sound, too. But now the campers all had outboards. In the daytime, in the hot mornings, these motors made a petulant, irritable sound; at night, in the still evening when the afterglow lit the water, they whined about one's ears like mosquitoes. My boy loved our rented outboard, and his great desire was to achieve single-handed mastery over it, and authority, and he soon learned the trick of choking it a little (but not too much), and the adjustment of the needle valve. Watching him I would remember the things you could do with the old one-cylinder engine with the heavy flywheel, how you could have it eating out of your hand if you got really close to it spiritually. Motorboats in those days didn't have clutches, and you would make a landing by shutting off the motor at the proper time and coasting in with a dead rudder. But there was a way of reversing them, if you learned the trick, by cutting the switch and putting it on again exactly on the final dying revolution of the flywheel, so that it would kick back against compression and begin reversing. Approaching a dock in a strong following breeze, it was difficult to slow up sufficiently by the ordinary coasting method, and if a boy felt he had complete mastery over his motor, he was tempted to keep it running beyond its time and then reverse it a few feet from the dock. It took a cool nerve, because if you threw the switch a twentieth of a second too soon you would catch the flywheel when it still had speed enough to go up past center, and the boat would leap ahead, charging bull-fashion at the dock.

We had a good week at the camp. The bass were biting well and the sun shone endlessly, day after day. We would be tired at night and lie down in the accumulated heat of the little bedrooms after the long hot day and the breeze would stir almost imperceptibly outside and the smell of the swamp drift in through the rusty screens. Sleep would come easily and in the morning the red squirrel would be on the roof, tapping out his gay routine. I kept remembering everything, lying in bed in the mornings—the small steamboat that had a long rounded stern like the lip of a Ubangi, and how quietly she ran on the moonlight sails, when the older boys played their mandolins and the girls sang and we ate doughnuts dipped in sugar, and how sweet the music was on the water in the shining night, and what it had felt like to think about girls then. After breakfast we would go up to the store and the things were in the same place—the minnows in a bottle, the plugs and spinners disarranged and pawed over by the youngsters from the boys' camp, the Fig Newtons and the Beeman's gum. Outside, the road was tarred and cars stood in front of the store. Inside, all was just as it had always been, except there was more Coca-Cola and not so much Moxie [1] and root beer and birch beer

11

1 Brand name of an old-fashioned soft drink.

and sarsaparilla. We would walk out with the bottle of pop apiece and sometimes the pop would backfire up our noses and hurt. We explored the streams, quietly, where the turtles slid off logs and dug their way into the soft bottom; and we lay on the town wharf and fed worms to the tame bass. Everywhere we went I had trouble making out which was I, the one walking at my side, the one walking in my pants.

One afternoon while we were there at that lake a thunderstorm   12
came up. It was like the revival of an old melodrama that I had seen long ago with childish awe. The second-act climax of the drama of the electrical disturbance over a lake in America has not changed in any important respect. This was the big scene, still the big scene. The whole thing was so familiar, the first feeling of oppression and heat and a general air around camp of not wanting to go very far away. In midafternoon (it was all the same) a curious darkening of the sky, and a lull in everything that had made life tick; and then the way the boats suddenly swung the other way at their moorings with the coming of a breeze out of the new quarter, and the premonitory rumble. Then the kettle drum, then the snare, then the bass drum and cymbals, then crackling light against the dark, and the gods grinning and licking their chops in the hills. Afterward the calm, the rain steadily rustling in the calm lake, the return of light and hope and spirits, and the campers running out in joy and relief to go swimming in the rain, their bright cries perpetuating the deathless joke about how they were getting simply drenched, and the children screaming with delight at the new sensation of bathing in the rain, and the joke about getting drenched linking the generations in a strong indestructible chain. And the comedian who waded in carrying an umbrella.

When the others went swimming, my son said he was going in,   13
too. He pulled his dripping trunks from the line where they had hung all through the shower and wrung them out. Languidly, and with no thought of going in, I watched him, his hard little body, skinny and bare, saw him wince slightly as he pulled up around his vitals the small, soggy, icy garment. As he buckled the swollen belt, suddenly my groin felt the chill of death.

Rachel Carson

The Obligation to Endure

Rachel Carson (1907–1964), a native of Springdale, Pennsylvania, was a marine biologist, conservationist, and award-winning science writer. From earliest childhood, she was intrigued with the ocean, and she dreamed of becoming a writer. She studied zoology at Pennsylvania College for Women and the Johns Hopkins University (M.A., 1932), taught briefly at the University of Maryland, and soon joined what is now the U.S. Fish and Wildlife Service. Then came the war, after which she returned to the Fisheries' office, becoming the editor of Fish and Wildlife in 1949. In 1952 she retired from government service to devote full time to writing. Most of her training in marine biology was acquired over the years in the laboratories at Woods Hole, Mass., and Beaufort, N.C. Carson's principal works are Under the Sea-Wind (1941); The Sea Around Us (1951, winner of the National Book Award); and Silent Spring (1962), a milestone in the literature of ecology. "The Obligation to Endure," a complete chapter from Silent Spring, makes the case against insecticides and other chemical pollutants.

The history of life on earth has been a history of interaction   1
between living things and their surroundings. To a large extent, the physical form and the habits of the earth's vegetation and its animal life have been molded by the environment. Considering the whole span of earthly time, the opposite effect, in which life actually modifies its surroundings, has been relatively slight. Only within the moment of time represented by the present century has one species—man—acquired significant power to alter the nature of his world.

During the past quarter century this power has not only increased to one of disturbing magnitude but it has changed in character. The most alarming of all man's assaults upon the environment is the contamination of air, earth, rivers, and sea with dangerous and even lethal materials. This pollution is for the most part irrecoverable, the chain of evil it initiates not only in the world that must support life but in living tissues is for the most part irreversible. In this now universal contamination of the environment, chemicals are the sinister and little-recognized partners of radiation in changing the very nature of the world—the very nature of its life. Strontium 90, released through nuclear explosions into the air, comes to earth in rain or drifts down as fallout, lodges in soil, enters into the grass or corn or wheat grown there, and in time takes up its abode in the bones of a human being, there to remain until his death. Similarly, chemicals sprayed on croplands or forests or gardens lie long in soils, entering into living organisms, passing from one to another in a chain of poisoning and death. Or they pass mysteriously by underground streams until they emerge and, through the alchemy of air and sunlight, combine into new forms that kill vegetation, sicken cattle, and work unknown harm on those who drink from once-pure wells. As Albert Schweitzer [1] has said, "Man can hardly even recognize the devils of his own creation."

It took hundreds of millions of years to produce the life that now inhabits the earth—eons of time in which that developing and evolving and diversifying life reached a state of adjustment and balance with its surroundings. The environment, rigorously shaping and directing the life it supported, contained elements that were hostile as well as supporting. Certain rocks gave out dangerous radiation; even within the light of the sun, from which all life draws its energy, there were short-wave radiations with power to injure. Given time—time not in years but in millennia—life adjusts, and a balance has been reached. For time is the essential ingredient; but in the modern world there is no time.

The rapidity of change and the speed with which new situations are created follow the impetuous and heedless pace of man rather

---

[1] (1875–1965), Alsatian philosopher, theologian, musician, and medical missionary to Africa.

than the deliberate pace of nature. Radiation is no longer merely the background radiation of rocks, the bombardment of cosmic rays, the ultraviolet of the sun that have existed before there was any life on earth; radiation is now the unnatural creation of man's tampering with the atom. The chemicals to which life is asked to make its adjustment are no longer merely the calcium and silica and copper and all the rest of the minerals washed out of the rocks and carried in rivers to the sea; they are the synthetic creations of man's inventive mind, brewed in his laboratories, and having no counterparts in nature.

To adjust to these chemicals would require time on the scale   5 that is nature's; it would require not merely the years of a man's life but the life of generations. And even this, were it by some miracle possible, would be futile, for the new chemicals come from our laboratories in an endless stream; almost five hundred annually find their way into actual use in the United States alone. The figure is staggering and its implications are not easily grasped—500 new chemicals to which the bodies of men and animals are required somehow to adapt each year, chemicals totally outside the limits of biologic experience.

Among them are many that are used in man's war against   6 nature. Since the mid-1940's over 200 basic chemicals have been created for use in killing insects, weeds, rodents, and other organisms described in the modern vernacular as "pests"; and they are sold under several thousand different brand names.

These sprays, dusts, and aerosols are now applied almost uni-   7 versally to farms, gardens, forests, and homes—nonselective chemicals that have the power to kill every insect, the "good" and the "bad," to still the song of birds and the leaping of fish in the streams, to coat the leaves with a deadly film, and to linger on in soil—all this though the intended target may be only a few weeds or insects. Can anyone believe it is possible to lay down such a barrage of poisons on the surface of the earth without making it unfit for all life? They should not be called "insecticides," but "biocides."

The whole process of spraying seems caught up in an endless   8 spiral. Since DDT was released for civilian use, a process of escalation has been going on in which ever more toxic materials must be found. This has happened because insects, in a triumphant vindication of Darwin's [2] principle of the survival of the fittest, have evolved super races immune to the particular insecticide used, hence a deadlier one has always to be developed—and then a deadlier one than that. It has happened also because, for reasons to be described later, destructive insects often undergo a "flare-back," or resurgence, after spraying, in numbers greater than before. Thus the chemical war is never won, and all life is caught in its violent crossfire.

Along with the possibility of the extinction of mankind by nuclear war, the central problem of our age has therefore become the contamination of man's total environment with such substances of incredible potential for harm—substances that accumulate in the tissues of plants and animals and even penetrate the germ cells to shatter or alter the very material of heredity upon which the shape of the future depends.

Some would-be architects of our future look toward a time when it will be possible to alter the human germ plasm by design. But we may easily be doing so now by inadvertence, for many chemicals, like radiation, bring about gene mutations. It is ironic to think that man might determine his own future by something so seemingly trivial as the choice of an insect spray.

All this has been risked—for what? Future historians may well be amazed by our distorted sense of proportion. How could intelligent beings seek to control a few unwanted species by a method that contaminated the entire environment and brought the threat of disease and death even to their own kind? Yet this is precisely what we have done. We have done it, moreover, for reasons that collapse the moment we examine them. We are told that the enormous and expanding use of pesticides is necessary to maintain farm production. Yet is our real problem not one of *overproduction?* Our farms, despite measures to remove acreages from production and to pay farmers *not* to produce, have yielded such a staggering excess of crops that the American taxpayer is paying out more than one billion dollars a year as the total carrying cost of the surplus-food storage program. And is the situation helped when one branch of the Agriculture Department tries to reduce

2 British naturalist Charles Darwin (1809–1882) based his theory of evolution upon "natural selection"; "survival of the fittest" was Herbert Spencer's (1820–1903) restatement of this idea.

production while another states, as it did in 1958, "It is believed generally that reduction of crop acreages under provisions of the Soil Bank will stimulate interest in use of chemicals to obtain maximum production on the land retained in crops."

All this is not to say there is no insect problem and no need of control. I am saying, rather, that control must be geared to realities, not to mythical situations, and that the methods employed must be such that they do not destroy us along with the insects.   12

The problem whose attempted solution has brought such a train of disaster in its wake is an accompaniment of our modern way of life. Long before the age of man, insects inhabited the earth—a group of extraordinarily varied and adaptable beings. Over the course of time since man's advent, a small percentage of the more than half a million species of insects have come into conflict with human welfare in two principal ways: as competitors for the food supply and as carriers of human disease.   13

Disease-carrying insects become important where human beings are crowded together, especially under conditions where sanitation is poor, as in time of natural disaster or war or in situations of extreme poverty and deprivation. Then control of some sort becomes necessary. It is a sobering fact, however, as we shall presently see, that the method of massive chemical control has had only limited success, and also threatens to worsen the very conditions it is intended to curb.   14

Under primitive agricultural conditions the farmer had few insect problems. These arose with the intensification of agriculture—the devotion of immense acreages to a single crop. Such a system set the stage for explosive increases in specific insect populations. Single-crop farming does not take advantage of the principles by which nature works; it is agriculture as an engineer might conceive it to be. Nature has introduced great variety into the landscape, but man has displayed a passion for simplifying it. Thus he undoes the built-in checks and balances by which nature holds the species within bounds. One important natural check is a limit on the amount of suitable habitat for each species. Obviously then, an insect that lives on wheat can build up its population to much higher levels on a farm devoted to wheat than on one in which wheat is intermingled with other crops to which the insect is not adapted.   15

The same thing happens in other situations. A generation or [16]
more ago, the towns of large areas of the United States lined
their streets with the noble elm tree. Now the beauty they hopefully created is threatened with complete destruction as disease
sweeps through the elms, carried by a beetle that would have only
limited chance to build up large populations and to spread from
tree to tree if the elms were only occasional trees in a richly
diversified planting.

Another factor in the modern insect problem is one that must be [17]
viewed against a background of geologic and human history: the
spreading of thousands of different kinds of organisms from their
native homes to invade new territories. This worldwide migration
has been studied and graphically described by the British ecologist
Charles Elton in his recent book *The Ecology of Invasions*. During the Cretaceous Period, some hundred million years ago, flood-
ing seas cut many land bridges between continents and living
things found themselves confined in what Elton calls "colossal
separate nature reserves." There, isolated from others of their kind,
they developed many new species. When some of the land masses
were joined again, about 15 million years ago, these species began
to move out into new territories—a movement that is not only
still in progress but is now receiving considerable assistance from
man.

The importation of plants is the primary agent in the modern [18]
spread of species, for animals have almost invariably gone along
with the plants, quarantine being a comparatively recent and not
completely effective innovation. The United States Office of Plant
Introduction alone has introduced almost 200,000 species and
varieties of plants from all over the world. Nearly half of the 180
or so major insect enemies of plants in the United States are
accidental imports from abroad, and most of them have come as
hitchhikers on plants.

In new territory, out of reach of the restraining hand of the [19]
natural enemies that kept down its numbers in its native land, an
invading plant or animal is able to become enormously abundant.
Thus it is no accident that our most troublesome insects are introduced species.

These invasions, both the naturally occurring and those depen- [20]
dent on human assistance, are likely to continue indefinitely.
Quarantine and massive chemical campaigns are only extremely

expensive ways of buying time. We are faced, according to Dr. Elton, "with a life-and-death need not just to find new technological means of suppressing this plant or that animal"; instead we need the basic knowledge of animal populations and their relations to their surroundings that will "promote an even balance and damp down the explosive power of outbreaks and new invasions."

Much of the necessary knowledge is now available but we do   21
not use it. We train ecologists in our universities and even employ them in our government agencies but we seldom take their advice. We allow the chemical death rain to fall as though there were no alternative, whereas in fact there are many, and our ingenuity could soon discover many more if given opportunity.

Have we fallen into a mesmerized state that makes us accept as   22
inevitable that which is inferior or detrimental, as though having lost the will or the vision to demand that which is good? Such thinking, in the words of the ecologist Paul Shepard, "idealizes life with only its head out of water, inches above the limits of toleration of the corruption of its own environment . . . Why should we tolerate a diet of weak poisons, a home in insipid surroundings, a circle of acquaintances who are not quite our enemies, the noise of motors with just enough relief to prevent insanity? Who would want to live in a world which is just not quite fatal?"

Yet such a world is pressed upon us. The crusade to create a   23
chemically sterile, insect-free world seems to have engendered a fanatic zeal on the part of many specialists and most of the so-called control agencies. On every hand there is evidence that those engaged in spraying operations exercise a ruthless power. "The regulatory entomologists . . . function as prosecutor, judge and jury, tax assessor and collector and sheriff to enforce their own orders," said Connecticut entomologist Neely Turner. The most flagrant abuses go unchecked in both state and federal agencies.

It is not my contention that chemical insecticides must never   24
be used. I do contend that we have put poisonous and biologically potent chemicals indiscriminately into the hands of persons largely or wholly ignorant of their potentials for harm. We have subjected enormous numbers of people to contact with these poisons, without their consent and often without their knowledge. If the Bill of Rights contains no guarantee that a citizen shall be secure against lethal poisons distributed either by private individuals or by public officials, it is surely only because our forefathers, despite

their considerable wisdom and foresight, could conceive of no such problem.

I contend, furthermore, that we have allowed these chemicals [25] to be used with little or no advance investigation of their effect on soil, water, wildlife, and man himself. Future generations are unlikely to condone our lack of prudent concern for the integrity of the natural world that supports all life.

There is still very limited awareness of the nature of the threat. [26] This is an era of specialists, each of whom sees his own problem and is unaware of or intolerant of the larger frame into which it fits. It is also an era dominated by industry, in which the right to make a dollar at whatever cost is seldom challenged. When the public protests, confronted with some obvious evidence of damaging results of pesticide applications, it is fed little tranquilizing pills of half truth. We urgently need an end to these false assurances, to the sugar coating of unpalatable facts. It is the public that is being asked to assume the risks that the insect controllers calculate. The public must decide whether it wishes to continue on the present road, and it can do so only when in full possession of the facts. In the words of Jean Rostand,[3] "The obligation to endure gives us the right to know."

[3] French biologist and essayist, born in 1894.

Ronald N. Bracewell
The Colonization of Space

Ronald Bracewell, professor of electrical engineering at Stanford University, is an expert on radar, radio astronomy, and celestial mechanics. He was born in Sydney, Australia, in 1921 and obtained degrees from the University of Sydney and Cambridge University, England (Ph.D., 1950). In 1955, after conducting laboratory research in Australia and England, he joined the faculty of Stanford, where he constructed a complex radio telescope that daily produced printed temperature maps of the sun. Bracewell is the author and co-author of many technical publications on wave propogation and radio astronomy, including The Fourier Transform and Its Applications *(1965). "The Colonization of Space" is a chapter of his latest book for nonspecialists,* The Galactic Club: Intelligent Life in Outer Space *(1974). It suggests where we go from the silent planet that Rachel Carson describes in the preceding essay.*

Man will not ultimately be content to be parasitic on the stars but will invade them and organize them for his own purposes.

> —J. D. Bernal, *The World, the Flesh, and the Devil* [1]

Although it is not possible to foresee what the specific [1]
motivation might be, earthly life may someday diffuse into
space. With the pressures of crowding and its attendant pollution, a part of society may consider space to be a better
habitat than earth. Or, as suggested by J. D. Bernal, the driving force for interplanetary colonization may turn out to be
competition for sunlight and meteoric matter.

When the colonists depart, what will their new home be? [2]
One might think first of a giant structure resembling Skylab. [2]
But, as self-sufficiency is a goal for a sustained colony in space,

---

[1] Published in 1929 by British physicist Joseph Desmond Bernal (1901–
1971).
[2] First manned space station, launched by the U.S. in May 1973.

we should keep in mind long-term requirements of self-support: agriculture, animal husbandry, a method for intercepting the necessary solar energy. Such a home in space must be large, but can be smaller than one might initially think. Bernal described space colonies of 20,000 to 30,000 inhabitants living in the interior of globes 10 miles in diameter.

A proposal for the colonization of space has been worked out   3 by Gerard K. O'Neill of Princeton University. He envisages a cylindrical vessel in space, 4 miles in diameter and 16 miles long. With air inside, it spins on its axis once in 1.9 minutes producing a centrifugal force exactly equivalent to gravity on earth. A person could stand up inside the cylinder, and feel that he was walking on level ground. However, his visual impression would be of standing at the bottom of a rounded valley. Trees growing on the sides of the valley would give the impression of leaning downhill (they would have grown up toward the axis, in the direction opposite to the centrifugal force). To brighten the habitat, O'Neill divides the curved surface of the cylinder into six long strips, each two miles wide, and makes three of them transparent windows, thus letting sunlight through onto the three solid strips of steel and soil which will form the inhabited valleys.

Because of the scattering of sunlight by the air molecules con-   4 tained within the cylinder, the sky will appear blue, giving a feeling of naturalness to the habitat. Since the whole cylinder is rotating once each 1.9 minutes, the sun would, however, be winked on and off in a most unnatural way as the three windows pass successively around. To keep the sun fixed in the habitat's sky we need three giant mirrors to deflect the sunlight through the windows, at the same time arranging to point the axis of the cylinder directly at the sun. To appreciate this arrangement consult the graphic depiction in the figure below.

If desired, sunrise and sunset, as well as seasons, can be simu-   5 lated by tilting the mirrors. One of O'Neill's purposes is to provide an attractive habitat—one perhaps preferable to what might be available on earth in years to come. In pursuit of this ideal, the valleys will be laid out as meadows, forests, lakes, villages, and mountains—even to the extent of copying areas of the earth that are celebrated for their scenic beauty. The ends of the cylinder will be sealed to keep the air in through the use of simulated mountains up to two miles high. They will be strange mountains

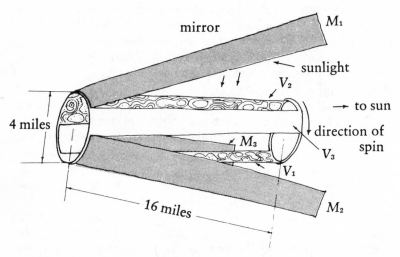

O'Neill's design for space colony, showing the arrangement of three valleys (V_1, V_2, V_3,) separated by windows. Valley V_1 is illuminated by sunlight reflected from mirror M_1, and so on.

to climb. The lack of oxygen noticed on two-mile-high mountains on earth will not be felt, and gravity will diminish as one climbs until a state of virtual weightlessness is at last reached. A vacation of mountain climbing would be a fascinating experience.

The first community would be built mainly from lunar surface materials, with only about 2 percent of the mass brought up from earth. Hydrogen from the earth, combined with oxygen from the lunar surface oxides, would provide water at a big saving in transport requirements. All the matter would be recycled. The later, bigger communities would obtain their materials from the asteroid belt—rich in hydrogen, carbon, and nitrogen as well as in the metals, minerals, and oxygen that are common on the moon.

Many details have been considered by O'Neill that must be omitted here, but may be consulted in the publication *Physics Today*, Sept. 1974. Interesting problems of structure and orbital mechanics arise. One of these is to prevent the spinning cylinder from gyrating like a top; to achieve this O'Neill counteracts the spin by building the cylinders in oppositely rotating pairs. Many biological decisions arise that will be intriguing to explore. How will the balance of nature be simulated and maintained? In O'Neill's plan, for example, birds will be introduced, but not flies and mosquitoes. What will the birds feed on, plants or insects? If insects, what will the insects feed on? Possibly an artificial ecology can be designed, but I wonder whether it will remain under control or develop a direction of its own.

So different are conditions in space from what we are accus- 8 tomed to on earth that it will come as a surprise to learn how the inhabitants of these two adjacent cylinders can visit each other. Calculation shows that a cylinder 4 miles in diameter rotating once in 1.9 minutes has a tangential speed of 400 miles-per-hour. A space shuttle parked on the outside of the clyinder would have to be tied down in order not to be flung off at this speed. However, if released while pointing in the right direction, the shuttle would take off at 400 miles-per-hour and could dock on the outer surface of its parallel and oppositely rotating cylinder nearby, touching down gently at the moment of arrival when the shuttle velocity would exactly equal that of the cylinder. No rocket engine would be required, and no fuel, just a good docking system and good timing.

Weather would result from the draft of warm air rising from 9 the sunlit valley bottoms, carrying moisture with it. Perhaps the moisture would condense into clouds or fog. Would rain fall only at night, and would the clouds form over the valleys? Would there be circulating winds? It is difficult to say what would happen in this system if left to itself. Perhaps the water would tend to condense on the cold windows where it would be pressed into place by centrifugal force, forming lakes which would be used as sources of irrigation water. If so, no rain need ever fall. If rain was desired, perhaps small modifications to the cylinder (making it more like a hexagonal prism, giving it a slight waist like an hour glass, or varying the sunlight by tilting the mirrors) might make it possible to choose and control the climate. Should cylinders continue to be constructed, the experience gained might lead to a diversity of habitats.

Although imitation of terrestrial environments may be a good 10 guiding principle, a cylinder with its broadside to the sun might be a perfectly satisfactory habitat, in which case the giant mirrors could be dispensed with. No dark shadows are to be expected within the cylinder even though the sun apparently races around outside—when any one valley is in shadow there will generally be some light reflected from sunlight strips of the other valleys just a few miles away. In addition, scattered light could be provided by making the windows of a diffusing substance. (Condensation on the interior of the windows would have the same softening effect on the shadows.) The net result could be similar to a day experienced on the North Atlantic coast when low patchy clouds racing overhead maintain a continual interplay of light and shade. While this is not the same as Mediterranean sunlight, it is pleasant to many people and is certainly natural to the earth. Another natural phenomenon is the long twilight of subarctic regions which, while confusing to visitors from temperate zones, is perfectly natural to the natives. In fact, man is so adaptable that great freedom is possible in arranging suitable habitats for him in space, austere as well as utopian. No doubt many ingenious designs will be pursued in coming years.

After this new miniworld becomes self-supporting, how will it   11
repay the loan that enabled it to be assembled with the aid of earth resources in the first place? It is conceivable that the inhabitants could finance their launching from their own capital, but it is hard to see how the earth could afford to spawn new offspring indefinitely. I feel that the urge to expand will lead, by one route or another, to continued colonization of space and utilization of its mass and energy resources. If a way could be formulated whereby the newly launched company could amortize its obligation to earth, I would expect it to be followed.

Since space is a high vacuum useful for special assembly tech-   12
niques, one might think of computer manufacture as a suitable industry in space. Computer manufacture requires high-vacuum conditions, and the computer market will be expanding for a long time. Tourism is another possible space industry. However, working against any commerce between the earth and space colonies will always be the heavy price of lifting or lowering material through the earth's gravitational field. Therefore, saleable services not involving transfer of mass to or from the earth's surface should be sought first.

The two candidates that occur to me are manufacture of space   13
structures and the supply of power. All sorts of space vehicles and space structures will be needed as the activity of space coloniza-

tion gathers momentum: space tugs for going to the asteroid belt and back, bringing iron and stone for the space factories; space shuttles for the trips to earth; the shipyards, the local vehicles, the town and its supporting services. The development of these facilities will take many years. But in time, as space mining delivers more and more raw material to the construction sites in space, dependence on earth material with its costly freight charges can be relieved.

Given the capital investment in means of production, the space [14] community can contribute an increasing share to the earth-originated venture. In the long run, the New Space World may exceed the earth in population and resources, just as on earth the Americas, after several hundred years of intense colonization, have caught up with and exceed, in many capacities, the communities that colonized them. However, it may be noted that shipbuilding, which received a tremendous stimulus from the colonization of the New World and the advent of world trade, has remained a major European activity over the half-millennium that has elapsed since the days of Prince Henry the Navigator.[3] I envisage an enduring phase in which space ventures remain a major earthly activity, while a growing space community makes welcome contributions. In a way, this may be likened to the American contribution to world shipping through the design and building of the clipper ships of 1833–69. However, the parallel would be closer if building materials in Europe had lain at the bottom of a hole hundreds of miles deep. The cost of transporting raw materials through space compared with that of lifting materials from earth favors an economy based on the mining of space.

While the power for manufactures in space should come di- [15] rectly from the sun, very large amounts of power will also be required on earth. How could the space community help with this? What the relative costs of nuclear fusion energy and solar energy will be is not known. But if solar energy is a substantial component of the terrestrial energy budget there will be one awkward feature: an extensive geographic area has to be covered with solar energy collectors. A given collecting area assembled in space would free the earth's surface for other use; the energy collected could

---

[3] (1394–1460), son of the king of Portugal, established an observatory and a school for navigation.

be radiated to earth in a condensed form that could be received on a much smaller collector.

With power handling and space manufacturing as an economic   16
base, the expansion of space colonies will be linked directly to the mining of materials in interplanetary space. In addition to the moon and asteroids there will be the numerous satellites of Jupiter and Saturn, and ultimately the planets themselves. *We live now on a satellite adrift in space—why would man not make more satellites to his taste if it came within his means?*

Should this colonization program proceed in the direction indi-   17
cated here, a great fleet of worlds will eventually accompany the earth in its orbit around the sun. At the very basis of this development is the possibility of obtaining more of the sun's energy and using more of the matter of the solar system. It is the same vision that Tsiolkovsky, the great Russian space pioneer, described in his book *Dreams of the Earth,* published in 1895. It is a step toward Dyson's world in which a shell ultimately envelops the sun to capture all its energy.

Glossary

ABSTRACT General, having to do with essences and ideas: Liberty, truth, and beauty are abstract concepts. Most writers depend upon abstractions to some degree; however, abstractions that are not fleshed out with vivid particulars are not likely to hold a reader's interest. See CONCRETE.

ALLUSION A passing reference, especially to a work of literature. C. G. Jung, the author of "Freud and Jung: Contrasts" (in "Essays for Further Reading"), is alluding to Goethe's dramatic poem *Faust* when he says, "Thou art conscious only of the single urge." This single brief reference carries the weight of Goethe's entire drama behind it. It implies thta Freud, like Goethe's worldly student, was moved only by base instincts and that Freud recognized no heavenly aspirations of the sort that moved Faust himself. Allusions, therefore, provide an efficient means of enlarging the scope of a statement; without Goethe's words behind his own, Jung would have required a whole paragraph to make his point. The most successful allusions are usually to works the reader knows; to most German readers, the line from Goethe would have been as familiar as Hamlet's "to be or not to be" speech to English readers.

ANALOGY A comparison that reveals a primary object or event by likening it to a secondary one, often more familiar than the first. In expository writing, analogies are used as aids to explanation and as organizing devices. In a persuasive essay, the author may argue that what is true in one case is also true in the similar case that he is advancing. An argument "by analogy" is only as strong as the terms of the analogy are similar. For examples of analogies and a discussion of their kinship with metaphors, see the introduction to Chapter 7.

APPEAL TO EMOTION, TO ETHICS, and TO REASON *See* Modes of Persuasion.

371

ARGUMENTATION *See* Persuasion.

CAUSE AND EFFECT A strategy of exposition. Writing a cause and effect essay is much like constructing a persuasive argument; it is a form of reasoning that carries the reader step by step through a proof. Instead of "proving" the validity of the author's reasoning in order to move the reader to action, however, an essay in cause and effect is concerned with analyzing why an event occurred and with tracing its consequences. See the introduction to Chapter 4 for further discussion of this strategy.

CLASSIFICATION A strategy of exposition that places an object (or person) within a group of similar objects and then focuses on the characteristics distinguishing it from others in the group. Classification is a mode of organizing an essay as well as a means of obtaining knowledge. The introduction to Chapter 2 defines this strategy in detail.

CLICHÉ A tired expression that has lost its original power to surprise because of overuse: *We came in on a wing and a prayer; The quarterback turned the tables and saved the day.*

COMPARISON AND CONTRAST A strategy of expository writing that explores the similarities and differences between two persons, places, things, or ideas. It differs from description in that it makes statements or propositions about its subjects. The introduction to Chapter 6 defines this kind of expository essay in some detail.

CONCRETE Definite, particular, capable of being perceived directly. Opposed to *abstract. Rose, Mississippi, pinch* are more concrete words than *flower, river, touch.* Five-miles-per-hour is a more concrete idea than slowness. It is a good practice, as a rule, to make your essays as concrete as possible, even when you are writing on a general topic. For example, if you are defining an ideal wife or husband, cite specific wives or husbands you have known or heard about.

CONNOTATIONS The implied meanings of a word; its overtones and associations over and above its literal, dictionary meaning. The strict meaning of *home,* for example, is "the place where one lives"; but the word connotes comfort, security, and love. The first word in each of the following pairs is the more neutral word; the second carries richer connotations: *like/adore; clothes/garb; fast/fleet; shy/coy; stout/obese; move about/skulk; interested/obsessed.* See DENOTATION.

DEDUCTION A form of logical reasoning or explaining that proceeds from general premises to specific conclusions. For example, from the general premises that all men are mortal and that Socrates is a man, we can deduce that Socrates is mortal. See the introduction to Chapter 9 for more examples.

DEDUCTIVE *See* Deduction.

DEFINITION A basic strategy of expository writing. Definitions set forth the essential meaning or properties of a thing or idea. "Extended" definitions enlarge upon that basic meaning by analyzing the qualities, recalling the history, explaining the purpose, or giving synonyms of whatever is being defined. Extended definitions often draw upon such other strategies of exposition as classification, comparison and contrast, and process analysis. See the introduction to Chapter 5 for a full treatment of definition.

DENOTATION The basic dictionary meaning of a word without any of its associated meanings. The denotation of *home*, for example, is simply "the place where one lives." *See* Connotations.

DESCRIPTION One of the four traditional modes of discourse. Description appeals to the senses: it tells how a person, place, thing, or idea looks, feels, sounds, smells, or tastes. "Scientific" description reports these qualities; "evocative" description recreates them. See the introduction to Chapter 8 for an extended definition of the descriptive mode.

DICTION Word choice. Mark Twain was talking about diction when he said that the difference between the almost right word and the right word is the difference "between the lightning bug and the lightning." "Standard" diction is defined by dictionaries and other authorities as the language that educated native speakers of English use in their formal writing. Some other *Levels of Diction* are as follows; when you find one of these labels attached to words or phrases in your dictionary, avoid them in your own formal writing:

Nonstandard: Words like *ain't* that would never be used by an educated speaker who was trying to impress a stranger.

Informal (or *Colloquial*): The language of conversation among those who write standard edited English. *I am crazy about you, Virginia,* is informal rather than nonstandard.

Slang: Either the figurative language of a specialized group (*moll, gat, heist*) or fashionable coined words (*boondoggle, weirdo*) and extended meanings (*dead soldier* for an empty bottle; *garbage* for nonsense). Slang words often pass quickly into standard English or just as quickly fade away.

Obsolete: Terms like *pantaloons* and *palfrey* (saddle horse) that were once standard but are no longer used.

Regional (or *Dialectal*): For example, *remuda*, meaning a herd of riding horses, is used only in the Southwest.

ETYMOLOGY A word history or the practice of tracing such histories. The modern English word *march*, for example, is derived from the French *marcher* ("to walk"), which in turn is derived from the Latin word *marcus* ("a hammer"). The etymological definition of *march* is thus "to walk with a measured tread, like the rhythmic pounding of a hammer." In most dictionaries, the derivation, or etymology, of a word is explained in parentheses or brackets before the first definition is given.

EXPOSITION One of the four modes of discourse. Expository writing is informative writing. It explains or gives directions. All the items in this glossary are written in the expository mode; and most of the practical prose that you write in the coming years will be— e.g., papers and examinations, job applications, business reports, insurance claims, your last will and testament. See the Introduction for a discussion of how exposition is related to the other modes of discourse.

EXPOSITORY *See* Exposition.

FIGURES OF SPEECH Colorful words and phrases used in a nonliteral sense. Some of the most common figures of speech are:
Simile: A stated comparison, usually with *like* or *as: He stood like a rock.*
Metaphor: A comparison that equates two objects without the use of a stated connecting word: *Throughout the battle, Sergeant Phillips was a rock.*
Metonymy: The use of one word or name in place of another commonly associated with it. *The White House* [for the president] *awarded the sergeant a medal.*
Personification: Assigning human traits to nonhuman objects: *The very walls have ears.*
Hyperbole: Conscious exaggeration: *The mountain reached to the sky.*
Understatement: The opposite of hyperbole, a conscious playing down: *After forty days of climbing the mountain, we felt that we had made a start.*
Rhetorical Question: A question to which the author either expects no answer or answers himself: *Why climb the mountain? Because it is there.*

HYPERBOLE Exaggeration. *See* Figures of Speech.

INDUCTION A form of logical reasoning or explaining that proceeds from specific examples to general principles. As a rule, an inductive argument is only as valid as its examples are representative. See the introduction to Chapter 9.

INDUCTIVE *See* Induction.

IRONY An ironic statement implies a way of looking at the subject that is different (not necessarily opposite) from the stated way. For example when Barbara G. Walker (in "For Women Mostly") says that spending an evening with "the Lover" is "like a nice quiet session with a boa constrictor," her irony tells us that such an evening is neither "nice" nor "quiet" from her point of view. (The Lover, of course, has a different point of view.) Irony of situation, as opposed to *verbal* irony, occurs when events in real life or in a narrative turn out differently than the characters or people had expected. It was ironic that Hitler, with his dream of world domination, committed suicide in the end.

METAPHOR A direct comparison that identifies one thing with another. *See* Figures of Speech.

MODES OF DISCOURSE Means or forms of writing or speaking. The four traditional modes of discourse are Narration, Exposition, Description, and Persuasion. This book is organized around these four modes. Chapter 1 gives examples of narration. Exposition is explained in Chapters 2–7; description, in Chapter 8; and persuasion (and argumentation), in Chapters 9 and 10.

MODES OF PERSUASION There are three traditional modes (or means) of persuading an audience to action or belief: the appeal to reason, the appeal to emotion, and the appeal to ethics. When applying the first of these, a writer convinces the reader by the force of logic; he or she constructs an argument which the reader finds to be correct or valid. When appealing to emotion, the writer tries to excite in the reader the same emotions the writer felt upon first considering the proposition he or she is advancing or some other emotion that will dispose the reader to accept that proposition. The appeal to ethics is an appeal to the reader's sense of what constitutes upright behavior. The writer convinces the reader that the writer is a good person who deserves to be heeded because of his or her admirable character. See the introductions to Chapters 9 and 10 for detailed discussions of these three modes.

NARRATION One of the four traditional modes of discourse. An accounting of actions and events that have befallen someone or something. Because narration is essentially story-telling, it is the mode most often used in fiction; however, it is also an important element in nonfictional writing and speaking. The opening of Lincoln's Gettysburg Address, for example, is in the narrative mode: "Fourscore and seven years ago our fathers brought forth on this continent a new nation. . . ."

PERSON The aspect of grammar that describes the person speaking, spoken to, or spoken about in a sentence or paragraph. There are three persons: first (I or we), second (you), and third (he, she, it, and they). *See also* Point of View.

PERSONIFICATION Attributing human characteristics to the nonhuman. *See* Figures of Speech.

PERSUASION The art of moving an audience to action or belief. According to traditional definitions, a writer can persuade a reader in one of three ways: by appealing to his or her reason, emotions, or sense of ethics. (*See* Modes of Persuasion.) *Argumentation*, as the term is understood in this book, is the form of persuasion that emphasizes the first of these appeals. An argument may be more concerned with pursuing a line of reasoning or stating the issued raised by a problem than with inciting someone to action. Nevertheless, an argument must persuade us that what it says is not only true but worthwhile; it must move us to believe if not to act. For a full explanation of persuasion and argumentation, see the introductions to Chapters 9 and 10.

PERSUASIVE ARGUMENT *See* Persuasion.

PLOT An aspect of narrative. Plot is the sequence of events in a story. It therefore has to do with actions rather than ideas.

POINT OF VIEW The vantage from which a story is told or an account given. Point of view is often described according to the grammatical person of a narrative. An "I" narrative, for example, is told from the "first person" point of view. A narrative that refers to "he" or "she" is told from the "third person" point of view. If the speaker of a third-person narrative seems to know everything about his or her subject, including their thoughts, the point of view is also "omniscient"; if the speaker's knowledge is incomplete, the point of view is third-person "limited." Sometimes point of view is described simply by characterizing the speaker of an essay. David E. Dubber's "Crossing the Bar on a Fiberglas Pole," for example, is told from the point of view of a dedicated college athlete as he arches over the horizontal bar in a pole-vaulting competition.

PROCESS ANALYSIS A form of expository writing that breaks a process into its component operations or that gives directions. Most "How To" essays are essays in process analysis: how to grow cotton; how to operate a fork lift; how to avoid shark bite. Process analyses are usually divided into stages or steps arranged in chronological order. They differ from narratives in that they tell *how* something functions rather than *what* happens to something or someone. See the introduction to Chapter 3 for further discussion of this expository technique.

RHETORIC The art of using language effectively in speech and in writing. The term originally belonged to oratory, and it implies the presence of both a speaker (or writer) and a listener (or reader). This book is a collection of the rhetorical techniques and strategies that some successful writers have found helpful for communicating effectively with an audience.

RHETORICAL QUESTION A question that is really a statement. *See* Figures of Speech.

SATIRE A form of writing that attacks a person or practice in hopes of improving either. For example, in "A Modest Proposal" ("Essays For Further Reading"), Jonathan Swift satirizes the materialism that had reduced his native Ireland to extreme poverty. His intent was to point out the greed of even his poorest countrymen and thereby shame them all into looking out for the public welfare instead of exploiting the country's last resources. This desire to correct vices and follies distinguishes *satire* from *sarcasm*, which is intended primarily to wound. *See also* Irony.

SATIRIZE *See* Satire.

SIMILE A comparison that likens one thing to another. *See* Figures of Speech.

SLANG Popular language that often originates in the speech of a particular group or subculture. *See* Diction.

SYNTAX The interrelationship among words. In the sentence, *The police chased the woman who had beaten her dog*, the phrase *the woman who had beaten her dog* is the "direct object." This term describes the syntax of the phrase because it defines the function of the phrase within the context of the entire sentence. In a larger sense, syntax refers to the total network of relationships, including meanings, among words in a discourse.

TENSE The time aspect of verbs. In the sentence, *He took the money and ran*, the past-tense forms indicate that the taking and running occurred at an earlier time than the writer's telling about those actions. There are six basic tenses in English: past, present, future, and the perfect forms of these three: past perfect, present perfect, and future perfect. (Here "perfect" means completed. An action in the future perfect—*He will have left*, for example— will be completed in the future before another stated future action: *He will have left before the police arrive*.) In writing, it is a good idea not to switch tenses unnecessarily. If you start an essay in the past tense, stick to that tense unless the sense of your remarks requires a change: *He took the money, but the police will catch him*.

TONE An author's revealed attitude toward his subject or audience: sympathy, longing, amusement, shock, sarcasm—the range is endless. When analyzing the tone of a passage, consider what quality of voice you should assume for reading it aloud. Nora Ephron's "A Few Words About Breasts," for example, should be read with a note of hysteria. The author's tone of voice indicates that the "I" of her essay was psychologically damaged by the experience it recounts.

TOPIC SENTENCE The sentence in a paragraph that comes closest to stating the topic of the paragraph as a whole. The topic sentence is often the first sentence, but it may appear anywhere in the paragraph. Some paragraphs do not have clear-cut topic sentences, especially if they function chiefly to link preceding paragraphs with those to follow.

TRANSITION The act of passing from one topic (or aspect of a topic) to another; the word, phrase, sentence, or paragraph that accomplishes such a passage. For an excellent example, see Alexander Petrunkevitch's "Intelligence vs. Instinct" in "Paragraphs for Analysis." Polished transitions are necessary if an essay is to be carefully organized and developed.

UNDERSTATEMENT A verbal playing down or softening for humorous or ironic effect. *See* Figures of Speech.